TAX Cafe®

Taxcafe.co.uk Tax Guides

How to Save Inheritance Tax

By Carl Bayley BSc FCA

Important Legal Notices:

Taxcafe®
TAX GUIDE – "How to Save Inheritance Tax"

Published by:
Taxcafe UK Limited
67 Milton Road
Kirkcaldy KY1 1TL
Tel: (01592) 560081
Email address: team@taxcafe.co.uk

Fourteenth Edition - January 2018

ISBN 978-1-911020-26-4

Pay Less Tax!

…with help from Taxcafe's unique tax guides

All products available online at

www.taxcafe.co.uk

Popular Taxcafe titles include:

- *How to Save Property Tax*
- *Using a Property Company to Save Tax*
- *How to Save Inheritance Tax*
- *Landlord Interest*
- *Salary versus Dividends*
- *Using a Company to Save Tax*
- *Small Business Tax Saving Tactics*
- *Keeping it Simple: Small Business Bookkeeping, Tax & VAT*
- *Tax Planning for Non-Residents & Non Doms*
- *Tax-Free Capital Gains*
- *Pension Magic*
- *Isle of Man Tax Saving Guide*
- *How to Save Tax*

Disclaimer

1. This guide is intended as general guidance only and does NOT constitute accountancy, tax, investment or other professional advice.

2. The author and Taxcafe UK Limited make no representations or warranties with respect to the accuracy or completeness of this publication and cannot accept any responsibility or liability for any loss or risk, personal or otherwise, which may arise, directly or indirectly, from reliance on information contained in this publication.

3. Please note that tax legislation, the law and practices of Government and regulatory authorities (e.g. HM Revenue & Customs) are constantly changing. We therefore recommend that for accountancy, tax, investment or other professional advice, you consult a suitably qualified accountant, tax advisor, financial adviser, or other professional adviser.

4. Please also note that your personal circumstances may vary from the general examples provided in this guide and your professional adviser will be able to provide specific advice based on your personal circumstances.

5. This guide covers UK taxation only and any references to 'tax' or 'taxation', unless the contrary is expressly stated, refer to UK taxation only. Please note that references to the 'UK' do not include the Channel Islands or the Isle of Man. Foreign tax implications are beyond the scope of this guide.

6. Whilst, in an effort to be helpful, this tax guide may refer to general guidance on matters other than UK taxation, Taxcafe UK Limited and the author are not expert in these matters and do not accept any responsibility or liability for loss which may arise from reliance on such information contained in this guide.

7. All persons described in the examples in this guide are entirely fictional. Any similarities to actual persons, living or dead, or to fictional characters created by any other author, are entirely coincidental.

8. The views expressed in this publication are the author's own personal views and do not necessarily reflect the views of any organisation which he may represent.

About the Author

Carl Bayley is the author of a series of 'Plain English' tax guides designed to help families, landlords, and other business owners understand the taxes they face and make savings through sensible planning and by having the confidence to know what they are entitled to claim. Carl's particular speciality is his ability to take the weird, complex and inexplicable world of taxation and set it out in the kind of clear, straightforward language that taxpayers themselves can understand. As he often says himself, "my job is to translate 'tax' into English".

Carl enjoys his role as a tax author, as he explains: "Writing these guides gives me the opportunity to use the skills and knowledge learned over more than thirty years in the tax profession for the benefit of a wider audience. The most satisfying part of my success as an author is the chance to give the average person the same standard of advice as the 'big guys' at a price which everyone can afford."

Carl takes the same approach when speaking on taxation, a role he frequently undertakes with great enthusiasm, including his highly acclaimed annual 'Budget Breakfast' for the Institute of Chartered Accountants.

In addition to being a recognised author and speaker on the subject, Carl has often spoken on taxation on radio and television, including the BBC's 'It's Your Money' programme and BBC Radio 2's Jeremy Vine Show.

Carl began his career as a Chartered Accountant in 1983 with one of the 'Big 4' accountancy firms. After qualifying as a double prize-winner, he immediately began specialising in taxation.

Having honed his skills with several major international firms, Carl began the new millennium by launching his own tax and accounting practice, Bayley Miller Limited, through which he provides advice on a wide variety of taxation issues; especially Inheritance Tax, property taxation and tax planning for small and medium-sized businesses.

Carl is the Chairman of the Tax Faculty of the Institute of Chartered Accountants in England and Wales and a member of the Institute's governing Council. He is also a former President of ICAEW Scotland and has co-organised the annual Practical Tax Conference for the last 16 years.

When he isn't working, Carl takes on the equally taxing challenges of hill walking and creative writing – his Munro tally is now 104, and he is currently putting the finishing touches to his first novel.

Carl lives in the Scottish Borders and has four children.

Dedications and Thanks

For the Past,

Firstly, given the subject matter of this book, it seems appropriate to dedicate it to the memory of those I have loved and lost:

First of all, to my beloved mother Diana – what would you think if you could see me now? The memory of your love warms me still. Thank you for bringing me into the light and making it all possible;

To my dear grandfather, Arthur - your wise words still come back to guide me; and to my loving grandmothers, Doris and Winifred;

Between you, you left me with nothing I could spend, but everything I need.

Also to my beloved friends: Mac, William, Edward, Rusty, Dawson, and the grand old lady, Morgan. Thank you for all those happy miles; I still miss you all.

For the Future,

I also dedicate this book to some very special young people who continue to provide me with a personal interest in this subject:

Robert – the 'chip off the old block', who is both cursed and blessed to have inherited a lot of my own character; luckily for him, there is a lot of his mother in him too!

James – the intellectual of the family, a true twenty-first century gentleman and one of the nicest guys I have ever met;

And lastly, and furthest from least:

Michelle – my truly wonderful daughter, I told her when she was just sixteen that she was one of the most interesting people I had ever met: since then she has grown more interesting, and more amazing, with every passing year!

I am so very proud of every one of you and I can only hope that I, in turn, will also be able to leave each of you with everything you need.

Thanks

Thanks are due to:

The Taxcafe team, past and present – for their help in making these books far more successful than I could ever have dreamed.

My old friend and mentor, Peter Rayney – for his inspiration and for showing me that tax and humour can mix.

Rebecca, Paul and David – for taking me into the 'fold' at the Tax Faculty and for their fantastic support at our Peebles conference over many years.

Gregor – for the 'brain-storming' sessions and those amazing ideas which sprang from his lateral thinking.

And last, but far from least, thanks to Nick for giving me the push!

C.B., Roxburghshire, January 2018

Contents

Appendices

Chapter 1

Introduction

1.1   THERE ARE TWO CERTAINTIES IN LIFE

Generally speaking, I find that the oldest sayings are the truest. One old saying is "There are only two certainties in life: Death and Taxes".

At the point where these two great 'certainties' meet lies 'Inheritance Tax', and it is through the medium of this tax that the Government will aim to get its final pound of flesh from you, just as you have departed this life.

Most people spend their lifetime trying to accumulate a reasonable amount of wealth, to take care of themselves in their old age and then to pass on any remaining surplus to their children. Much of the Government's fiscal policy is aimed at encouraging this type of behaviour.

It is somewhat unfair then, that without careful planning and a great deal of pre-emptive action, many families will ultimately face a huge Inheritance Tax bill.

Unchecked, this tax bill will rob your family of a significant proportion of their rightful inheritance – up to 40% of it, in fact.

Most people are absolutely appalled at this prospect, which, of course, is where Inheritance Tax planning comes in!

Some years ago, the Labour Party accused the previous Conservative Government of allowing Inheritance Tax to become a 'voluntary tax', paid only by the unwary, ill-advised and unprepared taxpayer, whilst wealthier taxpayers took expensive professional advice and avoided the tax.

Certainly, there was, and in fact still is, an element of truth in this accusation.

In recent years, however, it has become increasingly difficult to avoid this hated 'grave-robber's tax', with a host of measures introduced by Governments of all persuasions designed to block many of the popular methods used by families attempting to plan for the inevitable.

As we will see later in the guide, some Government attempts to block Inheritance Tax planning suffer from their well-known tendency to 'use a sledgehammer to crack a nut'. In fact, the scope of one particular charge (the 'Pre-Owned Assets Charge') is so wide that many innocent taxpayers are completely unaware that simple domestic arrangements like buying a house together may have led to a charge being technically due.

Not satisfied with getting this quite absurdly Draconian measure on the statute books, Gordon Brown turned up the heat even further in 2006, with a savage attack on trusts.

Help seemed to be at hand the following year when the Conservatives proposed a massive increase in the nil rate band exemption to £1m. Although this did not materialise for many years and, even then, it had been watered down beyond all recognition by a host of 'ifs', 'buts' and 'maybes', it did at least prompt the old Labour Government into making nil rate bands transferable between spouses and civil partners.

Suddenly, overnight, it seemed that almost every married couple, civil partnership, widow, widower and surviving civil partner had effectively doubled their nil rate band.

Since then, however, things have taken a turn for the worse: as it seems that all our politicians are happy to break their promises when it comes to Inheritance Tax.

Alistair Darling kicked off the 'season of broken promises' in 2009 when he announced that the planned increase in the nil rate band set for the following year would not go ahead. Worse still, he went on to announce a five year freeze in the nil rate band at its 2009 level of £325,000.

Soon afterwards, Labour were ousted and the Conservatives became the 'senior partner' in the first post-war Coalition Government. Sadly, however, their promised increase in the nil rate band was swiftly shelved and Labour's five year freeze retained instead: later extended to eight years; and then to twelve!

So, despite our change of Government, we are now stuck with a nil rate band of just £325,000 until at least 2021.

At the time of writing, we are nine years into the twelve year freeze period and inflation has already severely eroded the value of the nil rate band. A bout of high inflation before 2021 would reduce its value even further and could undo most of the benefit of the transferable nil rate band regime introduced in 2007 (and those who are single or divorced never even had that benefit in the first place).

Make no mistake about it; the twelve year freeze in the nil rate band is a significant tax-raising measure. As the value of the band decreases in real terms due to inflation, the Government's Inheritance Tax take is steadily increasing.

On top of all the broken promises about the nil rate band, the 2013 Budget brought yet more misery, as George Osborne announced a raft of new rules to restrict the deduction of liabilities for Inheritance Tax purposes.

As one might expect, the rules restricting the deduction of liabilities will block a number of popular planning techniques. However, what will be less apparent to most people is that the rules will also lead to some astonishingly unfair results, especially when a family business or family farm is passed on to the next generation.

We will look at the impact of these rules in more detail later in the guide, but it is clear to me that they severely undermine the original intention of helping small and medium-sized businesses to survive their owner's death. The additional Inheritance Tax burden which will now be placed on many families as a result of these new rules will inevitably reduce many businesses' chances of survival.

In the July 2015 'Summer Budget', Osborne finally returned to that promise of a £1m nil rate band. And what a mess he made of it!

Instead of the simple £1m nil rate band that he had originally promised in 2007, he created a new, additional, 'residence nil rate band', which is only available under certain very restricted circumstances: as we shall see later in the guide.

Claiming that the new residence nil rate band amounted to the equivalent of a £1m nil rate band: "Promise Made, Promise Delivered!", as he said; was somewhat disingenuous since, to get the required level of exemption, necessitates a complex combination of circumstances.

What Osborne did was rather like me promising to give one of my children £1,000 tomorrow – no strings attached, to do with as they please; but, instead of doing as I said, waiting eight years and then telling them that I would give them £1,000 in another five years' time, but only if they got married and bought a house.

That's what I call: "Promise Made, Promise Broken".

Despite all the changes to the Inheritance Tax regime over the last few years, what still remains true to this day is the fact that it is the moderately wealthy members of society who suffer the greatest proportionate burden when compared with their overall wealth. In fact, it seems to me that the new restrictions on deduction of liabilities are likely to further exacerbate this tendency.

In my experience, Inheritance Tax is predominantly paid by the modestly wealthy citizens of middle England (as well as middle Scotland, Wales and Northern Ireland too).

The problem for many people in the middle wealth bracket is that they face a fundamental dilemma.

On the one hand they have, on paper, sufficient wealth to leave their family with a very substantial tax burden when they pass away.

On the other hand, however, they do not really have a great deal of disposable income, despite leading reasonably modest lifestyles.

This means that the very simple expedient of just giving all their surplus wealth away is, in practical terms, simply not an option.

Recent trends have added to this problem. Massive increases in property values in some parts of the country have pushed more and more people into the Inheritance Tax bracket, especially in the 'hotspots' like London and the South East, and other desirable areas, such as Edinburgh or Bath.

The second factor adding impetus to the 'asset rich/cash poor' situation, which many people now find themselves in, is the current poor level of return on investments.

In short, what this means is that a lot of capital produces only a modest income, leaving a great many people with very little real wealth today but serious Inheritance Tax problems for tomorrow!

In my working life, I see the stress, worry and anxiety that this situation creates on a regular basis. I am firmly of the opinion that the emotional strain which Inheritance Tax places on so many people is so detrimental that it far outweighs any benefits that the Government may derive from collecting the tax.

Personally, I would dearly love to see this immoral, evil tax abolished as soon as possible.

Sadly, however, I am afraid to say that, in reality, we seem to be stuck with Inheritance Tax for the foreseeable future: as all of the major political parties now seem quite happy to play the role of 'grave robber' and at least two of them are content to abandon any promises they may have made in the past.

As ever, there remain two effective ways to avoid Inheritance Tax:

- Die poor, or
- Plan ahead

Most of us find the first option somewhat unpalatable and also quite difficult to achieve without a remarkable sense of timing!

Until recently, 'planning ahead' has also been seen as the prerogative of the very wealthiest members of society, leaving the moderately wealthy to pick up the bill!

However, my aim in this guide is to help put an end to this situation.

If the Government is still prepared to allow Inheritance Tax to be even partly 'voluntary', albeit to a far lesser extent than previously, then why should <u>anyone</u> volunteer?

Early and careful planning is the key to reducing the eventual Inheritance Tax burden on your family and you don't need to be a millionaire to do it. Or to <u>need</u> to do it either, for that matter!

Besides which, a great many people are surprised to discover that when they add up all of their assets they are, in fact, millionaires anyway – on paper, at least.

Whilst some tax can still be saved through 'last-minute' planning, a great deal more unnecessary tax can be avoided by planning for death and taxes throughout your lifetime. Read on and I will show you how.

1.2   GUIDE OVERVIEW

In this opening chapter, we will start by taking a brief look at some background issues important to an understanding of the rest of the guide.

Following that, in Chapter 2, we will cover some of the basics, including how the tax is calculated and who pays it. All of this comes under the general heading of 'know your enemy', because it is important to understand what you're up against before you start to make any plans to combat it.

We then move on, in Chapter 3, to look at the main exemptions which are available at any time, both during your lifetime and on death; as well as those which are only available on death.

Chapters 4 and 5 look at the area of lifetime transfers, including the additional exemptions available and how to maximise them.

The first five chapters prepare us for Chapter 6, which is devoted to Inheritance Tax planning for married couples, civil partners, widows, widowers and surviving civil partners.

The changes introduced in 2007 have fundamentally altered the entire Inheritance Tax planning landscape for all married couples and civil partners. In a great many cases, something which was the best advice before 2007 is now the very last thing you should do!

All married couples and civil partners therefore need to consider everything contained in the rest of this guide in the context of the issues and advice set out in Chapter 6.

Chapter 6 also includes a detailed analysis of the position now facing all widows, widowers and surviving civil partners, with advice on crucial tax-saving action which needs to be taken by the recently bereaved.

Even those who are currently single or divorced will benefit from Chapter 6 as it includes vital advice on the potential Inheritance Tax benefits of marriage.

Chapter 7 covers the important area of business property relief, perhaps the most valuable piece of equipment in our Inheritance Tax planning armoury.

We will then move into the realm of trusts in Chapters 8 and 9 and we will see what powerful tools these vehicles can provide in the battle against Inheritance Tax.

Chapter 10 reminds us that there is a 'bigger picture' than merely saving Inheritance Tax and here we will widen our sights to take in other aspects of estate preservation. This is reinforced in Chapter 11 with a look at the interaction between Inheritance Tax and Capital Gains Tax.

In Chapter 12, we look at the all-important issue of the family home. Here we will take a detailed look at some of the practical implications of the new residence nil rate band, as well as some of the other planning techniques available to shelter the family home from the Government's most despicable form of taxation.

The family home will then also dominate our review of the pre-owned assets charge in Chapter 13.

In Chapter 14, we cover perhaps the most drastic of all planning techniques, with a guide to emigration, as well as a look at the advantages available to those who have already done it.

Bringing things almost to a close, Chapter 15 provides a useful 'whole life' timetable for effective Inheritance Tax planning, which puts everything else we have learned into context and also reassures us that, whilst it's never too early to start planning, it's never too late either!

Finally, Chapter 16 covers the planning which a bereaved family can still carry out even after someone has died. Whilst this is not the ideal time for truly effective Inheritance Tax planning, it is surprising how much can still be achieved if the deceased's family acts quickly.

This expanded guide, fully updated for all of the drastic changes introduced over the last few years, must surely now have something of value for everyone and provides a useful tool in the battle against the Government's most despicable form of taxation.

1.3   A BRIEF HISTORY OF INHERITANCE TAX

Inheritance Tax, as we know it today, arrived in 1986, the brainchild of Margaret Thatcher and her then Chancellor, Nigel Lawson.

Inheritance Tax is actually little more than a re-branding of its predecessor, Capital Transfer Tax which, in turn, had replaced the earlier and rather more

Draconian Estate Duty, which, in its day, had played a major part in turning many of Britain's stately homes into amusement parks!

It is quite ironic that Inheritance Tax should have such a long lineage because it is, of course, one's descendants who will suffer its effects.

The principal difference between Inheritance Tax and its predecessors is the fact that there is a general exemption for most lifetime transfers to other individuals.

This is part of the reason behind the accusations that Inheritance Tax is a voluntary tax, since simply giving all of one's wealth away would initially seem to be an easy way to escape the tax altogether.

However, inevitably, as we will see later in this guide, Inheritance Tax is not quite that easy to avoid. You would have to survive for at least seven years after leaving yourself completely destitute (and homeless), for a start!

1.4   WHY WORRY?

Of course **you** won't actually have to pay any Inheritance Tax on your own estate. Furthermore, for most people, everything can safely be left to their spouse or civil partner free from any Inheritance Tax.

And, if you have no other dependants or potential beneficiaries to care about, but simply resent paying any unnecessary tax, you can simply leave it all to charity.

But most people **_do_** have someone they care about. Usually they have children or other family or friends whom they want to see benefit from the assets they have built up in their lifetime and they don't want to see the Government taking 40% of it away.

Even if, in the first instance, you are leaving everything tax free to your surviving spouse, your accumulated wealth will eventually be hit by Inheritance Tax if you don't plan ahead.

As we will see later in the guide, you need to take action **_now_** in order to safeguard your family's future prosperity.

Alternatively, you may be in the position of being the potential beneficiary yourself, trying to get an elderly relative to plan for the preservation of your inheritance.

Either way, there is plenty to worry about!

But Am I Wealthy Enough to Need to Worry?

Most people are quite surprised to discover just how much they are actually worth. How often have you heard someone say, "I'm worth more dead than alive"? Very often, especially as we get older, it's true (in pure financial terms only, of course).

This is basically because it takes an enormous amount of capital just to support one person. When that person dies, the capital that was previously tied up in supporting them is freed. (After the Government gets its share of it, that is!)

Hence, although you may not feel particularly wealthy, you may still find that you have a large potential Inheritance Tax bill.

You'd be amazed at just how many 'paper millionaires' there are these days. Take a look at this example:

Example
Rosemary is a divorcee with no children of her own: although she is very close to her two younger sisters and their children. She owns a fairly average sized detached house, which her ex-husband transferred to her under the terms of their divorce settlement. The house is bigger than she really needs, but she has fond memories of the many holidays her nephews and nieces spent there, so she is quite attached to it. She has been advised that its current market value is £450,000.

Rosemary is retired and lives off her savings and an investment portfolio that she managed to accumulate after her divorce. Although these produce an income of only £19,500 per annum, their total value is approximately £535,000.

Rosemary also has some jewellery, some silver and a few antiques. Altogether, these are worth £10,000. Lastly, she has a small car, worth £5,000.

Nobody would call Rosemary rich by any stretch of the imagination. She's living off only £19,500 a year. But add it all up and you will find that she is a millionaire! This means that Rosemary's family has a potential Inheritance Tax bill of £270,000!

And you don't need to be anywhere near as 'wealthy' as Rosemary to have an Inheritance Tax problem. Once your estate is worth over £325,000, you have a potential exposure to tax at 40% on the excess (subject to any transferable nil rate band: see Chapter 6; and any available residence nil rate band: see Section 3.4).

£325,000! What's that these days? A house, a car, a few savings and you're there!

So, yes, generally speaking, if you can afford to buy this guide there is a strong chance that you are wealthy enough to need to worry about Inheritance Tax!

1.5 MARRIED COUPLES & CIVIL PARTNERS

Throughout this guide, you will see me refer many times to 'married couples' and 'spouses', as well as to 'widows' and 'widowers'. In each case, the tax treatment being outlined applies equally to:

- Married couples of opposite sexes,
- Married couples of the same sex, and
- Registered civil partners

Hence, any references to 'married couples' throughout this guide should be taken to also include registered civil partnerships; any reference to the taxpayer's 'spouse' will also include their civil partner where relevant; and any reference to 'husbands' or 'wives' will include spouses of the same gender and civil partners. Similarly, any reference to 'widows' or 'widowers' will include surviving spouses or civil partners of the same sex.

For the avoidance of doubt, I would, in particular, point out that the spouse exemption covered in Section 3.3 and all of the planning issues covered in Chapter 6 apply equally to same sex spouses and civil partners.

However, it remains important to remember that, unless specified to the contrary, the tax treatment being outlined applies to legally married couples and legally registered civil partners only.

1.6 TAX YEARS

Inheritance Tax, like many other UK taxes, is administered by reference to the UK tax year, i.e. the period of twelve months ending on 5th April. Thus, for example, the 2018/19 tax year is the year ending 5th April 2019. Any references to the 'tax year' in this guide should be construed accordingly.

Other periods are, however, also important for Inheritance Tax purposes and a reference in this guide to a 'period of seven years' or a 'period of more than two years', for example, means a strict period of calendar years rather than tax years.

1.7 TRUST TERMINOLOGY

Trust concepts and terminology are key to an understanding of Inheritance Tax planning. As well as the various types of trust, we will encounter important concepts such as 'interest in possession' and 'life interest'. A full explanation of the trust terminology used throughout this guide will be given in Chapter 8.

1.8   PROPERTY TAXES

Inheritance Tax planning often involves the transfer of UK property. This will sometimes lead to tax charges arising on the transfer in the form of some variation of Stamp Duty. The type of Duty arising will depend on which part of the UK the property is located in, as follows:

England:	Stamp Duty Land Tax
Scotland:	Land and Buildings Transaction Tax
Wales:	Transfers before 1st April 2018: Stamp Duty Land Tax
	Transfers on or after 1st April 2018: Land Transaction Tax
Northern Ireland:	Stamp Duty Land Tax

The rules applying under each form of Duty are broadly similar. There are some variations in the rates applying, but these are fairly minor. Full details of the rates applying to all UK property are included in the Taxcafe.co.uk guide *'How to Save Property Tax'*.

For the sake of simplicity, I will refer only to Stamp Duty Land Tax, or 'SDLT', throughout the rest of this guide, but readers should note that similar charges will arise on property in Scotland or, from 1st April 2018, Wales: except that the Duty will have a different name and will be charged at slightly different rates.

1.9   A GUIDE TO EFFECTIVE INHERITANCE TAX PLANNING

All tax planning needs to be undertaken carefully and in full knowledge of the particular circumstances of the taxpayer's individual situation. This is probably never more true than in the case of Inheritance Tax planning, where a detailed review of the individual's situation is vital.

I have dealt with all of the recent changes to Inheritance Tax law on the basis of our current understanding. It is important to remember that further changes or restrictions could be introduced at any time and the precise meaning of some areas of law will only become apparent when tested in court: possibly many years from now.

Inheritance Tax law is constantly changing. This means no one can be sure of having avoided the tax until they are safely tucked up in their grave! In addition to taking professional advice when putting your plans into effect, you should also commission a regular professional review to determine whether your planning remains effective.

In this guide, I have highlighted some of the more popular planning techniques currently being used successfully by taxpayers wishing to protect their wealth from the scourge of Inheritance Tax, or which are at least currently believed to work.

HMRC does, however, have very wide powers to enable it to closely examine any Inheritance Tax planning technique and will do its utmost to overturn any planning strategy when the law permits it to.

The associated operations rules discussed in Section 10.21 and the general anti-abuse rule covered in Section 10.22 are both particularly wide-ranging in this regard.

Finally, the reader must also bear in mind the general nature of this guide. Individual circumstances vary and the tax implications of an individual's actions will vary with them. For this reason, it is always vital to get professional advice before undertaking any tax planning or other transactions that may have tax implications. The author and Taxcafe UK Ltd cannot accept any responsibility for any loss that may arise as a consequence of any action taken, or any decision to refrain from action taken, as a result of reading this guide.

1.10 ABOUT THE EXAMPLES

This guide is illustrated throughout by a number of examples. Unless specifically stated to the contrary, all persons described in the examples in this guide are UK resident and domiciled for tax purposes.

In preparing the examples in this guide, I have assumed that the UK tax regime will remain unchanged in the future except to the extent of any announcements already made at the time of publication. However, if there is one thing we can predict with any certainty, it is that change **will** occur. The reader must bear this in mind when reviewing the results of the examples.

All persons described in the examples in this guide are entirely fictional characters created specifically for the purposes of this guide. Any similarities to actual persons, living or dead, or to fictional characters created by any other author, are entirely coincidental.

1.11 ABBREVIATIONS

Generally, at Taxcafe, we don't like using abbreviations or jargon because we want to keep our guides as simple as possible. To save some space in this guide, however, we have allowed ourselves a few abbreviations. We think they are fairly obvious ones, so they should not cause any confusion. We will explain what each abbreviation means the first time that we use it and they are also set out again in Appendix I for your ease of reference.

Large numbers, such as £1,000,000 or more, are also abbreviated by use of the letter 'm'. For example, £2,500,000 will be written as £2.5m

Chapter 2

Inheritance Tax Principles

2.1 TRANSFERS OF VALUE

"Inheritance Tax is payable on death. Everyone knows that, don't they?"

Like so many things that 'everyone knows' (like "man will never fly" and "an iceberg will never sink a ship"), this is **WRONG**!

Now, admittedly, it is true that by far the biggest part of the Inheritance Tax ('IHT') that the Government collects arises on the occasion of someone's death. Furthermore, most of the remainder also arises due to attempts made by taxpayers to offload some of their wealth before then.

However, what actually triggers IHT is not death but any 'transfer of value'.

In principle, IHT is chargeable on any 'transfer of value' made by any person at any time. Thankfully, however, there are a number of exemptions and these help to ensure that we don't have to pay the Government 40% every time we give the kids their pocket money.

The reasons why we tend to think of IHT as applying mainly on death are really three-fold:

i)   On death, we are inevitably forced to transfer our entire wealth to others, thus causing, for most of us, the biggest 'transfer of value' of our lives.
ii) Most lifetime transfers to other individuals are exempt, or at least only become chargeable in the event of death within seven years.
iii) The name of the tax implies (falsely) that it is only related to death.

What is a 'Transfer of Value'?

A transfer of value occurs whenever you dispose of something and, as a result, your total net wealth is reduced. Your 'total net wealth' is referred to as your 'estate' and we will explore this concept further in Section 2.9.

What you are 'disposing of' may be money or may be any other asset with monetary value. Furthermore, it is the reduction in your own net wealth that generates the 'transfer of value', not necessarily the value of the asset disposed of. We will see an example of this a little later.

Any disposal of wealth by way of a 'transaction at arm's length' between unconnected persons is not treated as a 'transfer of value'.

Hence, the most basic transactions in life, such as buying the weekly groceries, will not be classed as a 'transfer of value', even though your total net wealth is inevitably reduced. Furthermore, when dealing at arm's length with unconnected persons, merely striking a 'poor bargain' will not be a transfer of value.

Example

John buys a car for £5,000 from Alexei, a second-hand car dealer. It turns out, however, that the car is an absolute wreck, worth at best around £800!

Poor John! However, at least there is no 'transfer of value' here, since John and Alexei are not connected.

If, on the other hand, John had bought the car from his sister, Janet, there would have been a transfer of value, as they are 'connected persons' (see Appendix C).

Nevertheless, a transaction with a connected person will still not give rise to any transfer of value, as long as it is carried out in the same way as it would have been if it had been an arm's length transaction with an unconnected person.

Example

Mick wants to buy his father's house. His father, Keith, obtains an independent valuation on the house, which indicates that it is worth £300,000. He therefore sells the house to Mick for this amount.

Unbeknown to Mick, Keith and the independent valuer, plans for a new bypass are just about to be announced, as a result of which the house's value will increase dramatically.

This may look like a 'transfer of value' but it isn't because Mick and Keith have struck the same bargain as would have been struck between unconnected persons.

The Amount of the 'Transfer of Value'

As stated above, a 'transfer of value' occurs whenever you make a disposal that is not at arm's length and, as a result, there is a reduction in your total net wealth (your estate). The simplest type of 'transfer of value' is therefore a straightforward gift.

If you give someone £10,000 in cash, that is a 'transfer of value' of £10,000, if you give someone a painting worth £5,000, that is a 'transfer of value' of £5,000.

A 'transfer of value' also occurs when sales take place between connected persons at an undervalue, or at an overvalue. If you sell your son a painting for £2,000 when it is, in fact, worth £10,000, that is a 'transfer of value' of £8,000. If you buy a car from your daughter and pay her £5,000, when the car is worth only £1,000, then that is a 'transfer of value' of £4,000.

But what is important to remember is that it is the reduction in the value of your overall estate that gives rise to the 'transfer of value'.

Example
Bjorn has a set of six antique chairs worth £20,000. He gives his son, Benny, one of the chairs. The value of a single chair, which is not part of a complete set, is only £1,500.

However, the 'transfer of value' here is not the value of Benny's single chair.

No, the 'transfer of value' is the reduction in the value of Bjorn's overall estate. Previously, he had a set of chairs worth £20,000. After the gift to Benny, he has five chairs worth £1,500 each, a total of £7,500.

Hence, the reduction in the value of Bjorn's estate, and thus the amount of the 'transfer of value', is £12,500.

2.2   WHO IS LIABLE FOR INHERITANCE TAX?

For UK domiciled individuals, IHT arises on:

- The net value of their entire estate (see Section 2.9) at the time of their death, wherever situated,
  Less:
  i)   The 'nil rate band' (£325,000 for deaths occurring between 6th April 2009 and 5th April 2021)
  ii) Any transferable nil rate band available (see Section 6.3)
  iii) Any other applicable exemptions & reliefs (see Chapter 3)

  AND

- Certain lifetime gifts and other transfers (Chapter 4)

What Does 'Domiciled' Mean?

Broadly speaking, 'domicile' is a concept similar to nationality and for most people it will be pretty obvious whether or not they are UK domiciled. Nevertheless, this analogy is not entirely accurate and 'domicile' can sometimes be a highly complex matter. We will therefore return to a detailed examination of it in Chapter 14.

The important thing to understand for UK tax purposes is that we first have to decide whether someone is UK domiciled under the general principles which we will examine in Chapter 14 and then also consider whether they are deemed to be UK domiciled for UK tax purposes under the principles outlined below.

Deemed Domicile

From 2017/18 onwards, any individual who has been resident in the UK for more than 15 out of the last 20 UK tax years is deemed to be UK domiciled for *all* UK tax purposes whilst they remain UK resident. This treatment generally starts at the beginning of the 16th year of UK tax residence within any 20 year period. (Or on 6th April 2017 for those who are caught by the new rule in 2017/18.)

Individuals with a UK domicile of origin who have acquired a non-UK domicile of choice, but who later return to the UK, will also be treated as UK domiciled for any year in which they are UK resident from 2017/18 onwards. (See Chapter 14 for the definitions of 'domicile of origin' and 'domicile of choice'.)

Prior to 2017/18, an individual was deemed to be UK domiciled for IHT purposes if they had been tax resident here for at least 17 out of the last 20 UK tax years. Before 2017/18, this did not affect their position in respect of Income Tax or Capital Gains Tax ('CGT').

From 2013/14 onwards, an individual's tax residence is determined under the statutory residence test. In some cases, this may effectively hasten, or prolong, their deemed UK domicile. For further details of the statutory residence test, see the Taxcafe.co.uk guide *'Tax Free Capital Gains'*.

Immigration

An 'excluded property trust' may be used to exclude from UK IHT any foreign property held for the benefit of a person who originally had foreign domicile but later becomes either UK domiciled or deemed UK domiciled. See Section 9.11 for more details.

Emigration

An individual who ceases to be UK domiciled under general principles will continue to have deemed UK domicile for IHT purposes for another five years thereafter. For those who left the UK before 6th April 2017, this additional period of deemed UK domicile was only three years.

Emigration is covered in more detail in Chapter 14.

Non-Domiciled Individuals

If you are neither UK domiciled, nor deemed to be UK domiciled, as explained above, then IHT will generally only arise on any UK assets that you hold, including land and buildings situated within the UK. Again, this liability arises on death or in the event of certain lifetime transfers which we will cover later in the guide.

Foreign currency bank accounts held by a non-UK domiciled individual at the time of their death are generally exempt from IHT, even when held with a UK bank or the Post Office. For the purpose of this exemption, the deceased must also be non-UK resident at the time of death.

Assets which are exempt from IHT by reason of a person's non-UK domiciled status are referred to as 'excluded property'.

From 6th April 2017, UK residential property held indirectly by non-UK domiciled individuals (e.g. through a company, trust or more complex structure) is subject to IHT. Minor interests in UK residential property which amount to less than 5% of the individual's worldwide property interests are disregarded however.

The countries listed in Appendix B have Double Tax Treaties with the UK, which may affect your position if you are domiciled there. This will sometimes also apply to the question of 'deemed domicile'.

2.3   WHO ACTUALLY PAYS THE TAX?

Despite my comments in Section 2.1, most IHT does still arise on death and, naturally, the deceased is not around to pick up the bill!

For specific bequests of real property, i.e. land and buildings (e.g. "I leave my house to my daughter Michelle"), there is a presumption that the beneficiary will bear the tax arising. Conversely, for bequests of cash and other assets (e.g. quoted shares, antiques, etc), there is a presumption that the personal representatives will settle the tax arising out of the assets of the estate.

In both cases, however, it is possible for the Will to direct that the tax arising should be borne in the opposite way (i.e. by the personal representatives or by the beneficiary, as the case may be).

A beneficiary becoming entitled to a life interest in property under the terms of a Will must generally bear the tax arising on their legacy.

For property already held in trust, but which is included in the beneficiary's estate for IHT purposes (as explained in Chapter 8), the tax may fall on the trustees or on a beneficiary of that trust, depending on the exact circumstances.

Subject to the above points, the liability for any further IHT arising on the residue of the estate will generally fall on the deceased's personal representatives who must again settle it out of the assets of the estate.

2.4   GROSSING UP

The amount of IHT payable on a specific asset or bequest may be affected by whether or not it is paid by the personal representatives. This is due to the procedure known as 'Grossing Up' and is best explained by way of a short example.

Example

John leaves his eldest son, Paul, a house worth £180,000, on condition that he settles any tax arising. He also leaves his younger son, George, the sum of £180,000 in cash, stating in his Will that this sum should be free of all taxes.

As Paul has to settle the IHT on his bequest directly, he will pay IHT at a straightforward rate of 40%, i.e. £72,000.

The IHT on George's bequest will, however, be paid by John's personal representatives, Ringo & Co. This brings 'Grossing Up' into play. In other words, George's bequest must be grossed up to account for the IHT being paid out of John's estate.

The 'Grossing Up' factor is two-thirds. Hence, an additional two-thirds must be added to George's bequest of £180,000, producing a grossed up amount of £300,000 (£180,000 PLUS two thirds of £180,000, i.e. £120,000).

The IHT due on this bequest is therefore £120,000 (i.e. £300,000 x 40%). As can readily be seen, this is equal to the amount of the 'Grossing Up', meaning that Ringo & Co. can now give the original sum of £180,000 to George free of any further tax liabilities.

NOTE: In this example, I have assumed that the remainder of the estate passes to an exempt beneficiary, such as John's widow or a charity.

Furthermore, for the sake of simplicity, I have ignored the impact of any applicable reliefs and exemptions, including the nil rate band. I have also assumed that there are sufficient other assets within the estate to enable the personal representatives to settle the IHT liability arising on George's bequest.

'Grossing Up' will only apply to the calculation of the tax payable on death when there is an exempt beneficiary entitled to some or all of the residue of the estate remaining after dealing with all of the specific bequests. It is of course that exempt person, or body, often the surviving spouse, who will ultimately suffer the impact of the 'Grossing Up' calculations.

In the absence of an exempt beneficiary, 'Grossing Up' cannot apply since the same total amount of IHT will always be payable out of the estate. The exact wording of each bequest may nevertheless still affect how much IHT is effectively borne by each beneficiary.

2.5   WHO ARE THE PERSONAL REPRESENTATIVES?

Where the deceased has left a Will, their executors are their personal representatives. In the case of a person dying intestate (i.e. without a valid Will), the person applying for a grant of representation (i.e. probate), or confirmation in Scotland, will be the personal representative.

Where no personal representative has been appointed by the court within twelve months after the end of the month of death then the deceased's beneficiaries will be required to fulfil the obligations regarding payment of IHT, delivery of accounts, etc, which would normally fall on the personal representatives.

2.6 WHO PAYS THE TAX ON LIFETIME TRANSFERS?

The primary responsibility for any IHT arising on lifetime transfers falls on the transferor. It is possible, however, to stipulate that the transferee should bear any IHT arising (see Memorandum 2 in Appendix D).

Additional IHT liabilities frequently arise when the transferor dies within seven years of a lifetime transfer. These liabilities usually fall on the transferee.

'Grossing Up' can also apply to lifetime transfers, although a lower 'grossing up' rate of one quarter applies. IHT on lifetime transfers is examined in more detail in Chapter 4.

2.7 COLLECTION OF TAX

As we can see from the preceding sections, the liability for IHT may fall on any of:

- The transferor,
- The transferee,
- The deceased's personal representatives, or
- The deceased's beneficiaries

Naturally, HMRC will, in the first instance, attempt to collect the tax due from the correct party. However, if they encounter any difficulty in collecting the tax from the correct party, they will look to any other party to the relevant transaction.

Hence, in the case of IHT arising on death, if a beneficiary is unable to pay their share of the tax, HMRC will then collect it from the personal representatives out of the remaining assets of the estate. Furthermore, the tax may then also have to be grossed up (see Section 2.4).

Conversely, a beneficiary who should have received a bequest free from IHT under the terms of the deceased's Will could end up having to bear part of the IHT arising when there are insufficient liquid funds left in the remaining estate.

Transferees should usually bear any extra tax arising when the transferor dies within seven years of making a gift (see Section 4.5) but this rule will also be overridden if HMRC finds it necessary to do so.

Example

In July 2017, George, a single man, gave his old friend Andrew £500,000 to help him out. Sadly, things continued to go from bad to worse for Andrew and, in 2018, he was declared bankrupt.

In March 2019, George dies and the earlier gift to Andrew becomes chargeable to IHT. George had also made earlier chargeable transfers in excess of his nil rate band during the seven years prior to July 2017, so the gift to Andrew is fully exposed to IHT (see Section 4.5).

As HMRC will be unable to collect the IHT due on Andrew's gift from him, they will look to George's personal representatives to pay the tax out of the assets of the estate. Instead of the original £200,000 (at 40%), however, the IHT due on this gift will now be £333,333 (two-thirds – see Section 2.4).

In short, HMRC doesn't really care who pays the tax, as long as it is collected. This is why it will often make sense to take out term assurance to cover IHT costs arising in the event of an unexpected early death and we will look at this further in Section 10.15.

2.8   HOW MUCH TAX IS PAYABLE?

On death, IHT is levied, generally at one single rate of 40%, on the entire value of your estate, less certain exemptions. The most important exemptions are the nil rate band, which is £325,000 for deaths occurring between 6th April 2009 and 5th April 2021, the exemption for transfers to spouses (see Section 3.3) and, for deaths occurring after 5th April 2017, the residence nil rate band (see Section 3.4).

Personal representatives of widows or widowers may be able to claim up to double the current nil rate band and residence nil rate band where the first spouse to die did not fully utilise their own nil rate band or residence nil rate band. We will cover this subject in detail in Chapter 6.

Lifetime Transfers

Where a lifetime transfer gives rise to an immediate IHT charge, the rate applying is 20%, sometimes known as 'the lifetime rate'. Extra tax will often become payable on lifetime transfers in the event of the taxpayer's subsequent death within seven years and we will look at this in detail in Section 4.5.

Transfers made directly to spouses are usually tax free. Furthermore, the £325,000 nil rate band can be deducted from the total value of transfers made in the last seven years. As we shall see in Chapter 4, this is very important because it means that tax-free transfers equivalent to the nil rate band can be made every seven years.

2.9   WHAT IS YOUR ESTATE?

Your 'estate' means everything you own, including land and property, shares and securities, savings accounts, cash, antiques, jewellery, paintings, your car, your furniture and anything else that has any monetary value whatsoever.

Income arising up to the date of death must also be included (e.g. unpaid pensions or salary, accrued bank interest, etc.). Also included in the deceased's estate will be:

i)   The net value of any assets held on their behalf in certain types of trust (see Chapter 8),

ii)   The value of any relevant 'gifts with reservation' (see Section 4.9), and

iii) The value of any assets that they elect to have included in their estate in order to prevent an Income Tax charge on a deemed benefit in kind (see Section 13.3)

For the purposes of IHT, any non-exempt transfers of value made in the seven years prior to death will also effectively be brought back into the deceased's estate. Reduced IHT rates do, however, apply to gifts made more than three, but less than seven, years prior to death.

Any liabilities, such as your mortgage, overdrafts, bank loans, credit card bills, outstanding utility bills, etc., may generally be deducted; although restrictions may sometimes apply (see Section 2.12). You may even deduct outstanding Income Tax and CGT liabilities!

'Reasonable' funeral expenses may also be deducted. What is 'reasonable' depends on your standard of living. (In one extreme case, the expense of a private army providing an honour guard at the funeral was deemed to be 'reasonable'.)

In other words, subject to a few adjustments, your 'estate' is basically your total net worth.

All of the property transferred on your death is subject to IHT in the same way, whether it transfers under the terms of your Will, by intestacy, by survivorship (for jointly held property) or by any other means.

Tax Tip

Many people take out insurance policies to cover outstanding liabilities, such as credit card bills or bank loans, if they should pass away unexpectedly. The result of this is that these liabilities would not be deductible from the value of the estate as they were automatically settled on the taxpayer's death.

It would be far better to make provision for such liabilities by other means (see Section 10.13) and thus ensure that they are deducted from the value of your estate for IHT purposes.

20

Wealth Warning

Many people assume that tax-advantaged products, such as Individual Savings Accounts are exempt from IHT because they are supposedly 'tax-free'. Unfortunately, this is not the case and *ALL* assets have to be included in your estate, regardless of their treatment for Income Tax or CGT purposes.

Wealth Warning

Household personal effects are generally overvalued, resulting in unnecessary overpayments of IHT. The valuations that most people have on their personal effects (jewellery, antiques, silverware, etc,) tend to be insurance valuations. However, the amount on which IHT is payable should only be the open market value of the assets and this is often considerably less.

2.10   THE BASIC CALCULATION ON DEATH

To illustrate the basic IHT calculation, let's take a look at a very simple example:

Example

Arthur has been very careful with his money all his life. At the time of his death in December 2018, his estate amounts to £3m.

Arthur has been divorced for many years and his Will leaves his entire estate to his son Tony. Hence, there are no exemptions available, other than the nil rate band.

The first £325,000 of Arthur's estate is exempt from IHT, as it is covered by the nil rate band. The remaining £2.675m is charged to IHT at 40%, giving rise to a tax charge of £1.07m!

2.11   MAKING THE PAYMENT

IHT arising on death is normally due six months after the end of the month of death. Hence, in the case of Arthur who died in December 2018, it will be due by 30th June 2019. Personal representatives may sometimes have to pay the tax earlier, however, as the liability is triggered when they deliver their accounts for probate or confirmation purposes.

This same payment date applies to all IHT arising on death, both on the deceased's estate itself and on gifts made within the previous seven years (see Section 4.5).

The personal representatives may elect for any tax on land or buildings within the deceased's estate to be paid in ten equal yearly instalments, commencing six months after the month of death.

If the property concerned is subsequently sold, however, then all of the remaining unpaid IHT relating to that property becomes payable immediately.

Interest is normally charged on, and added to, payments made by instalments. Interest is, of course, usually also charged on late payments under any other circumstances.

Since 2009, the interest rate applying has been 3%: the same as for most other major taxes. (Clearly, the Government has no sympathy for bereaved families suffering from both financial turmoil and emotional distress!)

When interest arises on either instalments or other late payments of IHT, there will be no Income Tax relief for it.

The beneficiaries could, instead, perhaps borrow the money to pay their IHT bills. Sadly, however, the IHT is regarded as a personal liability and the interest on such borrowings would generally therefore again be ineligible for Income Tax relief.

Tax Tip

> There is a potential way around this dilemma. If the beneficiary borrows the money to pay the IHT bill by re-mortgaging their own home then, if they subsequently move out of the house and turn it into a rental property, they will be eligible for Income Tax relief on the mortgage interest against their rental income. The beneficiary could then move into one of the inherited properties and adopt it as their new home.

Alternatively, the beneficiary could obtain Income Tax relief by re-mortgaging one or more rental properties up to the level of their market value at the time of introduction into the rental business.

The obvious step might therefore seem to be to re-mortgage an inherited property, use this to pay the tax and then rent that property out. The problem, however, is that the IHT generally has to be paid before the beneficiary can take title to the property.

The beneficiary's own home may provide the answer to this problem once more.

Example

Cheryl inherits her Aunt Sarah's house but has an IHT liability of £100,000 to settle. Cheryl therefore re-mortgages her own home and uses this money to pay the IHT.

After taking title to Sarah's old house, Cheryl mortgages that property and uses the funds to repay the mortgage on her own home. Cheryl then rents out Sarah's old house and is able to claim her mortgage interest against the rental income.

Wealth Warning 1

If an inherited property is already a rental property, interest relief may only be available on any borrowings against the property made up to the value of the property at the time when the deceased first rented it out.

Wealth Warning 2

Interest relief for borrowings on residential rental property is now being restricted for Income Tax purposes and will be progressively reduced to basic rate only over the next few years. See the Taxcafe.co.uk guide *'How to Save Property Tax'* for details.

Nonetheless, the techniques described above remain useful: after all, relief at the basic rate of 20% is still a lot better than no relief at all!

Selling Inherited Properties

If it becomes necessary to sell one or more inherited properties in order to pay IHT, there is one crumb of comfort in the fact that there is unlikely to be much CGT to pay, as we shall see in Section 11.2.

Paying Tax on Lifetime Transfers

Where IHT becomes payable on a lifetime transfer, it is due as follows:

i)   Gifts made between 6th April and 30th September – IHT is due on 30th April in the following year.

ii) Gifts made between 1st October and 5th April – IHT is due six months after the end of the month in which the gift is made.

From a pure cashflow point of view, therefore, the best day to make a chargeable gift is 6th April. (This may not always fit in with the rest of your planning though!)

Repayments

Where there is an overpayment of IHT, the rate of interest applying to the repayment of the excess is just 0.5%. This effectively means the Government is making an additional profit of 2.5% from the many bereaved families who are forced to make estimated IHT payments in an effort to meet the Government's own deadlines! (Any underpayments are charged with interest at 3%, whilst those who overpay receive a mere 0.5% in compensation.)

2.12   LOANS AND OTHER LIABILITIES

There are a number of restrictions applying to the deduction of liabilities for IHT purposes. In this section, I will cover the general principles of these restrictions and look at how they apply in a few practical scenarios. As we progress through the guide, I will also look at how the restrictions affect various IHT planning techniques.

Liabilities on Death

Liabilities may generally only be deducted from the value of the deceased's estate where the liability is actually discharged (i.e. paid) out of the assets of the estate.

The only exception to this rule arises where:

> i) There is a commercial reason for the non-payment of the liability, and

> ii) The non-payment does not give rise to any tax advantage (or any such advantage which arises was not a main purpose behind the non-payment).

For there to be a valid commercial reason for the non-payment, it is necessary to show either that:

> i) The liability was due to an unconnected party operating on an arms' length basis, or that

> ii) An unconnected party operating on an arms' length basis would have accepted the non-payment.

As far as tax advantages arising out of the non-payment are concerned, this provision is very wide-ranging and generally covers any situation where any person enjoys any saving or deferral of any kind of tax. However, it only applies where the non-payment of the liability gives rise to a tax advantage: not simply because the liability itself creates a tax advantage.

Example 1

Leona dies and leaves her house to her daughter Alexandra. The house is subject to a mortgage. The lender allows Alexandra to take over the mortgage so that it does not need to be repaid immediately.

The lender is an unconnected party operating on an arms' length basis so, although the mortgage has not been repaid out of the assets of Leona's estate, it may still be deducted from the value of her estate for IHT purposes.

Example 2

Gareth lends £20,000 to his father, Simon, on condition that it be repaid on the later of Simon's death or Simon's wife's death. Simon dies first. The loan is not repaid at that time.

Allowing a loan to be repaid on the second of a couple's deaths is a normal commercial arrangement. Hence, although Gareth is a connected party, the non-payment of the loan at the time of Simon's death does not prevent the loan from being deducted from the value of Simon's estate for IHT purposes.

This example shows that it is possible for a non-arms' length loan from a connected party to not be repaid immediately and still be deductible from the deceased borrower's estate: provided that the non-payment is permitted on a normal commercial basis.

It is, however, vital that the loan documentation is drawn up correctly. If, for example, the loan agreement only stated that 'the lender may permit the loan to be repaid on the second death' then an unconnected party operating on an arms' length basis would generally call for the loan to be repaid on the first death – unless the loan were secured (on the borrower's home or other property) and subject to interest at a commercial rate. (Such interest would of course give rise to Income Tax liabilities for the lender.)

Practical Implications

In practice, due to the spouse exemption (see Section 3.3), it is generally only on the second death in a married couple that it becomes important to be able to deduct outstanding liabilities from the estate.

At that stage, any liability is only likely to be deductible if:

- It is a secured loan on full commercial terms and one or more of the deceased's beneficiaries takes over the liability together with the asset on which the loan is secured,
- It is an arms' length commercial arrangement which one or more of the deceased's beneficiaries takes over (e.g. a business overdraft), or
- It is repaid out of the assets of the deceased's estate.

Paying Liabilities Out of the Estate

There are a number of ways in which liabilities may be paid out of the assets of the deceased's estate in order to qualify for deduction from the estate for IHT purposes.

Firstly, of course, the personal representatives can simply pay the liability out of cash held by the deceased or the proceeds of sale of the deceased's assets. There is no restriction where the cash or assets are themselves exempt (e.g. a foreign bank account held by a non-UK domiciled individual).

Alternatively, the deceased's personal representatives could take out a new loan and use it to repay the deceased's liabilities. The new loan would need to be charged against the assets of the estate.

It would then either need to be repaid by selling some of the assets of the estate before they are passed to the deceased's beneficiaries or taken over by one or more of the beneficiaries inheriting those assets.

A new loan used to repay the deceased's liabilities could come from any source: including the deceased's beneficiaries.

Wealth Warning

If a life insurance policy has been written in trust so that it falls outside the deceased's estate (see Section 10.14), it is vital that the proceeds aren't used directly to settle the deceased's liabilities, as these would then not have been paid out of the assets of the deceased's estate and would not be deductible.

Tax Tip

Life insurance proceeds could, however, be paid out to one of the deceased's beneficiaries who could then lend those funds to the deceased's personal representatives to enable them to pay the deceased's liabilities.

Example 3

Sharon dies leaving a house worth £800,000. She had a life insurance policy written in trust which yields £250,000 and she owed her son Jack £200,000: the total of a number of loans he had made to her in her latter years.

If Jack's loan is not repaid, it cannot be deducted from Sharon's estate and her IHT liability will be £190,000 (£800,000 - £325,000 = £475,000 x 40% = £190,000).

If the life insurance proceeds are paid directly to Jack in repayment of his loan then the loan will not have been settled out of the assets of Sharon's estate and her IHT liability will again be £190,000.

Instead, however, the life insurance proceeds are paid out to Sharon's daughter, Kelly. Kelly then lends £200,000 to Sharon's estate. The loan is charged against Sharon's house. Sharon's personal representatives use the £200,000 borrowed from Kelly to repay Jack meaning that his loan can be deducted from Sharon's estate for IHT purposes. This reduces Sharon's IHT liability to £110,000 (£800,000 - £200,000 - £325,000 = £275,000 x 40% = £110,000).

Sharon's house is then passed to Kelly subject to the £200,000 charge against it. Since the charge is in Kelly's name, she can then have it removed.

In theory, a similar strategy could be used where Jack was the sole beneficiary of both Sharon's estate and the life insurance policy. It would, however, be vital to ensure that Jack's original loan was repaid by way of a new loan from him to the estate and not repaid directly out of the insurance proceeds. In such a case, a good lawyer who knew their way around all of the necessary documentation would be essential!

Liabilities Incurred to Acquire Relievable Property

Certain types of business property, agricultural property and woodlands are eligible for relief from IHT. We will look at these types of 'relievable property' and the relevant reliefs in detail in Chapter 7.

Prior to 2013, it was not necessary to match relievable property with the liabilities incurred to acquire it. Hence, it was often possible to acquire an asset which was exempt from IHT and still get a full deduction for any borrowings used to acquire that asset.

However, for all transfers of value (whether arising on death or otherwise) taking place after 16th July 2013, any liabilities incurred to finance the acquisition, enhancement or maintenance of relievable property, must be taken to reduce the value attributed to that property (subject to the comments below regarding liabilities incurred before 6th April 2013).

A liability will be deemed to have financed relievable property where it is used directly or indirectly for that purpose. Guidance issued by HMRC indicates that they are taking a very broad view of what can be taken to have been used to indirectly finance relievable property. An example of some of their thinking on this subject is included in Section 7.29 although, as ever, it must be emphasised that HMRC guidance is not the law and it is for the courts to decide whether such a case would actually be caught in practice.

Liabilities Incurred Before 6th April 2013

Liabilities incurred before 6th April 2013 are exempt from being attributed to relievable property and may generally continue to be deducted in full from the general assets of the deceased's estate (subject to the other rules described in this section and the treatment of business liabilities discussed in Section 7.12).

However, where a liability incurred before 6th April 2013 is refinanced or varied on or after that date it will be treated as a new liability and it will then be caught by the new rules.

Wealth Warning

Replacing or varying any loans or other liabilities incurred before 6th April 2013 which have been used, directly or indirectly, to finance business property, agricultural property or woodlands, in any way, could lead to significant increases in your IHT liability.

27

I will look at the practical implications of the restriction on 'liabilities incurred to acquire relievable property' in more detail in Chapter 7.

Liabilities Incurred to Acquire Excluded Property

A similar restriction also operates where liabilities have been incurred to acquire 'excluded property'.

'Excluded property' means any assets which are exempt from UK IHT because they are non-UK assets and are owned by either:

- An individual who is non-UK domiciled and also not subject to deemed domicile (see Section 2.2 and Chapter 14), or
- An 'excluded property trust' (see Section 9.11)

For all transfers of value taking place after 16th July 2013, any liabilities incurred to finance the acquisition, enhancement or maintenance of excluded property, must be taken to reduce the value attributed to that property. In effect, this means that such liabilities are non-deductible for UK IHT purposes. This restriction applies to all liabilities incurred at any time: there is no exemption for liabilities incurred prior to 6th April 2013.

Once again, any liabilities which have indirectly financed the acquisition, enhancement or maintenance of excluded property are caught by this restriction and HMRC is taking a very broad view of the scope of this provision.

Example

Stuart is single and is domiciled in Germany. He owns a house in Liverpool worth £600,000. He mortgages his UK house for £400,000 and uses the money to buy some shares on the London Stock Exchange. A year later, Stuart sells all of his shares, realising an overall gain, and then uses all of the proceeds to buy a house in Germany.

A short time later, Stuart dies. He is subject to UK IHT on the full value of his house in Liverpool (after deducting his nil rate band and possibly also the residence nil rate band if the house qualifies). His mortgage cannot be deducted because it has been used indirectly to acquire excluded property (his German house).

In this example, Stuart has realised an overall gain on his shares and hence the entire £400,000 mortgage on his Liverpool house is deemed to have indirectly financed his German property. If he had made an overall loss on his shares, part of the mortgage would remain deductible from the value of his chargeable UK property.

For example, let's say that Stuart sold all his shares for £375,000 and used this sum to buy his German property. He would then be able to deduct £25,000 (his overall loss on the shares) from the value of his Liverpool property for UK IHT purposes.

Interest-Free Loans

HMRC's own IHT manual states: "The grant of an interest free loan repayable on demand is not a transfer of value (because the value of the loan is equal to the amount of it)." [IHTM 14317]

This opens up significant IHT planning opportunities and we will see several possible applications of this principle throughout this guide. The planning opportunities provided by interest free loans have, however, been severely curtailed since 2013 due to the restrictions discussed earlier in this section.

In most cases, it will now be essential for the loan to be repaid out of the assets of the deceased's estate in order for the planning to work as intended. This may not always be possible. Nevertheless, we will look at the practical implications arising as we consider the relevant planning techniques throughout the remainder of this guide.

2.13   QUICK SUCCESSION RELIEF

Back in the 'bad old days' of estate duty, families were often financially crippled when two generations died in quick succession. Imagine it: just as the family was struggling to recover from one set of death duties, they were landed with another lot. This happened so much in the First World War that the 'Death on Active Service' exemption (see Section 3.8) was brought in.

Thankfully, we now have quick succession relief, which provides some relief from IHT whenever a transferee dies within five years of having received an earlier transfer on which IHT was paid, or on which IHT subsequently becomes payable (bearing in mind that the tax can arise up to seven years after the original transfer).

Having said that, the value of quick succession relief declines pretty quickly and hence the crippling effects of IHT are therefore unfortunately still with us.

The amount of the relief is arrived at by way of the following formula:

QSR = 'Percentage' x Original Tax x Net Transfer/Gross Transfer

The 'Percentage' referred to above is as follows:

Period between original transfer and transferee's death	Percentage
One year or less:	100%
More than one year, but not more than two:	80%
More than two years, but not more than three:	60%
More than three years, but not more than four:	40%
More than four years, but not more than five:	20%

Example

On 5th May 2016, Ewan died and left £600,000 to his daughter, Kirsty. The IHT on this legacy was settled out of Ewan's estate. Grossing-up therefore applied (see Section 2.4), giving rise to an IHT bill of £400,000.

Sadly, in December 2018, Kirsty dies in an accident and leaves her estate to her friend Shane. Kirsty's executors can now claim quick succession relief. The relevant amounts for the calculation are as follows:

Percentage:	*60% (death between two and three years after original transfer)*
Original Tax:	*£400,000*
Net Transfer:	*£600,000*
Gross Transfer:	*£1,000,000 (after applying 'grossing up' on Ewan's death)*

The quick succession relief is therefore:

$$60\% \times £400,000 \times £600,000/£1,000,000 = £144,000$$

The reason for the 'Net Transfer/Gross Transfer' element of the formula is to ensure that the relief applies only to the net funds left in the transferee's estate after accounting for the IHT payable on the earlier transfer.

If you think about it, Kirsty only received £600,000 from Ewan's estate, so it would be illogical (although nice) for her to get relief for the tax paid on the entire £1m 'grossed-up' legacy.

Quick succession relief can also apply where either the first or second transfer (or both) was a lifetime transfer made within seven years of the transferor's death. It is not to be confused with taper relief (see Section 4.5), however, as the two reliefs operate independently of each other.

Chapter 3

The Main Exemptions

3.1 WHAT IS AN EXEMPTION?

IHT exemptions come in many different forms. Some exemptions are based on value, others on the relationship between the transferor and the transferee, still others on the nature of the transferee alone and some even on the circumstances of the transferor's demise.

Some exemptions have a general application, others apply only to lifetime transfers and others only to transfers made on death.

In Chapter 5, we will look at the IHT exemptions that apply only to lifetime transfers. In this chapter, we will concentrate on exemptions which apply regardless of whether the gift or transfer is made during the transferor's lifetime or on death; or which apply only on death.

In each case, there are a number of exceptions designed to prevent the exemption from being abused.

3.2 THE NIL RATE BAND

The nil rate band is probably the most important IHT exemption for the vast majority of people. As the name suggests, an IHT rate of nil is applied to the first part of your estate, which falls within this band.

The amount of nil rate band available depends on the date of death (or the date of transfer in the case of chargeable lifetime transfers – see Section 4.2). The current nil rate band applying to deaths or chargeable lifetime transfers between 6th April 2009 and 5th April 2021 is £325,000. The nil rate bands applying in previous years are set out in Appendix A.

Any part of the nil rate band which was not used on the earlier death of the deceased's spouse may additionally be claimed. This means that up to double the normal amount of the nil rate band may be available on the death of any widows, widowers or surviving civil partners. This has enormous implications for IHT planning for all married persons and we will look at this subject in detail in Chapter 6.

Despite this, it remains important to note that each individual has their own nil rate band. I will come back to this point, and explain its significance in IHT planning, later.

Up until 2009, the nil rate band, like many other tax exemptions, was generally increased on an annual basis, in line with inflation.

However, as is also the case with many other tax exemptions, the increase was generally only given by reference to retail price inflation.

In 2010, Labour Chancellor, Alistair Darling, announced a five year freeze in the nil rate band at its 2009/10 level of £325,000. This disgraceful departure from Gordon Brown's earlier promise to increase the nil rate band to £350,000 was later compounded by another despicable 'U-turn': this time from Conservative Chancellor, George Osborne, who abandoned his party's plans to increase the nil rate band to £1m by 2015 and adopted Darling's five year freeze instead; later extending it to eight years and then, in the Summer 2015 Budget, to twelve!

We are therefore now stuck with a nil rate band of just £325,000 until at least 5th April 2021.

When Tony Blair's 'New Labour' came to power in 1997, the nil rate band stood at £215,000. By the end of the 24 year period from then until 2021 it will still stand at just £325,000: a total increase over the period of just 51%. By contrast, in the period from May 1997 to August 2017, average UK house prices increased by **over 265%** (even after taking account of the fall in 2008 and 2009).

Hence, if the nil rate band had been increased, as seems appropriate, in line with house price inflation, it should have stood at over £785,000 by now.

What house prices will do over the next three years is anybody's guess but, even if we see a return to moderate annual growth rates of just 7.5%, an appropriate value for the nil rate band by 2021 might be something in the region of £1,050,000.

Even taking the residence nil rate band (see Section 3.4) into account, this will still leave many homeowners facing around £220,000 in extra IHT simply because of the Government's failure to keep pace with property prices. How's that for stealth tax!

The twelve year freeze in the nil rate band means that the Government's 'take' from IHT can be expected to steadily increase over the next few years. By 2007, the revenue raised by the Government through IHT on bereaved families was already **more than double** its 1997 equivalent; who knows how bad it could get by 2021?

The Future of the Nil Rate Band

Amongst the many contradictory announcements made about the nil rate band by various Chancellors was a proposal that it would be increased in line with the Consumer Prices Index ('CPI') once the current freeze period comes to an end.

Although the freeze period has been extended twice, the most likely prediction for the nil rate band beyond then would therefore still seem to be that it will begin to increase in line with the CPI from 2021/22 onwards.

The CPI takes absolutely no account of housing costs and has historically run at around 1% to 1.5% less than the Retail Prices Index. Using the lower index will therefore severely slow down the rate of increase in the nil rate band and lead to even greater shortfalls in future in comparison to house price inflation.

For the remainder of this guide, unless stated to the contrary, any predictions about the nil rate band beyond 2021 will be based on the assumption that it is increased annually in line with the CPI and that this lower inflation measure averages 2.5% per annum.

3.3   THE SPOUSE EXEMPTION

Except as noted below, all transfers of property made directly to your spouse are completely exempt from IHT. This covers both lifetime transfers and transfers made on death. The general exemption for transfers to a spouse opens up a wealth of planning opportunities and we will return to this subject in detail in Chapter 6.

Transfers to a Non-Domiciled Spouse or Civil Partner

The general exemption for transfers to a spouse usually operates without limit.

However, in the case of transfers from a UK domiciled person to their non-UK domiciled spouse, the exemption for transfers between spouses is restricted.

For transfers taking place after 5th April 2013, it is possible to remove this restriction if the foreign domiciled spouse elects to 'opt in' and be treated as UK domiciled for IHT purposes. We will look at this election, its benefits and pitfalls, in more detail in Section 6.19.

In the absence of any such election covering the time at which a transfer is made from a UK domiciled person to their non-UK domiciled spouse, only the following maximum amounts may be covered by the spouse exemption:

- For transfers made before 6th April 2013: £55,000
- For transfers made after 5th April 2013: an amount equal to the amount of the nil rate band (currently £325,000)

These limits apply on a cumulative basis and, once exceeded, any further transfers, both during the transferor's lifetime and on their death, will be treated just like any other transfer made to a person other than their spouse.

One single limit applies for the whole of the transferor's lifetime, even if they are divorced or widowed and later marry again to another foreign domiciled person.

Example

Donna is domiciled in the UK, but is married to Sean who is US domiciled. In 2012, Donna gave Sean £60,000 and, in 2018, she gave him a further £300,000.

£55,000 of Donna's first gift is covered by the spouse exemption, the remaining £5,000 is not.

£270,000 of Donna's second gift is covered by the spouse exemption, the remaining £30,000 is not. The exempt amount is derived by deducting the previous exempt amount (£55,000) from the new limit (£325,000).

In 2022, Donna divorces Sean and marries Guy who is domiciled in France. In June 2025, when the nil rate band is £371,000, Donna gives Guy £50,000.

£46,000 of this gift is covered by the spouse exemption, the remaining £4,000 is not. The exempt amount is derived by deducting Donna's previous cumulative total of exempt transfers (under the spouse exemption) from the current limit (which is equal to the current nil rate band in 2025/26). [£371,000 - £55,000 - £270,000 = £46,000]

The amounts not covered by the spouse exemption remain eligible for other exemptions in the same way as transfers to any other person. As these are lifetime transfers, many of the exemptions covered in Chapter 5 would be available. Any amounts still not covered by any exemption would be potentially exempt transfers and would only become chargeable to IHT in the event of Donna's death within seven years (see Chapter 4).

Furthermore, it is also important to note that I have assumed that each of the gifts in the example was a capital transfer of value. Many transfers between spouses will not be a capital transfer of value and would be exempted under the provisions covered in Sections 5.6, 5.8, 5.9, or sometimes even 5.10. Where these provisions apply, there is no capital transfer of value and any payments do not need to be counted towards the spouse exemption limit.

For transfers on death in excess of the limit, the nil rate band is available in the usual way, meaning that a UK domiciled spouse will often be able to leave up to £650,000 to a foreign domiciled spouse free from IHT where they have not previously used any of their spouse exemption.

This does, however, depend on whether they have any other beneficiaries and on whether they have made any other chargeable transfers in the previous seven years. In other words, once the spouse exemption has been exhausted, the non-domiciled spouse is in the same position as any other beneficiary (unless they 'opt-in' – see Section 6.19).

Where either spouse is deemed to be UK domiciled (see Section 2.2), they will be treated as UK domiciled in applying the above rules. We will look at IHT planning for married couples with mixed domicile in Section 6.18.

Transfers from a Non-Domiciled Spouse or Civil Partner

There is no restriction on transfers in the opposite direction: from a foreign domiciled spouse to a UK domiciled spouse. Why would there be - such transfers may eventually increase the tax haul. Beware, however, that these transfers might have foreign tax implications!

Other Exceptions to the Spouse Exemption

The general exemption for transfers between spouses is also restricted in a few other circumstances. The exemption may be lost where:

i) The transfer only takes effect after the expiry of another third party's interest in the asset or after the expiry of some other period of time.

Tax Tip

It is, however, acceptable to have a condition in your Will that your spouse must survive you by a certain period before becoming absolutely entitled to the asset.

ii) The transfer is dependent on a condition that is not satisfied within twelve months after the date of transfer.

iii) The transfer is only made as consideration for the transfer of a reversionary interest in some other property.

Transfers into Trust for the Benefit of a Spouse or Civil Partner

The spouse exemption does not generally apply to any transfer made into a trust during the donor's lifetime.

Transfers on death that confer an 'Immediate Post-Death Interest' (see Section 8.12) on a surviving spouse continue to be eligible for the spouse exemption.

What is a Spouse?

For IHT purposes, a spouse must be your legally married husband or wife or your legally registered civil partner.

A 'spouse' is not specifically defined in tax legislation but, for IHT purposes, HMRC takes the view that the exemption continues to apply to any transfer between persons who are still legally married at the time of that transfer.

Unlike CGT, therefore, the IHT exemption for transfers between spouses continues to apply to separated couples right up until the granting of a decree absolute.

Transfers between spouses on separation or as part of divorce proceedings will therefore be covered by the exemption if they are made before the granting of a decree absolute.

Generally speaking, a couple who are legally married under the laws of another country will similarly be recognised as legally married for tax purposes in the UK.

This will even include polygamous marriages when they are legally valid in the taxpayer's country of origin. In such cases, however, the spouse exemption limit discussed above must be applied to the cumulative value of transfers made to all of the transferor's non-UK domiciled spouses.

Wealth Warning

The spouse exemption applies only to married couples. There is no exemption for transfers to common-law partners!

Tax Tip

If you intend leaving most of your estate to a common-law partner then, if you can, try to get married (or enter a civil partnership) before you die. Deathbed marriages have been known to save **millions** of pounds in IHT and it is one planning device that is almost impossible for HMRC to overturn.

3.4   THE RESIDENCE NIL RATE BAND

For deaths occurring after 5th April 2017, the residence nil rate band provides an additional exemption on qualifying residential property. It operates in addition to the main, 'normal' nil rate band and is only available on death.

The amount of residence nil rate band available depends on the year of death, as follows:

2017/18:	£100,000
2018/19:	£125,000
2019/20:	£150,000
2020/21:	£175,000

Thereafter, we are told that the residence nil rate band will be increased in line with inflation, as measured by the slower-moving CPI. (Just as we were once told that the nil rate band would increase in line with the same index from 2015/16 onwards!)

Qualifying Property

In order to qualify for the exemption, a property must have been the deceased's private residence at some point during their ownership. Generally, the property will also need to be in their estate at the time of their death (i.e. still owned by them); except that:

- Property included in their estate under the 'gifts with reservation' rules (see Section 4.9) may qualify.
- There are 'downsizing' provisions to allow the exemption to be claimed where a more expensive qualifying residence has been sold in the past, or where the deceased no longer has a qualifying residence at the time of death. We will look at these provisions in more detail in Section 12.16.

If an individual dies still owning more than one qualifying property, their personal representatives may elect which property the exemption should apply to.

Where an individual resides in 'job-related accommodation', a property which they had acquired with the intention of adopting it as their private residence may qualify for the exemption. See the Taxcafe.co.uk guide *'How to Save Property Tax'* for further details regarding 'job-related accommodation'.

Closely Inherited

The residence nil rate band exemption only applies where the property is passed, on death, to a direct descendant of the deceased. Step children, adopted children and foster children are all accorded the same status as natural children for this purpose. A child who was the deceased's step-child at any time is included.

Generally, the property must pass directly to one or more direct descendants of the deceased in order to qualify.

However, the property may also qualify where it is passed to a trust for the benefit of one or more of the deceased's direct descendants. Only certain types of trust qualify for this purpose, as detailed in Section 8.6.

Example

Nicki divorced her husband many years before her death in June 2019. She leaves her estate, worth £600,000, to her daughter. Nicki's estate includes her former home, which is worth £250,000 at the time of her death.

The residence nil rate band available for 2019/20 exempts £150,000 of the value of Nicki's former home. This reduces her taxable estate to £450,000 before deduction of her main nil rate band of £325,000, which reduces it to £125,000. The IHT payable on Nicki's estate at 40% is thus £50,000.

Tapering

The residence nil rate band is withdrawn from estates worth in excess of £2m. This withdrawal is at the rate of £1 for every £2 by which the estate exceeds this threshold. We are told that the threshold itself will also be increased in line with the CPI from 2021/22 onwards.

Example

Ollie has an estate valued at £2.1m at the time of his death in January 2021. This exceeds the threshold by £100,000, so his available residence nil rate band is reduced by £50,000, from £175,000 to £125,000.

The withdrawal of the residence nil rate band means that, even by 2020/21, it may effectively be lost altogether where the deceased's estate exceeds £2.35m. This effective threshold may perhaps be as high as £2.7m where the deceased is a widow or widower, for the reasons explained below.

The value of the deceased's estate for the purpose of tapering is as detailed in Section 2.9, including items (i) to (iii), as listed in that section. Note that the estate is valued before deducting any reliefs: so even qualifying business property and assets that the deceased is leaving to their spouse will be counted.

Transfers of value in the seven years prior to death are not included for the purpose of tapering, however, and we will look at some of the potential planning implications of this in Section 15.14.

Unused Exemption Passing to Spouse

Like the main nil rate band, any unused proportion of the residence nil rate band passes to the deceased's spouse. This is not automatic, however: the additional transferred residence nil rate band must subsequently be **claimed** by the spouse's personal representatives when that spouse also dies.

Tapering still applies to the amount which may be transferred, however. Hence, for example, in Ollie's case (see above), only 71.4% (£125,000/£175,000 = 71.4%) of his residence nil rate band would transfer to his spouse if he did not use it himself.

Where a married individual died before 6th April 2017, their entire residence nil rate band is deemed to be unused and transfers to their widow or widower. This transfer also remains subject to tapering where the deceased spouse's estate was worth in excess of £2m.

It is important to remember that it is the unused **proportion** which transfers, not the unused **amount**. We will look at this issue in further detail in Chapter 6.

Mortgages and Loans

Any mortgages or other loans secured over a property may have to be taken into account when allocating the residence nil rate band. This is due to the simple fact that the value being transferred to the direct descendant will be the equity value only unless the mortgage or loan is repaid from other sources.

For example, where a property worth £250,000 is passed to the deceased's son subject to the son assuming liability for the outstanding mortgage of £180,000, the exemption will be limited to just £70,000.

Promises, Promises

In Section 1.1, I mentioned that Osborne had claimed that the introduction of the residence nil rate band had effectively fulfilled the promise he made in 2007 to increased the nil rate band to £1m. The word I would like to use here rhymes with 'rowlocks'.

Where:

- Both the main nil rate band and the residence nil rate band are completely unused on the death of a married individual, **and**
- The value of that individual's estate does not exceed £2m, **and**
- Their spouse dies after 5th April 2020, **and**
- The spouse's estate is also not worth in excess of £2m, **and**
- The spouse owns, or has owned, a private residence worth at least £350,000, **and**
- They leave that residence, or the funds arising on its sale, to a direct descendant,

Then, **and only then**, will their estate be eligible for a total exemption of £1m (2 x £325,000 + 2 x £175,000).

That is a million miles from a nil rate band of £1m!

3.5   GIFTS TO CHARITIES & OTHER EXEMPT BODIES

Generally, all gifts to charity are exempt from IHT. This covers both outright gifts and transfers into a Charitable Trust. A charity is defined as 'any body of persons established for charitable purposes only'.

The exemption applies to UK-registered charities and similar organisations based anywhere in the European Union (see Appendix G), Iceland, or Norway.

For charitable organisations based outside the UK to qualify, they must meet the same criteria as would apply to an organisation wishing to register as a charity in England.

Wealth Warning

Foreign charities based in other countries not referred to above are excluded!

Gifts to certain other bodies are also exempt from IHT:

- **Gifts to Housing Associations**
  Transfers of value that are attributable to land in the UK and are made to registered social landlords are exempt from IHT.

- **Gifts for National Purposes**
  Gifts to any of the bodies set out in Appendix E are exempt from IHT.

- **Gifts to Political Parties**
  Gifts to qualifying political parties are exempt from IHT. Funny that, isn't it?

  To qualify, the party must either have had at least two members elected to the House of Commons, or have received no fewer than 150,000 votes in total and had one member elected to the House of Commons, at the last General Election.

3.6   CHARITABLE LEGACIES

Charitable legacies are fully exempt from IHT: provided that the charity meets the criteria that we examined in Section 3.5. An additional relief also applies where the deceased leaves 10% or more of their 'net estate' to charity.

The 'net estate' for this purpose is the deceased's remaining estate after deducting the nil rate band and other applicable IHT exemptions and reliefs.

Where the estate qualifies for the additional relief, a discount of 10% applies to the IHT rate. In other words, the IHT rate on the remaining estate is reduced from 40% to 36%.

Example

Carter, a divorced man, dies in May 2018 leaving an estate valued at £1m. He leaves £67,500 to the local dog and cat home (a registered charity) and everything else to his daughter Yvonne.

Deducting the nil rate band of £325,000 from his estate leaves Carter with a 'net estate' chargeable to IHT of £675,000. He has given 10% of this amount to charity, so the IHT rate on Yvonne's inheritance is reduced to 36%.

After deducting the charitable legacy (which is exempt), and the nil rate band, the chargeable estate amounts to £607,500, so the IHT payable at 36% is £218,700.

Yvonne will therefore inherit a net sum of £713,800 (£1m - £67,500 - £218,700).

It is worth noting that, if Carter had not left anything to charity, the IHT bill would have been £270,000 and Yvonne would have received a net sum of £730,000. The relief does not leave the non-charitable beneficiary better off than they would have been without the charitable legacy so it is not worth contemplating such a legacy just to save IHT.

But, if you are planning to leave a sizeable amount to charity, it is certainly worth checking whether you will meet the 10% threshold.

If, in our example above, Carter had left £60,000 to charity, his chargeable estate would have amounted to £615,000 (£1m - £60,000 - £325,000), giving rise to an IHT bill, at 40%, of £246,000.

Yvonne's net inheritance after tax would then have been just £694,000 (£1m - £60,000 - £246,000). Hence, increasing the charitable legacy by £7,500 would actually leave her £19,800 better off overall!

Planning Issues

Initially, it had been hoped that it would be possible for charitable legacies to be 'topped up' to the required 10% threshold by way of a Deed of Variation (see Section 16.1).

Sadly, however, this does not appear to be the case and it seems that it is necessary for the deceased to have made the appropriate provisions within their Will.

As no-one can be quite sure exactly how much their 'net estate' will amount to, this requires a formula-based approach to ensure the correct result.

As we saw in our example, however, there is no point in making charitable legacies just for the sake of saving IHT: your main beneficiaries will still suffer an overall cost equal to at least 24% of the legacy, even after taking account of the relief.

But, as we also saw, where charitable legacies are already planned, there may actually be an overall saving for your main beneficiaries if you can 'top up' those legacies so that they reach the 10% threshold.

The question is: when does a 'top up' become worthwhile?

The answer to this is that your main beneficiaries will generally be better off overall by topping up your charitable legacies to the 10% threshold when you would otherwise have left charitable legacies equal to more than 4% of your 'net estate'.

Hence, for example, in Carter's case, he had a 'net estate' of £675,000, so Yvonne would benefit from an increase in his charitable legacies to the 10% threshold if he had already planned to give more than £27,000 to charity anyway.

3.7 NATIONAL HERITAGE PROPERTY

Have you ever wondered why so many stately homes are open to the public?

Well, just like the bricked-up windows in old Georgian houses and the roofless buildings we used to see back in the 1970s, it's all because of tax.

IHT arising on transfers of 'national heritage property' can be deferred when the owners give an undertaking to conserve and protect the property. They will also need to provide 'reasonable access to the public'.

The conditions to be satisfied in order to claim this exemption are somewhat complex, including, in most cases, the need for the property to be "pre-eminent for its national, scientific, historic or artistic interest".

So, simply allowing the punters to look at a couple of rusting chassis in your back garden will probably not qualify.

But, if your uncle leaves you his large collection of classic cars, a claim under the 'national heritage property' provisions might be worth thinking about.

3.8 DEATH ON ACTIVE SERVICE

There is a complete exemption from any IHT arising on the death of a person from wound, accident or disease contracted whilst on active military service. A certificate issued by the Ministry of Defence is required in support of any claim under this exemption.

From 6th April 2015, the same exemption has been extended to emergency service personnel who are killed in the line of duty, or whose death is accelerated due to injuries sustained in the line of duty. The exemption has also been extended to aid workers dying under similar circumstances or due to a disease contracted whilst providing aid.

Serving and former police officers or service personnel who are targeted because of their status are also now covered by the exemption.

The value of medals and certain other awards is also exempt from IHT.

Chapter 4

Lifetime Transfers

4.1   INHERITANCE TAX ON LIFETIME TRANSFERS

In Section 2.1, we established that what triggers IHT is not death, but any 'transfer of value'.

Despite this, however, very few transfers made during a person's lifetime actually give rise to any immediate IHT liability.

The reason for this seemingly contradictory position is the fact that any lifetime transfers to another individual are treated as 'Potentially Exempt Transfers' – free of IHT after seven years.

We will return to this concept in Section 4.3 because it remains important to realise that 'potentially exempt' effectively also means 'potentially taxable' and most lifetime transfers are therefore still potentially subject to IHT.

4.2   CHARGEABLE LIFETIME TRANSFERS

As explained above, many lifetime transfers are 'potentially exempt'. However, lifetime transfers of value by an individual to:

- A company, or
- Any trust other than:
    - A disabled trust,
    - A bare trust, or
    - A charitable trust,

will be chargeable (i.e. taxable) lifetime transfers.

Prior to March 2006, it was generally only transfers of value to a company or a discretionary trust that represented chargeable lifetime transfers.

Some readers unfamiliar with the nature of trusts may not feel that this change is particularly restrictive until I tell you that many insurance premiums represent a transfer of value into a trust. (Most of these are, however, exempt for other reasons, as we will see later.)

Chargeable lifetime transfers may be _immediately_ chargeable to IHT, depending on the cumulative value of such transfers made by the transferor within the last seven years.

Transfers of value into companies are rare and the main incidence of chargeable lifetime transfers are therefore transfers into trusts.

The amount of the chargeable transfer is arrived at by deducting any available exemptions (see Chapters 3 and 5) from the 'transfer of value'.

The amount on which IHT is actually chargeable is then the lower of the amount of the chargeable transfer, or the sum derived as follows:

Other chargeable transfers within the last seven years	X
PLUS	
This chargeable transfer	X
LESS	
Nil rate band	(X)

Wealth Warning

Only one nil rate band may be deducted when calculating the IHT on a chargeable lifetime transfer. The transferable nil rate band available to widows, etc, applies only on death.

IHT on lifetime transfers is charged at half death rates, i.e. 20%. Where other chargeable transfers made in the last seven years already equal or exceed the amount of the nil rate band, the tax due on the current chargeable transfer is simply a straight 20%.

Example

(In this example, I will ignore all exemptions and reliefs, other than the nil rate band)

Two years ago, Elvis gifted some investments worth £50,000 into a discretionary trust, thus giving rise to a chargeable transfer. No IHT was payable at the time, however, as this was well within his nil rate band.

Elvis now gifts his former home, Graceland, which is worth £375,000, into a discretionary trust (for the purposes of this example, it does not matter whether this is the same trust or not), on condition that the trust settles any IHT arising.

The trust's IHT liability is calculated as follows:

Previous Chargeable Transfers within last seven years:	*£50,000*
ADD	
This Chargeable Transfer	*£375,000*
EQUALS:	
Cumulative Chargeable Transfers	*£425,000*
LESS:	
Nil rate band	*£325,000*
EQUALS:	
Amount chargeable	*£100,000*
IHT Payable at lifetime rate (20%)	*£20,000*

Alternative Scenario – with 'Grossing Up'

Note that, if Elvis had settled the IHT himself, it would have been subject to 'Grossing Up', as follows:

Amount chargeable, as before	£100,000
Grossing Up factor – one quarter	£25,000
Grossed Up Amount	£125,000
IHT Payable at lifetime rate (20%)	£25,000

Wealth Warning

Note that, in this example, Graceland was Elvis's <u>former</u> home. This is a very important point since, as we will see later in the guide, it is very difficult to make an IHT-effective transfer of your current home.

Tax Tip

If Elvis were married, he could have avoided any IHT on his gift of Graceland by first transferring it into joint names with his wife before they both jointly gifted it to the discretionary trust. Each of them would then have made a chargeable transfer of only £187,500. Even after taking his previous chargeable transfer into account, Elvis would then have been covered by his nil rate band.

Elvis's wife would also be covered by her nil rate band as long as she had not made other chargeable transfers within the last seven years in excess of £137,500.

(As explained in Section 6.15, Elvis's wife must be under no obligation to make the subsequent transfer to the ultimate intended recipient.)

Avoiding 'Grossing Up'

In the above example, we have looked at the situation where the IHT is paid by the transferee (the Trust), as well as the situation where it is paid by the transferor (Elvis himself).

More tax is generally payable where the transferor is settling the liability. This is because the transferor is deemed to be making a gift not only of the original asset transferred, but also of the tax arising. This, in turn, is because the 'transfer of value' is once again calculated by reference to the reduction in value of the transferor's overall estate and the payment of the IHT arising naturally increases the amount of that reduction.

The bad news here is that, in the absence of any evidence to the contrary, the transferor is always assumed to be liable for any IHT. Hence, if care is not exercised, you may find that the value of any gifts that you make turns out to be 25% larger than you had expected!

The way to avoid this is to draw up a memorandum of your gift which stipulates that the transferee is to pay any IHT arising. An example of a suitable memorandum is included as Memorandum 2 in Appendix D.

4.3 POTENTIALLY EXEMPT TRANSFERS

As explained in Section 4.1, many lifetime transfers are potentially exempt transfers, which fall out of the IHT net after seven years. Lifetime transfers made by an individual to one of the following are usually potentially exempt transfers:

    i)   Another individual
    ii) A Bare Trust
    iii) A Disabled Trust

Transfers made *by* a trust are subject to different rules and we will explore these in Chapter 8.

Exceptions

The following transfers will not be treated as potentially exempt transfers:

- Any transfers to your UK-Domiciled spouse (these are fully exempt, except as noted in Section 3.3 above)

- Transfers to your non-UK Domiciled spouse which are covered by the spouse exemption (see Section 3.3)

- Any other transfer covered by another general or lifetime exemption (see Chapters 3 and 5). This will be of no practical consequence unless the transferor dies within seven years of making the transfer

- Any transfer which does not result in an increase in the value of the transferee's estate (see further in Section 4.4 below)

- Transfers of value caused by alterations to share capital, loan capital, or other rights in most private companies

- Deemed, as opposed to actual, transfers of value (e.g. on the cessation of a reservation of benefit on an earlier 'gift with reservation' – see Section 4.9)

- A transfer of value to a disabled trust that does not consist of a transfer of property into the trust (see further in Section 4.4 below)

So What Do We Mean By 'Potentially Exempt'?

Put simply, these transfers are <u>potentially</u> exempt because all the transferor has to do is to survive for seven years after making the transfer for it to then become fully exempt and completely free and clear of any possible IHT liability (subject to the 'gifts with reservation' rules – see Section 4.9).

In the meantime, the transfer is treated for all IHT purposes as if it is exempt (i.e. no IHT is due) and only becomes chargeable if and when the transferor dies within seven years of the date on which the transfer was made. If the transferor is still alive at the beginning of the seventh anniversary of the transfer, full exemption will have been achieved.

Example

On 4th August 2011, Chuck gave £1m to his little brother Richard. Sadly, on 11th August 2018, Chuck is electrocuted while playing his electric guitar in a rainstorm.

The gift to Richard was a potentially exempt transfer and, since Chuck survived the requisite seven years (just!), this sum is completely exempt from IHT on Chuck's death.

Tax Tip

If Chuck had died a week earlier, IHT would have been payable on his gift to Richard (see further in Section 4.5 below).

Hence, it is essential to have the documentary evidence to prove that the gift took place when it did. A memorandum along the lines of one of those shown in Appendix D should suffice for this purpose.

See also Section 4.7 below regarding the timing of gifts made by cheque.

4.4   PROBLEMS WITH PETS

One little known, but potentially important, point about potentially exempt transfers is that there must be an increase in the value of the transferee's estate in order for the transfer to qualify.

Furthermore, where the transferee is a disabled trust, there must be an actual gift of property into the trust.

Any transfers that do not qualify as potentially exempt transfers as a result of failing to meet these requirements will be chargeable lifetime transfers, unless some other exemption is available to cover them.

Examples of transfers of value which do not increase the transferee's estate might include:

i) A grandparent paying their grandchild's school fees. The grandchild, while receiving an indirect benefit, does not enjoy any increase in the value of their estate.

ii) Paying an insurance premium on a policy held for someone else's benefit. The value of the policy remains the same before and after payment of the premium, so there is no increase in the value of the transferee's estate.

iii) A parent paying the maintenance costs for their adult child's house. The value of the house may not necessarily be increased through routine maintenance, so neither is the child's estate.

Each of these payments might, of course, be exempt under the 'normal expenditure out of income' exemption (see Section 5.8). It therefore only matters that they are not potentially exempt transfers when they are not already exempt under that exemption or one of the other exemptions for lifetime transfers which we will examine in Chapter 5.

Nevertheless, in IHT planning, it is important to understand the status of every transfer of value. Remember that chargeable lifetime transfers must effectively be accumulated over a seven-year period and IHT charges will result if the cumulative total exceeds the nil rate band.

Hence, a transfer made today, which turns out to be a chargeable lifetime transfer instead of a potentially exempt transfer, could cause additional IHT charges to arise at any time over the next seven years even if the transferor survives throughout this period.

Looking after your PETS

In the first situation outlined above, the grandparent could avoid the problem by giving the necessary funds to cover the school fees to the child's parent, who would then pay the school fees themselves.

Alternatively, the parent could contract to pay the school fees, with the result that the payment by the grandparent gives rise to an increase in the value of the parent's estate, thus meaning that a potentially exempt transfer has taken place. The key point here is that the grandparent should not contract directly with the school unless they can be certain that the 'normal expenditure out of income' exemption will apply.

The second situation above is perhaps the one most likely to be covered by the 'normal expenditure out of income' exemption. In other cases, the position might be rectified by giving the money to pay the premium to the beneficiary, who then pays it themselves, although this does depend on who the policyholder is and whether the policy is held in trust. We will return to the subject of insurance premiums in Sections 10.13 and 10.14.

The position in the third situation above is perhaps arguable. In a case like this, there is a potentially exempt transfer to the extent that the value of the child's house is increased as a result of the work paid for by the parent. The remainder of the parent's expenditure, however, represents a chargeable lifetime transfer (unless it is covered by another exemption).

Example

Joe's daughter, Sam, would like to have her house completely redecorated. Joe offers to get the work done at his own expense. He contracts for a decorator to do the work, which is then carried out at a cost of £20,000. Joe has therefore made a transfer of value of £20,000.

Before the redecoration work, Sam's house was worth £300,000. Immediately after the work, it is worth £308,000. Joe has therefore made a potentially exempt transfer of £8,000 (the increase in the value of Sam's house), but the remaining £12,000 of his expenditure will be a chargeable lifetime transfer (unless covered by other exemptions).

Joe could have prevented any chargeable lifetime transfer very easily by simply giving all of the money for the work to Sam and leaving her to contract for the work and pay the bill herself.

Alternatively, if Sam had contracted for the work herself and was therefore liable for the decorator's bill, Joe could settle that bill and this would also be a potentially exempt transfer as Sam's estate increases when her liability is settled.

Either way, it is sensible for Sam to contract for the work!

Wealth Warning

If Joe were contractually liable for the work on Sam's house, but he gave Sam the money to pay the bill and she settled it, this could result in further potentially exempt transfers of £20,000 both from Joe to Sam and from Sam to Joe, as well as the transfers already described in the example above.

If **either** of them died within seven years, this could result in additional IHT liabilities arising.

The requirements for a transfer to qualify as a potentially exempt transfer where the transferee is a trust are even more restrictive.

If Sam's house was held by a disabled trust for her benefit, the only way for Joe to fund the redecoration work as a potentially exempt transfer would be for him to give the trust £20,000. The trustees could then contract and pay for the necessary work.

If Joe settled the decorating bill, then this would be a chargeable transfer regardless of who had contracted for the work.

Wealth Warning

Settling a debt on behalf of a disabled trust will not qualify as a potentially exempt transfer.

4.5   DEATH WITHIN SEVEN YEARS OF A LIFETIME TRANSFER

For CGT purposes, death is often a very good tax-planning strategy. The same cannot be said of IHT.

Both chargeable lifetime transfers and potentially exempt transfers made in the seven-year period prior to death are effectively brought back into the deceased's estate for IHT purposes. This applies whether any IHT was actually payable at the time of the original transfer or not.

Subject to the tapering provisions set out below, IHT becomes payable at the death rate (40%) on transfers made within the seven years prior to the transferor's death. Any IHT paid on the original transfer, however, may be deducted, so that it is just the excess that arises on death.

The additional IHT liabilities arising are usually the responsibility of the transferees. In other words, the situation may be like this:

> "I'm very sorry to hear about your father, son, but do you remember that gift of £10,000 that he gave you two years ago? Well, I'm afraid you're going to have to pay some tax on it now."

Now do you see why I call it an 'immoral and evil tax'?

The best way to avoid unwanted liabilities falling on transferees in the event of your death within seven years is to record your intention to bear any tax arising in a memorandum at the time of the gift (see Memorandum 3 in Appendix D). Alternatively, you can make a specific bequest in your Will in respect of the IHT falling on the transferee.

To avoid doubt, it is probably best to do both. There are two problems with both of these approaches, however:

i)   The payment of IHT arising at the time of your death from out of your estate will itself represent another transfer of value and hence 'grossing up' at full death rates will apply.

ii)   The primary responsibility for any IHT arising on death remains with the transferee. If there are insufficient funds remaining in your estate to cover the tax arising, the transferee will still have to foot the bill.

In practice, it often makes more sense for the transferee to take out term assurance on the life of the transferor in order to cover any potential IHT arising on the latter's death.

Conversely, the transferor will often be concerned to ensure that any IHT arising on earlier gifts does not come out of his or her estate and thus reduce the value of the net estate passing to their primary beneficiaries.

In theory, of course, the IHT arising on transfers made in the last seven years of the transferor's life should be paid by the transferees. However, as we saw in Section 2.7, HMRC is more concerned with collecting the tax than with who gets hurt. To put matters (reasonably) beyond doubt, it is therefore wise to use a memorandum specifying the transferee's responsibility for any IHT arising (see Memorandum 2 in Appendix D). Sadly, however, even this will not help if the transferee simply does not have the ability to pay the tax.

Tapering

Fortunately, there is some relief where death occurs more than three, but not more than seven, years after the lifetime transfer. In these cases, the rate of IHT arising on the death is tapered as follows:

No. of years after transfer before death occurs:	Proportion of 40% 'Death Rate' payable
Not more than 3	100% (=IHT @ 40%)
More than 3, not more than 4	80% (=IHT @ 32%)
More than 4, not more than 5	60% (=IHT @ 24%)
More than 5, not more than 6	40% (=IHT @ 16%)
More than 6, not more than 7	20% (=IHT @ 8%)

Tax Tip

Thanks to the tapering provisions, IHT savings may start to arise once the transferor has managed to survive just three years. Hence, even if you don't think that Great Aunt Maude stands any chance of lasting seven years, it may still be worth looking at getting her to make some gifts.

Note, however, that these savings only relate to the lifetime gifts made by the deceased. Tapering has no effect on the amount of IHT payable on the estate itself.

Tapering can therefore only produce a saving where the deceased has made lifetime gifts in excess of the nil rate band.

The reductions in the amount of IHT payable occur on the day of the relevant anniversary.

In the case of chargeable lifetime transfers (see Section 4.2), the tapering provisions could result in the final IHT liability on death actually being less than the amount already paid. Unfortunately, this simply means that no further IHT is due; it does not result in any repayment.

In calculating the IHT due on each transfer made within the seven years prior to death, any chargeable transfers in the seven years before that transfer must be taken into account. For this reason, chargeable lifetime transfers made up to 14 years previously may therefore continue to have an impact on the IHT arising on the transferor's death.

The calculation of the tax arising on transfers made within the seven years prior to death is almost a repeat of the calculation that we saw in Section 4.2 for a chargeable lifetime transfer, except that:

- The full death rate (40%) is used
- Tapering relief (as set out above) is applied
- The nil rate band available at the date of death is used in the calculations, rather than the nil rate band applying at the time of the transfer
- Any unused nil rate band on the earlier death of the deceased's spouse is also available (see Section 6.3 for further details)
- Potentially exempt transfers made in the seven years prior to death must be brought into the calculation

The effect of all this is best illustrated by way of an example.

Example

(As in previous examples, we will ignore any exemptions and reliefs, other than the nil rate band)

Roy, a lifelong bachelor and a kind, generous and rich old man, dies on 3rd December 2018. Roy had made no chargeable lifetime transfers prior to 2008 but, in the last few years of his life, he made the following gifts:

- *On 10th December 2008, he gave £200,000 in cash to the Wilbury Discretionary Trust.*
- *On 1st December 2011, he gave £50,000 in cash to his nephew George.*
- *On 13th January 2012, he gave another £145,000 in cash to the Wilbury Discretionary Trust. He paid £5,000 in IHT at that time (grossing up applied).*
- *On 8th May 2014, he gave his friend Jeff some shares in the Electric Light Company Inc. At that time, these shares were worth £50,000.*
- *On 4th December 2015, he gave his friend Tom some shares in Heartbreakers.com plc, which were worth £80,000 at that time.*
- *On 24th August 2016, he gave his friend Bob £100,000 in cash.*

The IHT payable by each of these transferees on Roy's death is as follows:

The Wilbury Discretionary Trust – First Gift

Roy's first gift to the Trust in December 2008 was made more than seven years prior to his death. This gift itself will therefore not be subject to IHT on his death. However, because gifts to discretionary trusts are chargeable transfers, it will continue to have an impact on later gifts made in the following seven years.

George

Roy's gift to George was a potentially exempt transfer made more than seven years prior to his death.

On the seventh anniversary of that gift, 1st December 2018, the gift became fully exempt and hence it can now be completely ignored for the purposes of calculating any IHT arising on Roy's death.

The Wilbury Discretionary Trust – Second Gift

Due to the grossing up provisions, Roy's second gift to the Trust in January 2012 was deemed to have been a gift of £150,000.

As this gift was within the last seven years of Roy's life, it is effectively pulled back into his estate for the purposes of his IHT calculation.

Furthermore, in calculating the IHT now due on this gift, we must also take account of his previous gift to the Trust, as that first gift was a chargeable transfer made within the seven-year period prior to the second gift.

The gift to George on 1st December 2011 can be ignored, however, as this has become fully exempt.

The cumulative total of chargeable lifetime transfers made by Roy up to the time of the second gift to the Trust was therefore £350,000. After deducting the nil rate band of £325,000 from this sum, there remains a chargeable sum of £25,000.

As the gift took place more than six, but less than seven, years before Roy's death, IHT is chargeable at only 20% of the death rate, i.e. 8%. Hence the IHT charge on this gift arising on Roy's death is £2,000. As this is less than the IHT already paid by Roy on the lifetime transfer (£5,000), no further IHT is payable.

Jeff

Roy's gift of shares to Jeff on 8th May 2014 was a potentially exempt transfer. Unfortunately, as Roy has died within seven years of making that gift, it has now become a chargeable transfer.

Both of the gifts to the Wilbury Discretionary Trust took place within the seven-year period prior to the gift to Jeff, so the cumulative value of chargeable transfers at this point is £350,000, meaning that the nil rate band has been fully exhausted and the gift to Jeff is now fully chargeable to IHT.

However, since the gift to Jeff took place more than four, but less than five, years before Roy's death, IHT is only chargeable at 60% of the death rate, i.e. 24%.

Jeff therefore has an IHT liability of £12,000 (£50,000 x 24%).

Tom

Tom really is going to be heartbroken. His gift took place just one day short of three years before Roy's death.

IHT is therefore payable at the full death rate, 40%. Furthermore, the cumulative value of total chargeable transfers within the previous seven years now amounts to £400,000, made up as follows:

	£
First gift to Wilbury Discretionary Trust	*200,000*
Second gift to Wilbury Discretionary Trust	*150,000*
Gift to Jeff	*50,000*
Total	*400,000*

Both gifts to the Wilbury Discretionary Trust are included as they both took place within the seven-year period prior to the gift to Tom.

The gift to Jeff is also included, as it has now become a chargeable transfer due to Roy's death within seven years. The gift to George is not included, however, as it took place more than seven years before Roy's death and has therefore become exempt.

Tom therefore has an IHT liability of £32,000 (40% x £80,000).

Bob

This gift took place within the last three years of Roy's life, so there is no tapering of the IHT liability.

The cumulative value of total chargeable transfers within the seven years prior to this gift amounts to £280,000, made up as follows:

	£
Second gift to Wilbury Discretionary Trust	*150,000*
Gift to Jeff	*50,000*
Gift to Tom	*80,000*
Total	*280,000*

The first gift to the Wilbury Discretionary Trust no longer needs to be included as it took place more than seven years prior to the gift to Bob. Adding Bob's own gift to the above figure gives a total of £380,000. From this, we are able to deduct the nil rate band of £325,000, leaving Bob with a chargeable transfer of £55,000.

Bob's IHT liability is therefore £22,000 (40% x £55,000).

Points to Note

Firstly, we can see that the total value of chargeable transfers in the last seven years of Roy's life amounts to £380,000. His nil rate band is therefore already exhausted before we even begin to look at his estate.

The next point to note is that the oldest gift in our example, which was made almost ten years before Roy's death, had a major impact on the recipients of his later gifts, despite the fact that it was made well before the critical seven-year period.

It is also interesting to note that the oldest gift within the seven-year period did not give rise to any more IHT for the recipients of that gift. This will often be the case for chargeable lifetime transfers made more than five years prior to the transferor's death.

This position may be altered, however, where there are significant amounts of potentially exempt transfers made within seven years of the transferor's death but prior to the chargeable transfer in question.

As we saw in the example, these two earlier gifts used up all of Roy's nil rate band, which had a major impact on some of the later transferees.

This was particularly unfortunate for Tom since a mere seven days' delay to his gift would have meant that the first gift to the Wilbury Discretionary Trust would then have been made more than seven years previously. Tom's own gift would then have been completely covered by the nil rate band.

> **Tax Tip**
>
> Where practical, it may make sense to leave a seven-year gap after making a large chargeable lifetime transfer before making further chargeable or potentially exempt transfers. Naturally, of course, delaying your gifts carries other conflicting risks, which you will need to weigh up.
>
> However, a delay of just seven days in order to bring the nil rate band back into play again would surely make sense!

By the time of Bob's gift on 24th August 2016, part of the nil rate band was available once more, thus giving him a lower IHT bill than Tom on a larger value gift.

This ably demonstrates the fact that, with careful planning:

The nil rate band is effectively available to each of us not just once a lifetime, but once every seven years!

Unforeseen Changes in Circumstances

In the case of a property which a transferor has gifted to a relative, there will not be a gift with reservation if the transferor is forced to move back into that property due to an unforeseen change in circumstances whereby he or she is unable to care for themselves due to ill health, old age or infirmity.

This, for example, may cover the situation where a person has transferred a property to their son or daughter and some years later has to move into the property so that their family can care for them.

The move back into the property must be for the provision of 'reasonable care and maintenance' by the transferee who must also be a relative. You can't just move back in because you'd like to see a bit more of the grandchildren.

This change must also be unforeseen. If you are already ill when you make the gift, the gift with reservation rules will still apply.

What's So Bad about Gifts with Reservation?

Plenty! Firstly, although the gift is ineffective when it comes to excluding the gifted asset from your estate, it is nevertheless still a transfer of value and could give rise to an IHT charge if you die within seven years.

Some relief is given to prevent an effective double charge but it does not entirely eliminate the problem. In this situation, two IHT calculations must be prepared. Firstly, IHT is calculated as if the transfer had never taken place and you still owned the gifted asset at the date of your death. A second IHT calculation must then be prepared on the basis that the transfer did take place.

The bad news is that it is the calculation that produces the greatest amount of IHT which is used. In other words, the tax payable is the greater of the amount payable on the transfer **or** the amount payable on the asset that is deemed to still be in your estate on death!

Generally, where the gifted asset is increasing in value, we would expect the greater tax to arise by including the asset in the estate on death. The overall effect of this is to render the gift ineffective for IHT purposes.

Wealth Warning

A gift with reservation where that reservation still applies at the time of the donor's death is at best ineffective and at worst may even increase the total IHT due.

Secondly, the gifted asset will also be included in the transferee's estate, thus giving rise to a possible double charge.

Thirdly, although the gift is ineffective for IHT purposes, it will still be a disposal for CGT purposes. This means that CGT liabilities may still arise on the gift. Furthermore, the transferee may not be entitled to the same reliefs as the transferor would have been if they had retained the asset. We will look further at the potential impact of this in Chapter 11.

What Happens When The 'Reservation' Ends?

The problems arising when a 'reservation' ends during the transferor's lifetime can be even worse. When the 'reservation' ends, a new transfer is deemed to take place.

For example, if a mother gave a house to her two sons in 1999 but continues to live in it until 2018, there is deemed to be a transfer of the house in 2018. This time the transfer **is** effective for IHT purposes but it brings a few problems.

The first problem is that the deemed transfer is treated as a chargeable lifetime transfer and not a potentially exempt transfer. Furthermore, the value of the deemed transfer will be the asset's value at the date the reservation ends, not the date of the original transfer. Deemed transfers on the cessation of a 'reservation' are also ineligible for a number of reliefs, including the annual exemption.

Generally speaking, therefore, the whole value of a property subject to a 'reservation' becomes a chargeable lifetime transfer when that 'reservation' comes to an end during the transferor's lifetime. Hence, if gifted property subject to a 'reservation' is worth more than the amount of the nil rate band when that reservation comes to an end, an immediate IHT charge will arise. Immediate charges may also arise when the transferor has made other chargeable lifetime transfers within the previous seven years.

Furthermore, as we saw in Section 4.5, chargeable lifetime transfers made within 14 years prior to the transferor's death may result in increased IHT liabilities for other transferees.

If the transferor dies within seven years of the cessation of a 'reservation', the property subject to the 'reservation' will effectively fall into the deceased's estate. Hence, the mother in our example would need to live until 2025 for her transfer of the house in 1999 to be exempt from IHT. If she should pass away before then, the value of the house when she moved out in 2018 will effectively be brought back into her estate.

Where both the original transfer and the deemed transfer on the cessation of the 'reservation' take place within the seven years prior to the transferor's death, it will again be necessary to prepare two IHT calculations: one including the original transfer and one including the deemed transfer. Once again, the calculation producing the greater amount of tax will be used.

4.10   WHY NOT JUST GIVE IT ALL AWAY?

After reading Section 4.3, you may have been thinking that avoiding IHT is simple. All you need to do is to give everything away to your family and then survive for seven years. Well, yes, in theory, in the right circumstances, simply giving your property away during your lifetime can be an effective way to avoid IHT.

Certainly there is no problem with giving away whatever parts of your estate you can afford to. Just remember to make sure that the gifts are potentially exempt transfers and then take good care of yourself for seven years. (Or take out some term insurance to cover the IHT risk – see Section 10.15.)

Unfortunately, however, in practice, there are a few 'catches'.

Firstly, as we have already seen, any gifts where you retain a beneficial interest are treated as still being part of your estate.

Secondly, even where a transfer appears to avoid the 'Gifts With Reservation' rules, there may be an Income Tax benefit-in-kind charge applying if the transferor continues to enjoy the use of the asset. This charge may also apply to any future use by the donor of an asset purchased with gifted funds. (See Chapter 13 for further details.)

Thirdly, when gifting assets other than cash during your lifetime, you may be exposed to CGT. Most lifetime gifts are treated like a sale at current market value for CGT purposes. (Here there is no problem with the family home, as it is generally exempt from CGT under the principal private residence relief provisions – these are fully explained in the Taxcafe.co.uk guide *'How to Save Property Tax'*.)

Lastly, in practice, you cannot simply give all your assets away because you will need something to live off for the rest of your life!

It's fine if you're happy to go and spend the rest of your days in a monastery or a nunnery, or to live off your last £325,000 (for at least seven years) but, in reality, very few people would be happy to follow such a drastic course of action.

Hence, at this point, we need to start looking at what exemptions and reliefs are available to you and how you can plan to use them to best effect.

Chapter 5

Lifetime Exemptions

5.1   ABSOLUTE EXEMPTION

There are a number of exemptions available to cover lifetime transfers. These are absolute exemptions, not dependent on whether you survive for any particular period.

Transfers covered by these exemptions would be free from IHT even if you were to pass away the very next day, or even on the way home from the lawyer's office. (Don't laugh: I know of one sad, but true, case where the taxpayer was knocked down by a bus outside the lawyer's office!)

These exemptions therefore provide very useful IHT planning tools under the right circumstances. Sadly though, the monetary values of the exemptions covered in Sections 5.2, to 5.5 have remained the same since 1981. These values are long overdue for an increase since retail price inflation alone would have increased them by a factor of more than three and a half times by now!

5.2   THE ANNUAL EXEMPTION

The first £3,000 of any transfers of value, which are not otherwise exempt, that each individual makes in each tax year are exempt from IHT. Married couples have an annual exemption of £3,000 <u>each</u>. If the annual exemption is not used one year, it may be carried forward and can be used in the next tax year if that following year's annual exemption is fully exhausted.

Example

Stevie makes the following gifts (having never made any before):

2018/19:	*£5,000 to his brother Marvin*
2019/20:	*£4,000 to his brother Smokey*
2020/21:	*£2,000 to his sister Dionne*
2021/22:	*£5,000 to his sister Aretha*

The first £3,000 of the gift to Marvin is covered by Stevie's annual exemption for 2018/19. His 2017/18 annual exemption is also still available, thus covering the remaining £2,000 of this gift. The gift to Marvin is therefore fully exempt from IHT.

The unused £1,000 of Stevie's 2017/18 annual exemption is simply lost, as it cannot be carried forward another year.

The first £3,000 of Stevie's gift to Smokey is covered by his 2019/20 annual exemption. The remaining £1,000 of this transfer is a potentially exempt transfer.

The gift to Dionne is fully covered by Stevie's 2020/21 annual exemption. Furthermore, the unused £1,000 of this exemption may be carried forward to 2021/22.

The first £3,000 of Stevie's gift to Aretha is covered by his 2021/22 annual exemption. The next £1,000 is covered by the unused balance of his 2020/21 annual exemption. The remaining balance of £1,000 is a potentially exempt transfer.

Tax Tip 1

If Stevie were married, he could have avoided the potentially exempt transfers to Smokey and Aretha by, in each case, first making a gift of £1,000 to his wife who could then have gifted this sum to the ultimate recipient.

As explained in Section 6.15, however, such interim gifts to a spouse must be free of any conditions so that the spouse would be free to refuse to hand the gift on to the intended recipient if they so wished.

Tax Tip 2

The annual exemption may not be very large, but it is important to bear it in mind when undertaking IHT planning. Making best use of the annual exemption is a matter of timing. The ability to carry it forward one year gives you an effective 'second chance', but the use of the annual exemption should nevertheless be reviewed at least every other year.

A couple who manage to make effective use of the annual exemption in the final few years of their lives will save around £20,000 in IHT.

Who Benefits From The Exemption?

According to HMRC, the taxpayer's annual exemption for each tax year must be applied on a strictly chronological basis. In their view, the exemption must be utilised against any potentially exempt transfers taking place before chargeable lifetime transfers made later in the same tax year.

This could have some most unfortunate consequences.

Example

Brian gives £6,000 to his brother Carl on 6th April 2018. This (according to HMRC) uses up Brian's annual exemptions for 2017/18 and 2018/19, despite being a potentially exempt transfer.

On 10th April 2018, Brian gives £338,000 to the Wilson Phillips Discretionary Trust for the benefit of his many nephews and nieces.

the total value of pension benefits is less than the Lifetime Allowance (£1 million in 2017/18). For death after age 75, income or lump sums payable to beneficiaries are subject to income tax at their highest marginal rate.

Many people still use some or all of their pension fund to buy an annuity to secure income in retirement. The death benefit from an annuity depends upon the type of annuity arranged at the outset. Commonly there are **widow(er)'s benefits** or guaranteed minimum payment periods, which are not subject to IHT but are potentially subject to income tax. Those annuities without these options stop paying income upon the death of the annuitant. This is **why it is important to shop around and make an informed decision. Visit www.hl.co.uk/annuities** for more information on annuity options.

Importance of nominating your beneficiaires

Personal pensions, SIPPs and drawdown plans are almost always written in trust. This means the death benefits are separate from your estate and Will, and normally IHT free. Investors should complete an expression of wish form to provide the trustees with details of to whom they would like the money paid in the event of death. Ultimately it is the trustees of the pension, not the investor, who decides who receives the value of the pension pot, although in practice, the beneficiary nomination is followed the vast majority of the time.

Pension death benefits

The death benefits of a pension depend upon many factors including the scheme rules, whether the benefits are in payment and the age at death. Normally pension death benefits are inheritance tax free. Final salary and defined benefit pensions usually pay a widow(er)'s pension which is taxed as income. Sometimes they pay a dependants' pension as well. If death occurs during employment, they might also pay a tax-free lump sum. The scheme booklet or administrators will have the details.

With personal pensions, stakeholder pensions, self-invested personal pensions (SIPPs) and drawdown plans, up until age 75, the value of the fund is normally paid free of any tax, providing

Unfortunately, this means that he has made a chargeable lif
Wilson Phillips Discretionary Trust. After deducting the nil ra[
the remaining £13,000 must be grossed up at the rate of one
an IHT bill of £3,250.

If, instead, Brian had made his two gifts in the opposi[e
exemptions for 2017/18 and 2018/19 would have been deducted ,.
chargeable transfer, leaving just £332,000, or £7,000 after deducting the nil ra[
band. Brian's IHT bill would then have been reduced to just £1,750: a saving of
£1,500.

HMRC's interpretation on this point is based entirely on a flaw in the drafting of the IHT law. What Parliament actually intended was for the annual exemption to be used first against any chargeable lifetime transfers, with any excess remaining available to cover potentially exempt transfers if they subsequently became chargeable on the transferor's death.

This difference in interpretation will affect not only those making large chargeable lifetime transfers in excess of the nil rate band, like Brian in the example above, but also the transferees calculating their own IHT bill in the event of the transferor's death within seven years. In the latter case there will be winners and losers but, in the former case, only HMRC can be the winner!

In practice, I would always advocate planning your affairs on the basis of HMRC's interpretation wherever possible.

Tax Tip

Chargeable lifetime transfers should be made earlier in the tax year than any potentially exempt transfers whenever possible.

But, if you find that you are already in the position where their interpretation is putting you at a disadvantage, you should argue for the law to be applied as it was quite clearly intended by Parliament.

Simultaneous Gifts

Transfers made on the same day are treated as being simultaneous for the purposes of the annual exemption. Any available annual exemption is divided between the 'same-day transfers' in proportion to their total value.

Example

On 9th October 2018, John gives £10,000 to his elder son Julian and £5,000 to his younger son Sean. John has made no previous gifts in the period since 5th April 2017.

John's 2017/18 and 2018/19 exemptions are therefore both available, enabling £6,000 of these gifts to be exempted.

ssuming the boys' cheques both clear the same day (if he makes his gifts in this way), and following HMRC's interpretation, John's annual exemptions will be divided as follows:

Julian:	*£6,000 x £10,000/£15,000 =*	*£4,000*
Sean:	*£6,000 x £5,000/£15,000 =*	*£2,000*

Julian will therefore have received a potentially exempt transfer of £6,000 (£10,000 - £4,000) and Sean will have received a potentially exempt transfer of £3,000 (£5,000 - £2,000).

Taking this point in conjunction with Section 4.7 above, one can imagine transferees racing each other to the bank! (Once again, it might be simpler if John makes his gifts by way of electronic transfer.)

5.3   THE SMALL GIFTS EXEMPTION

In addition to the annual exemption, there is also a general exemption for outright gifts of up to £250 to any one person each tax year.

This exemption applies to any number of such 'small gifts' to separate persons each year. It can, however, only apply to straightforward gifts to other individuals and cannot apply to transfers into trusts.

Again, a married couple may each utilise this exemption separately in their own right.

Wealth Warning

The small gifts exemption only covers gifts of up to £250. Unlike the annual exemption, it does not cover the first part of a larger gift. Hence, a gift of £251 is not covered by this exemption at all.

It should also be noted that the exemption has to cover all gifts to the same person in the whole tax year.

Furthermore, this exemption cannot be used in conjunction with the annual exemption. In other words, it is not possible to exempt gifts totalling £3,250 to the same person by using both exemptions together.

5.4   USING THE ANNUAL AND SMALL GIFTS EXEMPTIONS EFFECTIVELY

It is possible to combine these two exemptions in order to exempt a number of gifts to different family members. Using a cyclical basis, it will also be possible to even out any unfairness.

Example

Chris and Debbie have three sons: Scott, John and Gary; and wish to pass as much wealth to them as they can by using their annual and small gifts exemptions. On 5th April 2019, Chris gives Scott £6,000. This is covered by his annual exemptions for 2017/18 and 2018/19. On the same day, he also gives £250 each to John and Gary and these gifts are covered by the small gifts exemption.

Note that care would need to be taken here if other gifts had also been given to the sons earlier in the tax year – e.g. birthday and Xmas presents. Arguably, however, these other gifts would be covered by the 'habitual gifts out of income' exemption.

At the same time, Debbie gives John £6,000, which is covered by her annual exemptions for 2017/18 and 2018/19, and gives £250 each to Scott and Gary.

The next day, 6th April 2019, Chris and Debbie each give £3,000 to Gary. Both of these gifts are covered by their 2019/20 annual exemptions. Chris and Debbie also each give £250 to Scott and £250 to John.

In the space of 48 hours, Chris and Debbie have managed to give their sons a total of £20,000, which is completely exempt from IHT. If they should be unfortunate enough to die within seven years, this simple strategy will save the family £8,000.

*(**NB:** you may notice that Gary has received £250 less than his brothers. This can be evened out in later years.)*

In practice, Chris and Debbie might need to make their first gifts a few days earlier as, if made by cheque, the cheques would need to clear by 5th April 2019 in order for the gifts to fall into 2018/19 for IHT purposes.

Alternatively, as discussed in Section 4.7, it might be simpler and more certain if Chris and Debbie made their gifts by way of electronic transfer.

5.5   GIFTS IN CONSIDERATION OF MARRIAGE

It's an expensive business when the kids get married, but at least it does provide an extra opportunity to do some IHT planning. Gifts made in consideration of marriage are exempt from IHT up to the following limits:

- Parents: £5,000
- Grandparents, Great-Grandparents, etc: £2,500
- Bride to Groom or Groom to Bride: £2,500
- Other Donors: £1,000

All of the above limits apply on an individual basis and the relationships referred to must be to one of the parties to the marriage. Hence, for example, the groom could receive £5,000 from each of his parents, plus £2,500 from each of his grandparents and £1,000 from all of his aunts and uncles and the bride could receive the same from her family.

Alternatively, the bride's family could make their gifts to the groom or the groom's family could make their gifts to the bride.

Additionally, within this same exemption (and within the same overriding limits as set out above), gifts could be made into a trust for the benefit of:

i)   The bride and/or groom
ii) Children of either or both parties to the marriage
iii) Future spouses of children of either or both parties to the marriage
iv) A future spouse of either party to the marriage
v)   Children of any subsequent spouse of either party to this marriage and future spouses of those children

This all sounds terribly complicated but what it means is that the marriage provides an opportunity to put some money into trust for both living and unborn children of either or both parties to the marriage. The importance of this has greatly increased since 2006, owing to the fact that most lifetime transfers into trust are now chargeable lifetime transfers (see Chapter 8).

To fall within the exemption, gifts must be made on or shortly before the marriage and must be fully effective when the marriage takes place. For example, "I give you my property at Valotte on condition that you marry my daughter."

Where the gifts exceed the limits shown above, the excess may be covered by the annual exemption, if available. Otherwise, the excess will be treated like any other lifetime transfer, as explained in Chapter 4.

For the purpose of this exemption, a 'parent' includes the parent of an illegitimate child, adopted child or stepchild and, as explained in Section 1.5, all of the above applies equally to registered civil partnerships.

5.6   MAINTENANCE OF FAMILY

Anything you do for the maintenance of your 'family' is exempted from being a transfer of value for IHT purposes. Just as well since otherwise, every time you bought the weekly groceries you would be at risk of causing an IHT liability! This covers expenditure for the maintenance of your spouse, plus any expenditure for the maintenance, education or training of the following:

- A child of either you or your spouse who is either under 18 or still in full-time education or training on the last 5th April prior to the time of the relevant expenditure.

- Any other child who is not in the care of a parent and is under 18 on the last 5th April prior to the time of the relevant expenditure.

- Any other child who has been in your care for a substantial period and was still in full time education or training on the last 5th April prior to the time of the relevant expenditure.

Your 'child' for the purposes of this exemption includes a stepchild, adopted child or illegitimate child.

One major absentee from this list, however, is your unmarried partner and hence, technically, any expenditure for the maintenance of a common-law co-habiting partner would be a transfer of value.

Thankfully, however, such expenditure will often be covered by:

- The 'Normal Expenditure Out Of Income' exemption (Section 5.8), or
- The exemption for 'transfers not intended to confer a gratuitous benefit' (Section 5.9), since most 'transfers of value' in an unmarried couple are simply domestic cost-sharing arrangements.

Even so, this might still present a very significant problem, as a large part of a co-habiting partner's expenditure in the last seven years before their death could potentially be subject to IHT. Furthermore, since much of this 'maintenance' expenditure will not actually result in an increase in the value of the transferee's estate, it might even be considered to be a chargeable lifetime transfer!

5.7   DEPENDENT RELATIVES

This same exemption also extends to expenditure that represents a reasonable provision for the care or maintenance of a dependent relative. A 'dependent relative' for this purpose is:

i) Your widowed, separated or divorced mother or mother-in-law.
ii) Any other relative of yours or your spouse's who is incapacitated by old age or infirmity, as a consequence of which they are unable to maintain themselves.

By concession, an unmarried mother may also be included under heading (i) above, as long as she is genuinely financially dependent on the donor.

'Old' is usually taken to mean the current male state retirement age, i.e. 65.

It can be seen that sexism is alive and well and living in the UK tax legislation. I wonder when we will see a case being taken to court demanding equal treatment for widowed, separated or divorced fathers?

HMRC should, for example, accept that renting a property for your elderly and financially dependent relative to live in represents reasonable provision for their maintenance. They will not, however, accept buying a property for them and transferring it into their name to give them added security, as 'reasonable care or maintenance'.

This exemption is mostly only relevant when a person pre-deceases one of their parents. It could, however, also apply where a person is providing 'care or maintenance' for a disabled relative, such as a sibling or adult child.

5.8   NORMAL EXPENDITURE OUT OF INCOME

Lifetime transfers of value are exempt to the extent that:

i)   They are part of the normal, habitual, or typical, expenditure of the transferor,

ii) Taking one year with another, they are made out of income (i.e. not out of capital), and

iii) The transferor is left with sufficient net income to maintain his or her usual standard of living

This is an extremely useful exemption, since, unlike the annual exemption, there is no financial limit to the amount that can be covered by this exemption if the transferor can afford it.

The amount of gifts or other expenditure involved does not need to be exactly the same every year, as long as it is part of a regular pattern.

All of the following might potentially be covered as long as they meet the three tests set out above:

- Giving your son £10,000 every year
- Giving your granddaughter all of your ICI dividends every year
- Paying your nephew's school fees
- Buying your brother a new car every three years
- Passing all of the income you receive from a trust each year over to your elderly father
- Paying a monthly life assurance premium on a policy in favour of your daughter

Maintaining Your Usual Standard of Living

It has been suggested that the Capital Taxes Office (the HMRC department responsible for policing IHT) does not generally question the validity of gifts out of income if they do not, in total, exceed one third of the transferor's net annual after-tax income.

Nevertheless, I imagine they would still scrutinise any case where they had reason to think otherwise!

In some circumstances, the transferor might reasonably gift a far greater proportion of his or her income and still maintain their usual standard of living, e.g. a very wealthy person with a very frugal lifestyle.

It is generally accepted that this test is met if the transferor making the normal, habitual, expenditure is left with sufficient income to maintain his or her usual standard of living **on average**.

I have, however, met the 'chicken and egg' situation where HMRC has argued that the transferor's modest standard of living arose **because** of the expenditure in question. To avoid this argument, there will clearly need to be some surplus income remaining.

What Is Income?

The first point to note is that HMRC regards 'income' for the purposes of this exemption as net after-tax income.

Furthermore, not everything that is treated as 'income' for Income Tax purposes will be regarded as 'income' for the purposes of the exemption. (Yet another example of HMRC having their cake and eating it!)

There are, for example, cases where the proceeds of sale of company shares may be treated as income for Income Tax purposes. This often occurs as a result of specific statutory provisions relating to employee shares.

The underlying nature of this 'income', however, would remain capital and hence this would not be 'income' which could be relied upon for the purposes of the 'normal expenditure out of income' exemption.

For a self-employed transferor, 'income' for the purposes of the exemption would generally be based on the results shown in their business accounts.

Hence, 'income' will be arrived at after deducting items such as depreciation and business entertaining, even though these are not allowed for Income Tax purposes. As stated above, however, the full Income Tax charge will need to be deducted from the accounts income in order to arrive at the net after-tax income available for the purposes of the exemption.

Habitual Gifts

Establishing a gift as being part of your normal, habitual expenditure is a question of fact.

The matter will be determined by looking at the particular facts of each individual case and considering the actual behaviour of the transferor over a number of years.

HMRC will usually consider expenditure to have become normal, or habitual, when it has been made three times, with the intention of continuing to make further similar payments.

It is, however, possible to establish that a gift has become part of your normal, habitual expenditure even if you should die after only one such gift. This is because the exemption will still apply if it can be shown that it was the transferor's intention to make the gift regularly on a habitual basis.

A contractual commitment to make regular payments will usually be accepted as evidence of an intention to make the expenditure part of the transferor's normal pattern of expenditure. In the absence of such a commitment, some other documentary evidence of the transferor's intentions is advisable.

Tax Tip

Establishing an intention to make a gift on a habitual basis will require some evidence to prove it. For example, if you intend paying your niece's school fees on a regular basis, it would be wise to write a letter to the school confirming this fact.

If you should then unfortunately pass away soon after paying the first set of fees, the letter will confirm that this payment was intended to be normal habitual expenditure and thus exempt from IHT (as long as the other requirements set out above are also met).

Wealth Warning

To be covered by this exemption, the relevant gifts or expenditure must be maintained on a regular basis.

Hence, you must be sure to keep making your 'habitual' gifts every year (or such other period as is your habit). Unlike the annual exemption, there is no scope for carrying this exemption forward!

The Danger of Irrelevance

Where the gifts concerned are made directly to another individual, this all only becomes relevant when the transferor has died within seven years since, otherwise, the gifts will be potentially exempt transfers in any case (see Section 4.3).

Unfortunately, what this means in practice is that the true status of these transfers is generally never established until after the transferor's death, leaving a great deal of uncertainty for their beneficiaries. It is vital, therefore, to maintain appropriate records of your normal expenditure out of income throughout your lifetime, to assist your executors in establishing the correct position when dealing with your estate after your death.

5.9   TRANSFERS NOT INTENDED TO CONFER GRATUITOUS BENEFIT

There is a general exemption for any transfer of value that is not intended to confer a gratuitous benefit on the transferee.

One very important example of such a transfer is one made as part of a divorce settlement (when made in circumstances where the spouse exemption does not apply).

Tax Tip

This provides the opportunity to put property into trust as part of a divorce settlement without creating a chargeable lifetime transfer. Not only is this probably preferable from a practical perspective (e.g. the ex-spouse's interest can be terminated in the event of their re-marrying), it also means that the property will not fall into the ex-spouse's estate and can later pass to the children without a 40% charge on the ex-spouse's death.

Note that, whilst the property can pass into the trust free from IHT under this exemption, anniversary and exit charges will still apply (see Chapter 8). Nevertheless, on balance, the technique will very often be beneficial overall.

Settlements between common-law partners might also be covered under this exemption, as well as simple transactions, such as friends sharing the cost of a holiday or a restaurant bill.

5.10   TRANSFERS ALLOWABLE FOR INCOME TAX OR CONFERRING RETIREMENT BENEFITS

'Transfers of value' that are made for the purposes of a trade, and are thus allowable for Income Tax, are exempt from IHT. This covers paying your employees' wages, for example; including employees who are also family members, provided that they genuinely earn those wages through the effort they put into your business.

There is also an exemption for payments securing pension or other retirement benefits for:
  i)   any employee of the transferor, who is not otherwise connected with the transferor, or
  ii)   the widow, widower or dependants of a person within (i) above

Payments securing pension benefits for family members are not covered by this exemption (but could be covered by other exemptions).

Chapter 6

IHT Planning for Married Persons

6.1   SCOPE OF THIS CHAPTER

In this chapter, we are going to take a detailed look at the IHT planning opportunities available as a consequence of marriage or civil partnership. We will cover people who are married or in a civil partnership now; widows, widowers and surviving civil partners; and those contemplating marriage or civil partnership in the future.

Everything that applies to married people in this chapter applies equally to civil partners and everything that applies to a widow or widower applies equally to a surviving civil partner.

Unless expressly stated to the contrary, it is assumed throughout this chapter that both spouses are (or were) UK domiciled, deemed UK domiciled (see Section 2.2), or have (or had) elected to be treated as UK domiciled at the relevant time (see Section 6.19).

6.2   A BRAVE NEW WORLD?

On your death, your personal representatives may claim any unused part of an earlier deceased spouse's nil rate band. In simple terms, this means that all widows and widowers are potentially entitled to a double nil rate band.

Furthermore, since we all have the potential to become a widow or widower one day, it actually means that we all have the potential to double our nil rate band. This has turned a great deal of IHT planning on its head!

Before October 2007, a great deal of IHT planning centred around ensuring that the first member of a married couple to die fully utilised their nil rate band since it would otherwise go to waste. Now, however, we often find that it is better to ensure that none of the first spouse to die's nil rate band is used on their death.

Many of the planning techniques which were often used to ensure that the first spouse's nil rate band was fully utilised would now appear to be highly disadvantageous in many cases. We will look at when and how to undo such planning in Section 6.13.

Any person dying after 5th April 2017 will also be entitled to any unused part of an earlier deceased spouse's residence nil rate band. Further details on the amount available are included in Sections 3.4 and 12.16.

6.3 THE TRANSFERABLE NIL RATE BAND & RESIDENCE NIL RATE BAND

Any part of the nil rate band which is unused on a married person's death is transferable to their spouse.

The transferable nil rate band must be claimed by the widow or widower's personal representatives within two years of the widow or widower's death. No claim is necessary on the first spouse's death and it does not matter how long ago the first spouse died.

Furthermore, it does not matter whether the first spouse actually had any assets at the time of their death. Even if they died penniless, their widow or widower can still claim a transferable nil rate band.

It is the **proportion** of the nil rate band unused on the first death which transfers, not the amount. This means that the widow or widower benefits from any increase in the nil rate band since their spouse's death.

In the simplest case, where none of the nil rate band was used on the first spouse's death, the widow or widower will be entitled to a double nil rate band. For widows or widowers dying between 6th April 2009 and 5th April 2021, this amounts to £650,000 (regardless of when the first spouse died).

Where, however, some of the first spouse's nil rate band was used, the amount transferred to the survivor will be reduced.

Example

Lee died on 1st September 2002 when the nil rate band was £250,000. Lee left a legacy of £100,000 to her son Peter and the remainder of her estate to her husband Lenny. 60% of Lee's nil rate band was therefore unused (£150,000/£250,000) and transfers to Lenny.

Lenny dies on 1st May 2018 and is entitled to his own nil rate band plus a further 60% transferred from Lee. His total nil rate band is thus as follows:

Own nil rate band:	*£325,000*
Nil rate band transferred from Lee (£325,000 x 60%):	*£195,000*
Total nil rate band available	*£520,000*

The Transferable Residence Nil Rate Band

Similar principles will apply to the transfer of a deceased spouse's residence nil rate band, although this will only apply where the surviving widow or widower dies after 5th April 2017 and will be subject to the tapering provisions explained in Section 3.4.

Example Continued

As Lee died in 2002, she would not have used any of her residence nil rate band. If her estate was worth no more than £2m at the time of her death, her entire residence nil rate band will therefore transfer to Lenny, giving him a total residence nil rate band at the time of his death in May 2018 of £250,000: made up of his own residence nil rate band of £125,000 and Lee's unused residence nil rate band of £125,000.

Combining his residence nil rate band of £250,000 with his enhanced nil rate band of £520,000 (see above) gives Lenny a total potential exemption of £770,000. He will, however, have to meet the rules outlined in Section 3.4 in order to benefit from the residence nil rate band element of this exemption.

Using the Residence Nil Rate Band on First Death

As explained in Section 3.4, tapering provisions apply to reduce the amount of residence nil rate band available on the death of an individual with an estate worth in excess of £2m.

Where a married couple's **combined** net assets exceed £2m, it may be worth ensuring that the residence nil rate band is utilised on the first spouse's death since, otherwise, it will be reduced or eliminated through the tapering that will apply on the second spouse's death.

Where a married couple's combined net assets exceed £4m, there are also potential savings to be made by keeping one spouse's estate to no more than £2m. In that way, the 'poorer' spouse will retain their full residence nil rate band entitlement.

To use that entitlement, it may also be necessary to leave some property which qualifies for the residence nil rate band directly to a 'direct descendant' on the 'poorer' spouse's death. For this reason, it would generally be preferable for the 'poorer' spouse to be the one with the shorter life expectancy, although this may require a little 'negotiation' amongst the family!

6.4   NIL RATE BAND TRANSFERS IN PRACTICE

Applying the transferable nil rate band system in practice is fraught with problems.

The first spouse may have died many years ago with a total estate which was clearly nowhere near the amount of the nil rate band. No-one will have given much thought to IHT at that time since it was clearly irrelevant.

Now, many years later, we will be faced with the prospect of attempting to ascertain how much of the nil rate band was used at that time.

The first question is 'how much was the nil rate band?' Here, at least, HMRC has been helpful and has published the nil rate bands going back to 1914. These are reproduced in Appendix A.

Where the first spouse died before 1986, they will have been subject to a different death tax regime but the previous equivalent of the nil rate band, as shown in Appendix A, is used for the purposes of calculating the transferable nil rate band.

There is a particularly nasty problem for widows and widowers whose spouse died before 13th March 1975 under the Estate Duty regime.

Under Estate Duty, there was no general exemption for transfers to spouses. For deaths occurring between 21st March 1972 and 12th March 1975 there was a limited exemption of just £15,000. Prior to 21st March 1972, there was no spouse exemption at all.

Hence, where the first spouse died before 13th March 1975, there may be little or no transferable nil rate band available even if the first spouse's entire estate passed to their widow or widower.

The families of those who have been widows or widowers for a long time could be badly affected by this.

Example

Vera has been a widow since her husband Glen went missing during a fishing trip in late 1945. Glen left his entire estate, worth just £30, to Vera.

Despite the size of Glen's small estate, this nevertheless used up 30% of his nil rate band (see Appendix A).

Only 70% of Glen's nil rate band will be available to Vera. At today's rates this means that she has lost £97,500 of transferable nil rate band, resulting in a potential additional IHT burden for her family of £39,000, or 1,300 times the value of Glen's estate!

There will of course be some straightforward cases where the first spouse did not use any of their nil rate band. This will include cases where the first spouse:

- Died after 12th March 1975 and left their entire estate to the surviving spouse,
- Left everything to charity,
- Had nothing of any financial value, or
- Died on active service (see Section 3.8)

Remember, however, that the first spouse may have used some of their nil rate band if they:

a) Made any transfers of value in the last seven years of their life (see Section 4.5),
b) Made any gifts with reservation (see Section 4.9), or
c) Elected to include an asset in their estate in order to prevent an Income Tax charge (see Section 13.3)

Example

When Pete died in March 2006, he left everything to his civil partner Roger. However, Pete had also given £100,000 to his friend Keith in 2002.

The gift to Keith in 2002 became chargeable on Pete's death. This was not important at the time as Pete left his entire estate to his civil partner but it meant that Pete used £100,000, or 36.36% (£100,000/£275,000), of his nil rate band.

Only 63.64% of Pete's nil rate band therefore transfers to Roger, or £206,818 at current rates.

Practical Problems

As we have already seen, the impact of even small gifts and legacies made by the first spouse could be quite significant. In practice, we may therefore see some extensive queries from HMRC whenever a transferable nil rate band is claimed.

In other words, whenever a widow or widower dies with an estate worth more than the nil rate band, we can expect to face detailed enquiries regarding the first spouse's estate and any transfers they may have made in the last seven years of their life.

For married couples who are both still alive, it will be vital to keep accurate records of all transfers which take place.

6.5   REMARRIAGE

It is, of course, not unusual for a widow or widower to remarry. Furthermore, some people (particularly widows) go on to outlive two or more spouses.

Sadly, however, a widow or widower can only be entitled to a maximum of one transferable nil rate band regardless of how many husbands or wives they have buried.

Example

In 1987, Liz married Eddie. He died in 1995 leaving Liz his entire estate. She remarried in 1998, to Richard, who died in 2001 and also left her his entire estate.

Although Liz has survived two husbands, neither of whom used any of their nil rate band, she is only entitled to one transferable nil rate band. Liz herself dies in March 2019. Her personal representatives may therefore claim a nil rate band of £650,000, comprising her own nil rate band plus one transferable nil rate band.

A widow or widower whose spouse used part of their nil rate band may, however, continue to accumulate further transferable nil rate band through remarriage until such point as they have accumulated a total of one additional nil rate band.

Example

Kurt died in 1991 when the nil rate band was £140,000, leaving a legacy of £70,000 to his cousin Dave and the remainder of his estate to his wife, Courtney. Courtney is thus entitled to a transferable nil rate band of 50% from Kurt.

In 1998, Courtney remarried to Michael. Sadly, in May 2018, Michael died, leaving a house worth £260,000 to his sister Kylie and the rest of his estate to Courtney. Kylie's legacy used up 80% of Michael's nil rate band so, this time, Courtney is only entitled to a transferable nil rate band of 20%.

Courtney can, however, add her two transferable nil rate bands together to give her a total 70% of transferable nil rate band. If she should die before 6th April 2021, her personal representatives could therefore claim an additional transferable nil rate band of £227,500 (£325,000 x 70%) in addition to her own nil rate band of £325,000.

If Courtney were to remarry again and subsequently be widowed for a third time, she would be entitled to claim any unused nil rate band on the death of her third husband up to a maximum of 30% (since a further 30% would bring her up to a total of one transferable nil rate band).

The key planning point to emerge here is that many widows and widowers will already have their maximum amount of transferable nil rate band when they remarry.

A simple way to ensure that you retain the full benefit of an existing transferable nil rate band entitlement is simply not to remarry. This does mean that you will not be able to benefit from the spouse exemption but, if you are already entitled to a full transferable nil rate band and you intend to leave your estate to your children rather than to any new partner (who may already be financially comfortable), then this will sometimes make sense.

Taking the Residence Nil Rate Band into Account

Similar principles apply to ensure that a widow or widower who remarries can only ever be entitled to a maximum of one additional residence nil rate band. Those who outlive more than one spouse will again be able to accumulate additional proportionate amounts of residence nil rate band until they reach an additional 100%.

At first glance, one might expect someone like Courtney, in our example above, to already be entitled to a full additional residence nil rate band since both of her husbands died before the new exemption became available on 6th April 2017. However, it is important to remember that if either of their estates were worth in excess of £2m at the time of their death, then tapering would apply and the proportion of residence nil rate band passing to Courtney would be reduced (see Section 3.4 for more details).

6.6   SEPARATION & DIVORCE

As we saw in Section 3.3, for the purposes of the spouse exemption a couple continue to be regarded as married for IHT purposes throughout any period of separation and right up until the granting of a decree absolute.

As far as we know, it is reasonable to assume that the same definition of marriage can be used in applying the transferable nil rate band system.

In other words, even if the couple were separated at the time of the first spouse's death, it appears that the surviving spouse will still be entitled to claim any part of the first spouse's nil rate band or residence nil rate band which is unused.

Example

Mick and Marianne met in the 1960s and led a wild life together for a few weeks. One drunken night in Las Vegas they got married. Shortly afterwards they drifted apart. They never got divorced.

Marianne continued to lead a wild life and eventually died penniless in the 1990s.

Mick got his act together and eventually went on to become very rich. Despite the fact that it has been over 50 years since their brief marriage, Mick would appear to be entitled to claim Marianne's unused nil rate band and residence nil rate band. That drunken night in Las Vegas could therefore save his family up to £200,000!

(Based on the nil rate band and residence nil rate band applying in 2020/21: £325,000 + £175,000 = £500,000 x 40% = £200,000)

There is a major practical problem with this situation. An estranged spouse like Mick may find it very difficult to ascertain how much of Marianne's nil rate band is available for him to claim. This will make any tax planning more difficult. Mick's personal representatives will also face difficulties when the time comes to claim the unused proportion of Marianne's nil rate band.

In an extreme case like Mick and Marianne's, the survivor may not even know that their spouse has died!

There is also the danger of more detailed legislation designed to restrict the use of transferable nil rate bands. It is possible that the CGT definition of 'married' may be applied to IHT. This would mean that a couple would cease to be treated as married when they separated. If the IHT rules were changed in this way then a separated spouse would not benefit from the two transferable nil rate bands.

We can only speculate about the precise nature of any future detailed rules. In the meantime, however, there remains a fair possibility that the transferable nil rate band and residence nil rate band will have the wide application suggested by the example above. We will return to some of the other implications of this in Section 6.17.

Divorce

Divorce was already a costly business! Now, there is effectively a further cost: the loss of the two transferable nil rate bands.

If the IHT definition of 'married' continues to apply as set out in Section 3.3, then both members of a separated couple will continue to have the potential to claim any part of their estranged spouse's nil rate band or residence nil rate band which is unused on the spouse's death.

If the couple divorce, however, the two transferable nil rate bands will no longer be available to either of them.

Hence, for IHT purposes, it makes sense for separated couples to stay married. If your ex is not that well off when they die, you may benefit!

In fact, in many cases, it is the couple's children who will ultimately benefit from any transferable nil rate band or residence nil rate band, which provides even more incentive to stay married for their benefit.

6.7   INHERITANCE TAX PLANNING FOR MARRIED COUPLES

The transferable nil rate band has completely changed the IHT planning landscape for all married couples.

Before October 2007, the first step was always to ensure that the first spouse to die would use their nil rate band effectively. Now we know this is no longer necessary, as any unused nil rate band will transfer to the surviving spouse.

In fact, there is a case for saying that the best planning now is to ensure that none of the nil rate band is used on the first spouse's death.

'But surely it doesn't make any difference', I hear you say. This is certainly the impression that the old Labour Government tried to give when Alistair

Darling first announced the transferable nil rate band in 2007 by suggesting that those who had already taken steps to utilise their nil rate band would be 'unaffected'.

I suppose this was true in a strict literal sense but a more accurate statement would have been to say that 'those who have already taken steps to utilise their nil rate band will not benefit'.

Am I just splitting hairs? No!

The important point is that the surviving spouse is able to claim whatever **proportion** of the nil rate band is unused on the first spouse's death. The **amount** of that claim, however, will depend on the amount of the nil rate band at the time of the widow or widower's death.

This means that some former IHT planning techniques may sometimes now have a disadvantageous effect.

Example

John and Dee were a married couple. Some years ago, they took some professional advice on their IHT position. Following this advice, they amended their Wills in order to implement a 'Widow's Loan Scheme' (see Section 6.12) when the first one of them died.

The effect of the scheme was to ensure that the first of them to die would utilise their nil rate band. The survivor would then be able to deduct an amount equal to that nil rate band from their estate. This was good planning at the time since, as things stood, this was likely to save John and Dee's family over £100,000 in IHT.

John died in May 2018 and the 'Widow's Loan Scheme' was put into action. A sum of £325,000 was left to a discretionary trust. Dee inherited the remainder of John's estate and, following one of the mechanisms explained in Section 6.12, was left owing a sum of £325,000 to the discretionary trust.

At this point everything seems fine. Dee still has her own nil rate band and will also be able to deduct her debt of £325,000 to the discretionary trust from her estate (provided the debt is repaid out of the assets of her estate - see Section 2.12). This provides a total effective exemption of £650,000 and, if Dee herself were to die before 6th April 2021, the effect would be the same as under the transferable nil rate band system.

Let us suppose, however, that Dee lives on for many years, through many changes of Government and much political manoeuvring and eventually dies when the nil rate band is £1.5m. On her death, Dee's nil rate band and her debt to the discretionary trust add up to a total of £1.825m of effective exemption from IHT.

If John and Dee had not implemented the 'Widow's Loan Scheme', however, John's nil rate band would have been unused and would have transferred to Dee. On Dee's death, her personal representatives would have been able to claim a transferable nil rate band of £1.5m in addition to her own nil rate band, giving her estate a total effective IHT exemption of £3m.

In this example, the earlier planning has resulted in the loss of £1.175m worth of IHT exemption for John and Dee's family. This would cost the family up to £470,000 in additional IHT at today's rates. The reason for this is the fact that the nil rate band increased by £1.175m during the period between John and Dee's deaths.

This gives us the general principle that a married couple's family will lose out to the extent of:

- The proportion of the nil rate band used on the first spouse's death
  TIMES
- The increase in the nil rate band between the first spouse's death and the second spouse's death
  TIMES
- The rate of IHT at the time of the second spouse's death

What Does All This Mean for Inheritance Tax Planning for Married Couples?

Any use of any part of the nil rate band on the first spouse's death may potentially have a detrimental effect on the second spouse's death.

The first spouse may use part of their nil rate band through any of the following:

- Legacies to anyone other than their spouse or one of the exempt bodies set out in Section 3.5
- Chargeable lifetime transfers in the last seven years of their life
- Potentially exempt transfers in the last seven years of their life
- Gifts with reservation of benefit (Section 4.9)
- An election to include an asset in their estate in order to prevent an Income Tax charge (Section 13.3)

Any of the above now put some or all of any married person's nil rate band in jeopardy and may have a detrimental effect on their spouse's IHT position.

This means that any transfer of value by a married person which does not carry an immediate complete exemption now carries an element of risk. This is particularly relevant to potentially exempt transfers, as well as chargeable lifetime transfers which are covered by the transferor's nil rate band (see Chapter 4 for further details).

Prior to October 2007, it was fair to say that such lifetime transfers could generally be made with an attitude of 'there's nothing to lose'. If you survived seven years, you were free of any problem, if you survived three, there might still be some benefit and, if you died within three years, the position was probably no worse than it would have been anyway.

Now, however, every lifetime transfer by a married person which is not covered by one of the absolute exemptions set out in Chapter 5, puts their spouse's transferable nil rate band at risk.

Example

On 5th January 2013, Richard gave his son Zak a gift of £32,500. This was a potentially exempt transfer as Richard had already used up any other available exemptions.

Sadly, Richard dies on 1st April 2019 and leaves his entire estate to his wife Barbara. The earlier gift to Zak becomes chargeable and uses up 10% of Richard's nil rate band. This means that Barbara receives a transferable nil rate band of only 90%.

Whatever the nil rate band may be when Barbara dies, she will lose out on 10% of it because of Richard's gift to Zak in 2013.

Lifetime Transfers by Married People

At this point, it is tempting to suggest that all married people should avoid making any lifetime transfers which are not covered by an immediate exemption.

This is not the case; it only means that many such transfers now carry a degree of risk that they might actually make the position worse.

Lifetime transfers by married people will often still be beneficial, such as when:

- The transferor survives for at least seven years
- The transferor's spouse already has a transferable nil rate band from a previous marriage (see Section 6.5)
- The transferred assets grow in value faster than the increase in the nil rate band

Example Revisited

Let us suppose that the gift from Richard to Zak in our previous example comprised quoted shares worth £32,500. Let us also suppose that these shares increase in value at a compound rate of 5% every year until Barbara's death in early 2033.

This means that Zak's shares will be worth £86,200 at the time of Barbara's death.

If the shares had not been transferred to Zak, they would still have been in Barbara's estate and would thus increase her IHT liability.

Instead, the gift to Zak means that the shares are not in Barbara's estate. However, the same gift also means that Barbara loses 10% of the transferable nil rate band.

Hence, if the nil rate band for 2032/33 is less than £862,000, the family will be better off overall because of Richard's original gift to Zak.

It may still be worthwhile for a married person to use part of their nil rate band on the transfer of funds or assets which will grow in value faster than the rate at which the nil rate band increases.

Following this principle in practice may be difficult as it involves a good deal of 'crystal ball gazing'. However, we know for a start that the nil rate band is to remain frozen at its current level of £325,000 until at least 5th April 2021. This will certainly provide a good 'head start' for the funds within any lifetime transfers made now!

Beyond that, however, it is hard to know what might happen. Will a future Government increase the nil rate band more significantly at some stage in the future? Will we be stuck with simple inflationary increases for many years to come after 2021? At present, no-one can say.

It may be worth reflecting on the table in Appendix A to remind us of how the nil rate band has grown historically. For the period from 1996 to 2009, the growth in the amount of the nil rate band was equivalent to an annual compound rate of around 3.57%. However, it has risen more steeply on some previous occasions.

For a lifetime transfer, there is the added bonus that any growth in value of the transferred asset up to the point of the transferor's death is effectively free of any IHT cost. In our example, for instance, it was the value of the shares when they were transferred in 2013 which was used to calculate the restriction in Barbara's transferable nil rate band, not their value at the date of Richard's death (which would have been around £43,500).

Planning On the First Death

At this point, it seems fairly reasonable to say that most married couples will now be better off if they **do not** use any of the planning schemes previously designed to utilise the first spouse's nil rate band on their death without actually passing on any wealth to other beneficiaries at that time.

We saw an example of the detrimental effect which such planning could now have in John and Dee's case above. Note that the planning techniques set out in Sections 6.9 to 6.12 are therefore no longer beneficial for most married couples. (We will look at how and when such planning carried out in the past can be undone in Section 6.13.) The position may differ, however, where one or both members of the couple have remarried following the death of a previous spouse.

We will look at planning for these couples in Section 6.8. It is mainly for the benefit of these couples that the techniques set out in Sections 6.9 to 6.12 are still included in this guide.

Those couples aside, any other married couple should now generally avoid using any scheme which simply uses up the first spouse's nil rate band without actually passing any assets or funds to other family members.

What is less certain is whether it remains worth using the first spouse's nil rate band on genuine legacies to other family members. Here, we must go back to the principle set out above, i.e. such legacies may be worthwhile if they consist of funds or assets which will grow in value faster than the rate at which the nil rate band increases.

In the case of a legacy, however, the proportion of transferable nil rate band lost will be based on the value of the relevant asset at the date of the first spouse's death. This means that the growth rate must be greater than in the case of a lifetime transfer before the legacy is worthwhile for IHT purposes.

Remember also that the reduction in the surviving spouse's transferable nil rate band caused by a legacy to another beneficiary is permanent. A gift of the same asset from the surviving spouse to another person would instead be a potentially exempt transfer and would be exempt if that spouse survives another seven years thereafter.

In many cases, therefore, and especially where the survivor still has a long life expectancy, it may be preferable to avoid any legacies to other beneficiaries. Subject to the comments below, the family will often achieve a better overall result if the surviving spouse makes lifetime transfers instead.

Passing on Wealth Tax Efficiently

Of course, it is all very well me telling you not to give your children (or other beneficiaries) anything unless they are going to invest it at better rates of growth than the nil rate band, but what if they need money or you simply want to help them out?

In most such cases, you will probably give them money during your lifetime and this will be a potentially exempt transfer. As we know, this will lead to a reduction in the transferable nil rate band if the person making the potentially exempt transfer dies within seven years.

You will therefore reduce the risk of a reduction in the transferable nil rate band if the spouse with the longer life expectancy makes the potentially exempt transfer. This is not foolproof, but it improves your chances.

Remember, you can pass wealth to your spouse first free from any IHT risk (subject to the points below) and they can then make the potentially exempt transfer if they choose to do so.

Wealth Warnings

There are two very important points to note here. Firstly, you cannot make it a pre-condition of any gift to your spouse that they will then pass that gift on to another person. If any such condition existed, then the first gift is ignored and you will be treated as having made the gift directly to the ultimate recipient, meaning that you will have made the potentially exempt transfer.

There is no problem, however, if your spouse chooses to pass the gift on of their own free will.

The second point to note is that the transfer to your spouse may itself be a potentially exempt transfer if they are non-UK domiciled (see Section 3.3).

Alternatively, you may wish to pass some wealth on to some person other than your spouse after you have died. As we have already discussed, a direct legacy has the drawback of causing a permanent reduction in the amount of transferable nil rate band which can ultimately be claimed against your spouse's estate.

You may therefore wish to consider passing the wealth to your spouse and leaving it in their hands to decide what to do.

This would enable the surviving spouse to make appropriate gifts as potentially exempt transfers. If the survivor lives for another seven years, these will be exempt from IHT and the full transferable nil rate band will be available against the rest of their estate.

As with a lifetime transfer, however, it is imperative that there is no prior agreement that your spouse will pass the assets or funds on to another person. You **must** leave the decision entirely in their hands. This point is crucial and is explored in further detail in Section 6.15.

6.8   THE SECOND TIME AROUND

Where one or both members of a married couple have remarried following the death of an earlier spouse, the position may be different to that outlined in the previous section. This is because one or both of the couple may already have an entitlement to claim all or part of a transferable nil rate band which was unused on the death of their previous spouse.

If, however, the whole of the previous spouse's nil rate band was used on their death (and this cannot be undone – see Section 6.13), then the current married couple will still be in the same position as any 'first time' couple and should go back to Section 6.7 for advice on their IHT planning position.

This leaves us with those who already have some entitlement to a transferable nil rate band. As explained in Section 6.5, a widow or widower cannot claim more than one additional nil rate band. This, in turn, means that we are back in the position where some or all of the nil rate band of the first of the spouses in the current couple to die will effectively go to waste unless we undertake some appropriate planning. Let me explain this further with an example.

Example

When George died a few years ago, he left a sum equal to half of the nil rate band to his son Ravi and the rest of his estate to his wife Patti. Patti is therefore already entitled to claim an additional 50% transferable nil rate band, or £162,500 at current rates. Patti is now married to Eric (who has never been married before). At the moment, Eric and Patti's Wills both leave everything to each other.

If Patti should die first, her nil rate band will go unused and will transfer to Eric. The additional half nil rate band which transferred from George to Patti will, however, go to waste.

If Eric should die first, his nil rate band will go unused and will be available to transfer to Patti. However, as Patti already has half a transferable nil rate band, she will only be able to claim half of Eric's unused nil rate band and the other half will go to waste.

Either way, whether Eric or Patti dies first, half a nil rate band will go to waste!

As we can see from the example, where one member of a couple already has an entitlement to part of a previous spouse's unused nil rate band, that entitlement will go to waste if the couple do not plan effectively.

Where the previous spouse's nil rate band was completely unused, we are back into familiar territory, as that whole nil rate band may potentially go to waste. At current rates, that amounts to £130,000 worth of wasted tax relief.

Whatever amount of transferable nil rate band is already available, the current couple will achieve the best result by ensuring that this same proportion of nil rate band is used on the first of their deaths. We will look at how this can be done over the next few sections.

Double Second-Timers

Where both of the current couple already have some entitlement to a transferable nil rate band, the amount potentially going to waste on the first of their deaths will be the sum of their two existing entitlements.

Preserving all of both existing entitlements in this case will necessitate the first spouse to die using all of their existing transferable nil rate band plus all or part of their own nil rate band.

Example

Buddy died some years ago and used 25% of his nil rate band.

Buddy's widow, Holly, later remarried to Waylon, who was a widower himself. Waylon's previous wife Jenny had used 60% of her nil rate band when she died.

As things stand, therefore, Holly is entitled to a 75% transferable nil rate band and Waylon is entitled to a 40% transferable nil rate band. The couple's existing entitlements total 115% and this is how much will go to waste without effective planning.

Holly and Waylon therefore both draw up Wills to put a 'Widow's Loan Scheme' into effect on their death which will utilise 115% of the value of the nil rate band at that time. (I am assuming that each of them has enough wealth to do this.)

If Holly dies first, the 'Widow's Loan Scheme' will use up all of her existing transferable nil rate band entitlement, plus 40% of her own nil rate band, leaving a further 60% transferable nil rate band entitlement to transfer to Waylon.

If Waylon dies first, the 'Widow's Loan Scheme' will use up all of his existing transferable nil rate band entitlement, plus 75% of his own nil rate band, leaving a further 25% transferable nil rate band entitlement to transfer to Holly.

Either way, the survivor will end up with a full transferable nil rate band entitlement and none of the couple's existing entitlement will have gone to waste.

In the case of a couple who both already have an existing entitlement to a full transferable nil rate band, the amount of additional relief which can be preserved in this way will be equal to double the amount of the nil rate band. At current rates, this amounts to £260,000 worth of tax relief.

Is It Worth It?

Before we look at how to use an existing transferable nil rate band entitlement effectively, it is worth pausing to consider whether we think it is 'worth the effort'.

Before October 2007, any married couple had a potential exposure to IHT whenever their combined total wealth exceeded £300,000. The purpose of any planning designed to utilise the nil rate band on the first death was to effectively double the point at which that IHT exposure began, to an effective £600,000, and thus save the couple's family up to £120,000 (at 2007/8 rates).

Now we have a starting position where most married couples will only have a potential exposure to IHT when their combined total wealth exceeds £650,000. In some cases, where there is a suitable qualifying property and the couple intend to leave it, or its eventual sale proceeds, to their children, the potential exposure, after 5ᵗʰ April 2020, will only be on wealth in excess of £1m (due to the residence nil rate band – see Section 3.4 for details).

The planning which we are now considering is designed to increase the point at which the couple's IHT exposure begins to an even greater level, often as much as £975,000 or even £1.3m: PLUS whatever further exemption they can achieve with the residence nil rate band.

Whether this is worthwhile really depends on how great an estate you anticipate the second spouse to die having at the time of their death. I can only leave you to judge that, but I will leave you with an example to think about.

Example

Aaliyah and Marshall are a married couple who have both been married before and both already have an existing entitlement to a full transferable nil rate band.

When Marshall dies in December 2018, Aaliyah is advised that there is no need to carry out any IHT planning since the property which she has just inherited is worth £650,000 and is therefore covered by her own nil rate band plus her existing transferable nil rate band entitlement.

However, between 2018 and Aaliyah's death in March 2029, house prices triple. [This is the same as the increase which occurred during the period of equal length, from June 1997 to September 2007, so this is entirely possible!]

Following the twelve year freeze to 5th April 2021, the nil rate band is increased by just 2.5% each year thereafter (see Section 3.2). We will also assume that the residence nil rate band is increased at the same rate from 2021/22 onwards.

When Aaliyah dies, her property is worth £1.95m, but the nil rate band is just £401,000 and the residence nil rate band is £217,000. Even after claiming her two transferable nil rate bands, this leaves £714,000 (£1.95m – 2 x £401,000 – 2 x £217,000) of Aaliyah's estate exposed to IHT, costing her family £285,600.

Worse still, if Aaliyah has no direct descendants that she wishes to pass her property to (not everyone does Mr Osborne!), then £1.148m (£1.95m – 2 x £401,000) of her estate will be exposed to IHT, robbing her beneficiaries of £459,200 of their rightful inheritance.

If only they had done some planning when Marshall died!

Why a nephew, niece, lifelong friend, or step-child from an unmarried partnership should suffer an extra £173,600 in IHT defies all understanding!

6.9   USING THE TRANSFERABLE NIL RATE BAND

As explained in the previous section, many 'second time around' couples will still benefit from using all or part of the first spouse to die's nil rate band plus, in some cases, their existing entitlement to a transferable nil rate band. The amount of additional relief which may be generated in this way will be up to double the amount of the nil rate band, producing savings of up to £260,000 in some cases.

Example

Thomas died in March 2019, leaving his net estate worth £3m to his son Arthur (who is also Thomas's executor). Thomas was a widower who had survived two wives: Alice who had died in 1985, without using any of her nil rate band, and Doris, who had died in November 2018.

After claiming the transferable nil rate band to which Thomas was entitled, as well as Thomas's own nil rate band, Arthur is left to bear IHT at 40% on £2.35m (£3m – 2 x £325,000), i.e. £940,000.

However, within Thomas's estate there was a property worth £650,000 that he had inherited from his second wife Doris. Doris herself had been entitled to a transferable nil rate band as a result of a previous marriage to Tony, who had died some years ago without using any of his nil rate band.

Since Doris left the property to her husband and it was therefore exempt anyway, both her nil rate band and her transferable nil rate band (from Tony) were never used. What Doris should have done, instead, was to leave her property to Arthur. No IHT would have been payable on her death, as her property was covered by the sum of her nil rate band and her transferable nil rate band entitlement.

But when Thomas died later, his estate would have been worth £650,000 less, i.e. £2.35m. After deducting Thomas's nil rate band and transferable nil rate band entitlement, Arthur would have had to pay IHT at 40% on just £1.7m. Arthur's IHT bill would thus have been £680,000, giving him a saving of £260,000.

In effect, Arthur would have benefited from four nil rate bands instead of just two!

Non-Spousal Legacies

The non-spousal legacy (e.g. the one from Doris to Arthur in the above example) does not need to be one specific property. It could be a whole group of assets, or simply worded as a legacy equal to the appropriate multiple of the nil rate band to be paid out of the general assets of the estate.

But What if You're Not That Well Off?

The non-spousal legacy strategy is pretty simple to follow when, like Thomas and Doris above, there are plenty of assets around.

The problem for some 'second time around' married couples, however, is that they can't afford to simply give their children, or other beneficiaries, up to £650,000 when one of them dies.

The surviving spouse will need to retain sufficient assets to support them for the rest of their life including, in most cases, the family home.

Fortunately, as we shall see in the next few sections, there are some planning strategies available to deal with this dilemma.

Too Much of a Good Thing?

When including a non-spousal legacy, or any other technique designed to use all or part of your nil rate band, in your Will, it is usually best not to word the legacy as a specific sum.

What you may wish to do instead is to draft your Will so that it includes a legacy equal to the appropriate proportion of whatever the nil rate band happens to be at the time of your death.

That way, the amount of the legacy will automatically adjust in line with the nil rate band (when the happy day does *finally* come at last that the nil rate band starts to increase again!)

This may have some practical drawbacks, however. If any future Government were to drastically increase the value of the nil rate band, this strategy could cause some practical problems for your family.

'What's the problem', you say: after all you can just amend your Will if that happens. Probably, yes, and if you keep the situation under review you will be able to do this.

But what happens if you no longer have legal capacity (see Section 15.13) at that time?

To guard against this possibility, you may also wish to place a 'cap' on the maximum value of the legacy.

What About the Residence Nil Rate Band?

You will also need to factor in the residence nil rate band into your planning.

It is likely, in most cases, that anyone with an existing transferable nil rate band entitlement will also have an entitlement to their former spouse's residence nil rate band: although this will not always be the case, for the reasons we explored in Section 3.4.

Nonetheless, where one or both of the current spouses have an existing entitlement to a previous deceased spouse's unused residence nil rate band, this may provide scope for some further savings.

Example Revisited

Let's take the same facts as before, except that:

- *Thomas does not die until March 2021, when the residence nil rate band is £175,000*
- *Doris died in November 2020*
- *The property that Doris had left to Arthur was worth £1m and was a qualifying property for residence nil rate band purposes*

Let us also assume that the former spouses, Alice and Tony, had each died with estates worth less than £2m.

None of this would alter Arthur's IHT liability of £940,000 if Doris had left her entire estate to Thomas.

However, if Doris had left her property worth £1m to Arthur (instead of Thomas), it would have been fully exempted by her own nil rate band, her transferable nil rate band (from Tony), her residence nil rate band and the residence nil rate band transferred to her from Tony (£325,000 x 2 + £175,000 x 2 = £1m).

Thomas's estate would now be worth £2m, meaning that, he would now be entitled to his own residence nil rate band and the one transferred to him from his first wife, Alice. If his estate included a qualifying property worth at least £350,000, or the sale proceeds from such a property (see Sections 3.4 and 12.16 for further details), this would provide a further exemption of £350,000, leaving him exposed to IHT on just £1m (£2m - £325,000 x 2 - £350,000) and giving Arthur an IHT liability of just £400,000.

In conclusion, by 6th April 2020, a non-spousal legacy on the first death in a 'second time around' couple could produce savings of up to £540,000!

If Only We'd Known About This Before!

Don't despair if you think you've left it too late. Any of the methods available to utilise a transferable nil rate band or a former spouse's residence nil rate band which are described in this guide can be put in place through a Deed of Variation made within two years of the relevant spouse's death. See Section 16.1 for further details.

6.10   ESTATE EQUALISATION

One thing that you cannot do, even with a Deed of Variation, is to put more money into the hands of the deceased!

For a 'second time around' married couple with some existing transferable nil rate band entitlement, it is therefore vital to ensure that both spouses have sufficient net assets in their own right to utilise the appropriate proportion of the nil rate band on their death (plus the residence nil rate band where appropriate). As you do not know which one of you will die first, nor even when this will be, it is usually advisable to share your assets equally throughout your marriage, or at least until you each have net personal assets well in excess of the required amount.

This strategy is known as 'estate equalisation' and makes perfect sense as long as you are happy that your marriage will last 'Until Death Do Us Part'!

For a number of reasons, it is generally preferable for the couple to equalise their estates throughout their married life rather than rely on large transfers between them as they get older. Such transfers may render some IHT planning techniques void, although in Section 15.14 we will also look at situations where they can still be effective.

As explained in Section 6.3, however, there may now be an exception to all this in cases where a married couple's combined net assets exceed £4m.

6.11   WILL TRUSTS

One method for using an existing transferable nil rate band is to set up a discretionary trust through your Will (see Chapter 8 for an explanation of discretionary trusts).

Assets with a value equal to the appropriate proportion of the nil rate band (which will otherwise go to waste - see Section 6.8), are left to the trust. The surviving spouse will be one of the beneficiaries of the trust and, in practice, can actually retain all the benefits of ownership of the assets in the trust.

This can be achieved by ensuring that the trustees exercise their 'discretion' in such a way as to ensure that the surviving spouse receives the income from, and enjoyment of, the assets.

There is, however, a danger that HMRC may attack this type of discretionary trust on the basis that it is really a 'de facto' interest in possession trust. This would mean that the trust constituted an 'Immediate Post-Death Interest' (see Section 8.12).

This, in turn, would mean that the assets of the trust will remain in the surviving spouse's estate for IHT purposes, thus rendering this planning void.

Nevertheless, this type of Will trust should still work where the trust is genuinely discretionary in nature.

This would necessitate avoiding the usual 'Letter of Instruction' to the trustees stating that the surviving spouse is to receive all income from the trust. It would also be wise to ensure that other beneficiaries did, indeed, receive some trust income.

This method is therefore probably unsuitable for IHT planning with the family home, but we will see some variations that may still be suitable in Chapter 12.

Wealth Warning

Some standard 'off the shelf' Will trusts will actually give rise to an interest in possession and are thus of no use for this type of planning. This can even apply to standard Will trusts provided by some quite reputable organisations. As usual, this just goes to show that there is no substitute for taking proper professional advice.

This method cannot be used to utilise a transferred residence nil rate band.

6.12 THE WIDOW'S LOAN SCHEME

Another method for utilising an existing transferable nil rate band is to leave a specific legacy of a sum equal to the appropriate proportion of the nil rate band (see Section 6.8) to a discretionary trust in your Will and the remainder of your estate (or most of it) to your spouse.

Your spouse would be a beneficiary of the trust, together with other family members (usually).

There are a number of variations to this method but, in essence, the basic principle is that all (or most) of the deceased's assets are passed to the surviving spouse who therefore ends up owing a sum equal to the appropriate proportion of the nil rate band to the trust.

The 'charge scheme' is one such variation and, unlike the simple Will Trust (see Section 6.11), it is well suited to IHT planning with the family home. Under this scheme, the trust initially takes possession of the deceased's share of the family home and then takes a charge over it for a sum equal to the required proportion of the nil rate band. The deceased's share of the property is then passed to the surviving spouse subject to the charge.

When the surviving spouse subsequently dies, the amount of this charge is deductible from their estate (subject to the points below regarding payment of the debt), thus effectively providing relief for the transferable nil rate band which would otherwise have gone to waste (see Section 6.8).

Some experts suggest that where the 'charge scheme' is being used, the surviving spouse should not be an executor of the deceased's estate. It is not absolutely clear if this would actually be a problem, but it is certainly wise to 'play it safe' in these matters.

The so-called 'debt scheme' is a simpler variation of the 'Widow's Loan Scheme', but has some technical problems which can lead to difficulties if the main 'bread-winner' turns out to be the survivor.

Another variation which appears to avoid such technical problems is to leave the appropriate proportion of the nil rate band to a discretionary trust and leave the remainder of your estate to an interest in possession trust for the benefit of your spouse, rather than to your spouse directly.

As explained in Section 8.12, the interest in possession trust is entitled to the spouse exemption, but will be left owing the appropriate sum (which you need in order to utilise the existing transferable nil rate band) to the discretionary trust.

Once again, the debt due to the discretionary trust will be deductible from the surviving spouse's estate on their subsequent death (subject to the points below regarding payment of the debt).

Despite its name, whichever variation of the 'Widow's Loan Scheme' is used, it should work equally well in principle for a widower, but professional advice remains essential in all cases!

Wealth Warning

There is a school of thought that it may be necessary for the discretionary trust to charge interest on the loan to the surviving spouse in order to make the 'Widow's Loan Scheme' effective. Although some of the interest charged could be passed back to the surviving spouse (as a beneficiary of the trust), this would still lead to an Income Tax cost (see Section 8.22). Once again, professional advice is essential!

Payment of the Debt

In most cases, it will be essential that the debt due to the discretionary trust is actually repaid out of the assets of the surviving spouse's estate (see Section 2.12). Where an interest in possession trust is used (as described above) the debt will need to be repaid from the assets of that trust.

In many cases, this will be easy to achieve by simply selling some or all of the assets of the estate (or the interest in possession trust, as the case may be) and making a suitable cash payment to the discretionary trust.

In other cases, one of the alternative techniques outlined in Section 2.12 may be used instead.

As discussed in Section 2.12, there may also be some cases where the debt is structured on a sufficiently commercial basis that it can be left outstanding. This would generally require, as a bare minimum, that:

- The loan is subject to interest at a commercial rate
- The interest is actually paid to the discretionary trust (see Section 8.22 regarding the Income Tax consequences of this)
- The loan is secured
- The loan is taken over by a person or persons who do not pose a greater risk than an arms' length lender would generally be willing to accept

Once again, professional advice is essential!

Again, this method cannot be used to utilise a transferred residence nil rate band.

6.13   WHEN AND HOW TO UNDO OBSOLETE PLANNING

For a long time before October 2007, the main emphasis in IHT planning for all married couples was to ensure that the nil rate band was fully utilised on the first spouse's death.

As discussed in Section 6.7, however, this is now the very last thing which most married couples should do. (Although there are exceptions to this, as we have already seen in Section 6.8.)

Many people are therefore in the position that they have implemented some form of IHT planning which now looks to be disadvantageous. What should these people do now?

Married Couples

Where both members of the couple are still alive and have undertaken some IHT planning through their Wills, the answer is simple: rewrite your Wills to revise your planning along the lines set out in Section 6.7.

If, however, you have undertaken some planning which involved making lifetime transfers to use up your nil rate band, you will be unable to reverse this and will need to wait seven years before your nil rate band is available again.

Widows and Widowers

Your position depends on a number of things.

Firstly, if you have outlived two or more previous spouses, you may find that you already have the maximum transferable nil rate band entitlement even if one of your previous spouses undertook some planning to utilise their nil rate band. If so, the planning already carried out remains effective and should probably be left in place.

Similarly, if you were a widow or widower but have remarried since the earlier IHT planning was implemented by your previous spouse, you still have the potential to acquire a transferable nil rate band from your current spouse and the earlier planning again probably remains effective. As far as any further planning is concerned, you will be in the same position as a 'first time' couple which we examined in Section 6.7.

The same can be said if you are expecting to remarry again in the near future.

In any other cases, any previous steps put in place to utilise your late spouse's nil rate band may now be disadvantageous to your position.

If, however, your estate will clearly never exceed the nil rate band this will probably never be of any consequence unless, perhaps, you should win the lottery (see Section 10.17 for important advice if you play the lottery).

If earlier planning has put you at a disadvantage, you may be able to undo it if your spouse died within the last two years.

A widow or widower whose spouse died within the last two years may be able to enter a Deed of Variation (see Section 16.1) to alter the terms of their spouse's Will in order to benefit from the transferable nil rate band regime. This, of course, will only help if the deceased spouse utilised their nil rate band on death; it will not be possible to alter any lifetime transfers which they made.

6.14   THE DAUGHTER-IN-LAW PLAN

I am not sure how many people would be prepared to follow this plan in practice but, in theory, it should work. I will illustrate the plan with an example.

Example

Frank, a widower, is almost 90 years old. He has a huge estate, which he wishes to leave to his son, Frank Junior. Unfortunately, Frank has done no IHT planning and now realises that relying on surviving for seven years may not be good enough.

Frank Junior is engaged to Mia, a 30-year-old, UK-domiciled, actress.

However, what the family decides is that, instead of marrying Frank Junior, Mia should marry 90-year-old Frank.

Shortly after the marriage, Frank gives everything he owns to Mia. This transfer is exempt under the spouse exemption.

A little while later, Mia divorces Frank and marries Frank Junior. She can now (if she wishes) transfer everything to Frank Junior and it will again be exempt from IHT under the spouse exemption.

As I said, this works in theory. Like any other tax-planning strategy, this probably depends on how well it is done. To date, HMRC has not had any success challenging the validity of a marriage.

But the real problem with this plan lies in the phrase 'if she wishes'. What is there to stop Mia from running off with all of the family's money?

The above strategy can easily be adapted to pass wealth from a mother to her daughter, from father to daughter, or from mother to son.

6.15   THE SPOUSE BRIDGE

A spouse with a longer life expectancy can be used as a 'bridge' to transfer assets to children or other beneficiaries.

Assets are transferred to the spouse either during lifetime or on death and this transfer is tax free (subject to the points set out in Section 3.3). The spouse can then transfer the assets to the children as a potentially exempt transfer (see Section 4.3) and, as long as the spouse survives for seven years after that transfer, IHT is avoided.

In theory, any spouse will do for this strategy, including an estranged spouse who the transferor has not yet divorced, or a spouse who is not actually a parent of the children who are ultimately supposed to benefit.

Example

Tremela divorced her ex-husband many years ago and has single-handedly managed to raise her daughter Alisha, as well as building up a large portfolio of investment properties. Tragically, Tremela has now found out that she has only a short time to live and wishes to leave everything she owns to Alisha, who is now a young adult.

Tremela has been friends with Brian for many years and now decides to marry him.

When Tremela tragically dies a short time later, she leaves £325,000 to Alisha but leaves the rest of her estate to Brian. No IHT is due as everything is covered by either the nil rate band or the spouse exemption.

Brian can then give Alisha all of the property received from Tremela and, as long as he survives seven years, IHT will be avoided.

There are a few possible problems with this strategy, however.

Firstly, potentially exempt transfers of anything other than cash may give rise to CGT liabilities (see Chapter 11).

Secondly, where there is an informal request asking the beneficiary under a Will to transfer inherited property to another person and the beneficiary does indeed make the requested transfer within two years of the deceased's death, the transfer is treated as a direct transfer from the deceased to that other person.

This particular provision can be side-stepped by either making a lifetime transfer to the spouse or by the spouse waiting two years and a day after the deceased's death before passing the assets on to the ultimate recipient.

Thirdly, and perhaps more importantly, there is the question of whether the transferee spouse will behave as the transferor hopes. They cannot be forced to pass the assets on to the children, or the initial transfer will be ignored.

Preliminary transfers to a spouse are a perfectly good way to avoid or reduce IHT liabilities, as long as there is no obligation on the transferee spouse to make the subsequent transfer to the ultimate recipient.

If, however, the arrangement for the second transfer is already in place, the initial transfer to the spouse would be disregarded and the position would revert to that given by a single transfer direct from the transferor spouse to the ultimate recipient. The spouse exemption would then be lost and IHT would be payable in full on the original transferor's death within seven years.

This is why in the previous section we had to leave Mia to transfer assets to Frank Junior 'if she wishes'.

Even with no fixed arrangements for the assets to be passed on to the children, there is still some risk that HMRC might invoke the associated operations rules (see Section 10.21) or the general anti-abuse rule (see Section 10.22). The initial transfer would then again be ignored, resulting in the loss of the spouse exemption. How anyone could do this in the face of such a terrible tragedy as poor Tremela's premature death escapes me, but that is the nature of IHT!

In the more usual case of a married couple who are still living together at the time of the initial transfer (or until the transferor's death), this risk would generally be much lower, as HMRC does not usually attack arrangements between married couples still living together.

In the case of a separated couple, or a 'marriage of convenience' like Tremela and Brian, the risk of such an attack is probably far greater, but may possibly be avoided if the transferee retains the assets for a few years before passing them on to the ultimate recipient.

As explained in Section 6.14, HMRC has not had any success in challenging the validity of a marriage itself to date.

A similar method that might be used to pass assets to a minor child is set out in Section 8.12.

6.16   THE FAMILY DEBT SCHEME

A sale of an investment asset to your spouse can be used as a means to reduce the value of your estate for IHT purposes without increasing the value of theirs to the same extent.

The asset, such as an investment property for example, is sold to the spouse for any price up to its full market value. Although the transfer is not a gift, the sale still represents a transfer between spouses and is therefore exempt from both IHT and CGT.

Some form of Stamp Duty will be payable in most cases, however, and the rates involved can be quite prohibitive where residential property is used (see the Taxcafe.co.uk guide 'How to Save Property Tax' for details).

Nonetheless, SDLT can be avoided if the property is a non-residential property and is sold for a consideration not exceeding £150,000.

If you sell shares to your spouse, Stamp Duty will be payable on the sale consideration at the rate of 0.5%.

The sale consideration due from the purchasing spouse is left outstanding as a loan; or an 'IOU' if you like.

The vendor spouse then gives the 'IOU' to their children or other intended beneficiaries. This is a potentially exempt transfer, meaning that the value of the 'IOU' will be exempt from IHT as long as the vendor spouse survives for seven years. This provides the reduction in the vendor spouse's estate since they no longer hold either the original asset or the 'IOU'.

On the purchasing spouse's death, the value of the 'IOU' will be deducted from their estate: ***provided*** that the sum due under the 'IOU' is actually paid out of the assets of their estate (see Section 2.12). This will cancel out some or all of the value of the transferred property.

This method is generally only used for investment assets which do not qualify for business property relief (see Chapter 7).

6.17   GRAB A GRANNY

As explained in Section 6.6, it is possible that we may in future see some more detailed provisions designed to restrict the transferable nil rate band and perhaps, in particular, to prevent separated couples from benefitting. This would reduce the attractiveness of some potential planning ideas.

In the meantime, however, the transferable nil rate band system currently appears to open up some interesting planning ideas for people who are currently single.

Firstly, as things stand, it appears that a surviving spouse will benefit from any unused nil rate band on the death of a spouse at any time, even many years before their own death.

Example

Dave is a single young man with great ambitions. One day, he hopes to die rich and he would like to pay as little IHT as possible.

Visiting a local nursing home, Dave meets Elsie, one of the residents. He announces that he has fallen in love and he marries Elsie, who is living off a state pension and barely has two pennies to rub together. Dave is grief stricken when Elsie dies shortly after their marriage. His one consolation is that he has just acquired full entitlement to a transferable nil rate band. Permanently!

Secondly, once a person has a transferable nil rate band, they can remarry and can still preserve the benefit of their transferable nil rate band by following the planning strategies set out in Sections 6.9 to 6.12. Furthermore, where both members of a couple are already entitled to a transferable nil rate band, the full benefit of both existing entitlements can be preserved.

A short time after Elsie's death, Dave meets Sam and Dave proposes. However, what Dave proposes is that Sam should pop down to the local nursing home and see if there is anyone there that Sam fancies marrying: it worked for him, after all!

Sure enough, Sam finds Bill, who is penniless, announces that this is true love and marries him.

Just like Dave, Sam is consoled after Bill's death a short time later by the knowledge that Bill's unused nil rate band now transfers and may be claimed against Sam's own estate.

A little while after Bill's death, Sam and Dave, both recently bereaved, seek solace in each other by getting married. Many years later, Sam and Dave prepare to pass on their wealth to their children. The couple are now very wealthy and are each able to include legacies to their children equal to twice the amount of the nil rate band.

Sam and Dave's children will therefore be able to benefit from no less than four nil rate bands!

6.18 MARRIED COUPLES WITH MIXED DOMICILE

In Section 2.2, we saw that, from 6th April 2017, a non-UK domiciled person acquires deemed UK domicile when they have been resident in the UK for more than 15 out of the last 20 UK tax years.

In Section 3.3, we also saw that the limit on exempt transfers to a non-UK domiciled spouse would cease to apply if that spouse acquired deemed UK domicile.

This may open up some interesting planning ideas for any married couples with mixed domicile.

Example

Mary is UK domiciled but has significant foreign assets. Her husband Farrokh is domiciled in Zanzibar but has lived in the UK for the last 18 years and therefore has deemed UK domicile for tax purposes.

Mary can transfer all her foreign assets to Farrokh and this transfer will be fully exempt from IHT. Farrokh could then leave the UK and would automatically lose his deemed UK domicile five years later.

All of Mary's foreign assets, now held by Farrokh, would then be free from UK IHT.

"Couldn't Mary achieve the same result just by emigrating herself?" you may ask. Yes, she could, but, as we shall see in Chapter 14, it would be much harder for her to shed her UK domicile whereas, for Farrokh, it will be automatic.

Wealth Warning
This strategy is effective for IHT purposes, but may not be for CGT. If Farrokh is still UK resident at the time of the transfer, Mary would continue to be subject to UK CGT on the transferred assets after Farrokh left the UK for as long as she remained UK resident herself.

Tax Tip
One way around this might be to make the transfer after Farrokh has ceased to be UK resident but before the end of the period that he continues to have deemed UK domicile.

The example above is based on the assumption that Farrokh has not elected to 'opt in' for UK IHT purposes. In the next section, we will look at the advantages and disadvantages of an 'opt in' election. We will also revisit the above planning strategy to see a variation which works where an election has been made.

6.19 THE OPT-IN ELECTION

A non-UK domiciled person with a UK domiciled spouse may elect to 'opt-in' and be treated as UK domiciled for UK IHT purposes.

A non-UK domiciled widow or widower who had a recently deceased UK domiciled spouse may also make an election.

Where the UK domiciled spouse is still alive, the election may be backdated by up to seven years; but can never apply to a date earlier than 6th April 2013.

Where the UK domiciled spouse is deceased, the election must be made within two years of their date of death and may be backdated by up to seven years prior to that date. Once again, however, the election cannot apply to a date earlier than 6th April 2013.

The person making the election must be non-UK domiciled under general principles but they are not barred from making it if they have deemed UK domicile (see Section 2.2).

Where both spouses are deceased, the personal representatives of the non-UK domiciled spouse may make the election on their behalf (subject to the time limits described above).

Impact of Election

The basic effect of the 'opt-in' election is that the non-UK domiciled spouse is treated as UK domiciled for IHT purposes with effect from whichever date the election is specified to apply from (subject to the limits described above).

The election is irrevocable and hence will apply for the remainder of the electing spouse's lifetime and on their death – unless they become non-UK resident for a period of four consecutive tax years, in which case the election automatically ceases to apply.

Whilst the election generally means that the non-UK domiciled spouse is treated as UK domiciled for most UK IHT purposes, there are a few exceptions:

- Certain Government securities and other similar assets with 'excluded property' status (see Section 2.2), will retain that status

- The provisions of any applicable Double Tax Treaty (see Section 2.2 and Appendix B) are unaffected

- Double tax relief will continue to be available where the person is also subject to IHT (or a similar tax) in another country

The election does not alter the non-UK domiciled spouse's status for the purposes of Income Tax or CGT.

Advantages of Making the Election

- Complete exemption from IHT on all transfers from the UK domiciled spouse to the non-UK domiciled spouse during lifetime (from date on which the election becomes effective) and on death

- The ability to use an unlimited spouse exemption to transfer assets into an immediate post-death interest trust free from IHT (see Section 8.12)

- The ability to obtain a full transferable nil rate band on the UK domiciled spouse's death (where the entire estate is left to the non-UK domiciled spouse)

- Other exemptions, such as the annual exemption (see Section 5.2) will not be used up by lifetime transfers to the non-UK domiciled spouse after the election becomes effective

- The ability to carry out any planning mechanisms which are available to UK domiciled spouses (e.g. the 'spouse bridge' – see Section 6.15)

- Unlimited exemption from the 'gifts with reservation of benefit' rules (see Section 4.9) on any transfers between spouses after the election becomes effective

Disadvantages of Making the Election

Disadvantages include:

- The non-UK domiciled spouse's entire worldwide estate will be subject to UK IHT (subject to the terms of any applicable Double Tax Treaty)

- Any transfers of assets, including foreign assets, by the non-UK domiciled spouse to anyone other than the UK domiciled spouse may potentially use part of the non-UK domiciled spouse's nil rate band and reduce the transferable nil rate band available

- The non-UK domiciled spouse would be unable to set up an excluded property trust (see Section 9.11) to shelter any of the assets which they held on or after the date on which the election becomes effective

Tax Tip

The non-UK domiciled spouse could set up an excluded property trust before the date on which the election becomes effective. When considering this option, it will be vital to ensure that the election is not backdated prior to the date on which assets are transferred into the trust.

- The pre-owned assets charge (see Chapter 13) may potentially apply to foreign assets enjoyed by the non-UK domiciled spouse (unless held within an excluded property trust before the election becomes effective)

- Lifetime transfers of foreign assets by the non-UK domiciled spouse may be chargeable lifetime transfers or may become chargeable lifetime transfers in the event of their death within seven years

Tax Tip

It is important to consider the impact of backdating any 'opt-in' election where the non-UK domiciled spouse has made any transfers of foreign assets, or funds held abroad, to any person other than their UK domiciled spouse.

It may also be worth considering making such transfers before making an 'opt-in' election.

In Summary

Whilst the decision whether or not to make an 'opt-in' election is something which really requires professional advice, it seems fair to say that, in general terms, an 'opt-in' election is likely to be beneficial where the UK domiciled spouse has the majority of the couple's assets.

On the other hand, the election is likely to be disadvantageous where the non-UK domiciled spouse has substantial foreign assets, or may acquire them in the future (e.g. by way of their own inheritance).

Planning Revisited

In some cases, it will be possible to adapt the planning set out in Section 6.18 so that it works where the non-UK domiciled spouse has previously made an 'opt-in' election.

Example

Whitney is UK domiciled but has significant foreign assets. Her husband Bobby had a 'domicile of origin' (see Section 14.2) in Massachusetts but elected to 'opt-in' and be treated as UK domiciled with effect from 6th April 2013.

Some years later, Whitney transferred all of her foreign assets to Bobby.

In March 2020, Bobby moved to Jamaica and ceased to be UK resident. On 6th April 2024, after four consecutive years of being non-UK resident, Bobby's 'opt-in' election automatically ceases to apply. As a result, all of Whitney's former foreign assets are now exempt from UK IHT.

Wealth Warning 1
See Section 6.18 regarding the potential CGT drawbacks of this strategy which apply equally here.

Wealth Warning 2
Following the introduction of the statutory residence test with effect from 6th April 2013, it is now generally more difficult to achieve non-UK residence: especially if you still have a UK resident spouse!

Having said that, it probably remains easier for Bobby to achieve non-UK residence for four years than for Whitney to achieve non-UK domicile!

Wealth Warning 3
The strategy outlined in the example is appropriate for those who have made an 'opt-in' election some time earlier: well before leaving the UK.

If the election were made only a short time before the non-UK domiciled spouse left the UK, it is likely that HMRC would seek to block this planning strategy.

Chapter 7

The Tax Benefits of Business Property

7.1   INTRODUCTION

Where the appropriate conditions are satisfied, relief from IHT is available on the transfer of relevant business property or agricultural property. As a result, it is possible to pass on many family businesses free from IHT.

Care must be exercised, however, as there are a great many pitfalls awaiting the unwary! In particular, the rules relating to the deduction of liabilities (see Section 2.12) have led to a whole extra set of problems for business owners looking to pass their business on to the next generation. In some cases, these rules may effectively wipe out the benefit of the relief. We will see an example of this in Section 7.11.

The reliefs for business and agricultural property apply, in principle, to both lifetime transfers and transfers on death, although, as we shall see in Section 7.19, there are a few more conditions to be met in the case of lifetime transfers.

In many cases, where available, the relief is given at 100%, meaning that the transfer of the business or agricultural property may potentially escape IHT altogether.

In those cases where relief is given at a rate less than 100%, the relief is given before applying any other exemptions (such as the annual exemption or the nil rate band). Where relief is available at 50%, this effectively doubles the value of these other exemptions.

Example

Cliff has an industrial building worth £662,000 on which business property relief is available at the rate of 50%. He wishes to transfer the building to the Marvin-Welch Discretionary Trust. This will be Cliff's first chargeable lifetime transfer. After business property relief at 50%, the chargeable transfer is reduced to £331,000. Cliff's annual exemptions for the current and previous years are still available. Deducting these (at £3,000 each) leaves a chargeable transfer of £325,000, which is covered by Cliff's nil rate band.

Note that, in the above example, there is a risk that IHT liabilities will arise if Cliff dies within seven years of making this transfer. We will return to the subject of business property relief on lifetime transfers in Section 7.19. Technically, no actual 'claim' is required, as these reliefs apply automatically when the relevant conditions are met. In practice, one does still have to 'claim' that the conditions have been met.

Trusts

These reliefs also apply to the tenth anniversary and exit charges for trusts (see Chapter 8). Naturally, the trust will need to meet all of the necessary conditions, including the minimum ownership period (see Section 7.17). In practice, the trust will generally need to hold any business or agricultural property for at least two years before passing it on to a beneficiary in order to obtain the relief.

7.2   WHEN IS BUSINESS PROPERTY RELIEF AVAILABLE?

Business property relief is available on transfers of business property that meet each of the following three conditions:

i) The business concerned is a qualifying business (see Sections 7.4 to 7.7),

ii) The asset itself is relevant business property (see Section 7.8), and

iii) The asset has been owned by the transferor for at least the relevant minimum period (see Section 7.17)

There is no requirement for the business to be located in the UK (but see Section 7.30 regarding agricultural property).

7.3   JUST HOW USEFUL IS BUSINESS PROPERTY RELIEF?

There is absolutely no limit to the amount of business property relief that a taxpayer may claim where the qualifying conditions are met. The relief could potentially be used to completely exempt an estate worth **billions** of pounds from IHT!

An obvious, and vital, piece of IHT planning is therefore to maximise the value of any assets qualifying for business property relief within your estate. We will come back to this in Section 7.22.

But business property relief isn't just for those with an existing business. The relief provides a useful mechanism to give IHT-exempt funds to family and friends, as we shall see in Section 7.27. There are even some types of investments which may qualify, as we shall see in Section 7.28.

Furthermore, it generally takes just two years for assets to achieve exemption through business property relief, which is much better than the seven-year waiting period for potentially exempt transfers.

Sadly, however, it is all too easy to lose business property relief by failing to meet the qualifying conditions at the appropriate time. There are some particularly nasty pitfalls to watch out for with business property relief. In fact, not only is the relief very easy to lose, but this also has a tendency to happen at the point in life when IHT planning is becoming most important.

There is also the problem that some quite normal commercial structures will leave the business owner with business property relief at just 50% on their most valuable asset when they could so easily have had 100%.

Furthermore, the rules on liabilities incurred to finance relievable property (see Section 7.11) mean that some business owners will enjoy little or no benefit from business property relief. Worst of all, refinancing an existing loan could lead to the loss of relief in some cases (see Section 7.15).

Given the importance of this relief and the ease with which it can be lost, we will now take a long and detailed look at the relevant qualifying conditions. Some of this gets quite technical but is important for anyone wanting to benefit from what is arguably the most powerful way to save IHT.

7.4   QUALIFYING BUSINESSES – BASIC PRINCIPLES

For this purpose, any business is a 'qualifying business' as long as it is being carried on with a view to profit and does not consist wholly or mainly of dealing in securities, stocks or shares or land and buildings, nor of making or holding investments (except for the holding company of a trading group).

This may not initially sound too restrictive but, as we shall see, the definition of what constitutes 'making or holding investments' can be a great deal broader than what one might normally think.

Despite this, however, Lloyd's underwriters generally qualify for at least some business property relief. The businesses of 'market makers' or 'discount houses' on the Stock Exchange will also generally qualify. As in many other fields of taxation, special rules apply to each of these businesses.

What is a Business?

Case law suggests that a business will exist where at least some of the following six tests apply to the activity being undertaken:

    i)   The activity is a 'serious undertaking earnestly pursued' or a 'serious occupation'.

    ii)   The activity is 'an occupation or function actively pursued with reasonable or recognisable continuity'.

    iii) The activity has 'a certain measure of substance as measured by the value of supplies made'.

    iv) The activity is 'conducted in a regular manner and on sound and recognised business principles'.

    v)   The activity is 'predominantly concerned with the making of supplies to consumers'.

    vi) The goods or services supplied 'are of a kind which, subject to differences in detail, are commonly made by those who seek to profit by them'.

Where some or all of the above tests are satisfied, the activity will constitute a business and will generally qualify for business property relief purposes unless it falls under one of the statutory exclusions outlined above.

The Importance of the Profit Motive

Nevertheless, even though it may be accepted that a business exists, the intention to make a profit remains essential. The profit motive requirement means that businesses like stud farms or the business activities of artists or authors may sometimes be ineligible for the relief.

Tax Tip

Preparing a credible business plan would provide valuable supporting evidence that you had a reasonable expectation of making a profit from your business.

A documented annual review of the plan will also be useful, as the 'profit expectation' test must be met at the time of the eventual transfer.

Note, however, that a business plan will not help you if it clearly bears no resemblance to your actual behaviour in respect of the business.

7.5   PROPERTY INVESTMENT OR LETTING BUSINESSES

Unfortunately, as so often seems to be the case in UK taxation, property investment or letting businesses are generally not accepted by HMRC as being qualifying businesses for the purpose of business property relief.

The HMRC view is that the mere holding of investment property and collection of rent does not constitute a business for business property relief purposes. (Although this does not seem to stop them from collecting Income Tax on profits generated by this 'non-business' activity!)

Sadly, HMRC's view is supported by the fact that it was specifically stated that the letting of land would not qualify for business property relief during the parliamentary debates when the relevant rules were first enacted.

Doubtless, those of you with property letting businesses will think that this is unfair. This is certainly what the executor of a certain Mrs Burkinyoung thought in 1995 when he made a claim for business property relief on the furnished flats that Mrs Burkinyoung had been letting.

Unfortunately, when the case got to court, the judge decided otherwise, holding that Mrs Burkinyoung's properties were only investments and did not constitute a 'business' for IHT purposes.

It also turns out that it would not have helped the Burkinyoung family if the late Mrs Burkinyoung had instead been letting out commercial property. In another case, business property relief was also denied where the deceased's business consisted of letting out small industrial units. Once again, the judge held that the lettings amounted to the mere holding of investments.

Ancillary Services

That same judge went on to say that the provision of security services, heating or cleaning services as part of the terms of the lease would still not be sufficient, in his opinion, to create a qualifying business. The judge felt that these services would be merely incidental to the holding of investments, even though he acknowledged that such services would constitute a qualifying business if provided independently of the letting business.

Tax Tip

Separating out ancillary services into a separate business may provide landlords with some scope to get business property relief on at least part of their business.

In a later case, property maintenance services were also added to the list of ancillary services that would be regarded as merely incidental to the holding of investments. Again, therefore, it might be helpful to separate these out into a separate business.

Does Size Matter?

You may think, perhaps, that the reason the cases referred to above were lost may be that the letting businesses concerned were too small. Sadly, this is not the case since, in yet another case, a company letting out more than 100 properties was still not regarded as having a qualifying business.

Furnished Holiday Letting

I don't know where they get these judges from, or why it is that they persist in regarding property letting as an easy and completely passive way to make a living.

Nevertheless, as the law stands, it appears that the only type of rental properties that might sometimes attract business property relief are furnished holiday lettings (as described in the Taxcafe.co.uk guide 'How to Save Property Tax').

Qualifying furnished holiday letting may be accepted to be a 'business' for IHT purposes when the lettings are generally short-term (e.g. a week or fortnight) and the owner was substantially involved with the holidaymakers' activities.

This last test does not necessarily mean that the owner must personally cook all of their tenants' meals and take them on guided tours every day (although this might suffice). The necessary services may be provided by an agent, employee, friend or relative of the owner.

However, recent developments suggest a hardening of attitude on this issue from both HMRC and the courts. Hence, whoever actually provides the services, they will really need to be quite substantial in order for the business to qualify for business property relief.

Services provided to tenants will need to be far beyond the 'normal' level where landlords merely provide maintenance and cleaning services. Significant additional facilities will need to be available to the holidaymakers before the business can qualify.

Landlords with furnished holiday lettings should therefore never assume that they will be eligible for business property relief just because they meet the necessary rules for other tax reliefs (as set out in the Taxcafe.co.uk guide 'How to Save Property Tax'). A far greater level of business activity will be required in order to obtain relief. Anyone planning to rely on business property relief for a furnished holiday let should seek professional advice. (But see also Section 7.32 for a good way of testing the position where the availability of business property relief remains in doubt.)

In Conclusion

Investment property is generally unlikely to qualify for business property relief and you will usually need to be using property in some sort of qualifying trading business in order to be able to claim the relief. A few furnished holiday letting properties may qualify for the relief, however.

7.6   BUSINESSES EXPLOITING LAND

A great many businesses involve some form of 'exploitation of land'. This is a legal term to cover any situation where the use, by customers, of land and buildings is a vital component of the business.

When it comes to claims for business property relief whenever there is some 'exploitation of land' involved in the business, difficulty often arises when HMRC perceives the income from the business to be derived from the use of the land rather than the provision of services. In these cases, HMRC will often attempt to argue that the business consists merely of the 'holding of an investment'.

The best defence against this argument is to show that the business income is derived mainly from the provision of services or sale of goods and not from any form of rent or other payment for the use of land.

Let's now take a look at how the 'exploitation of land' argument has been interpreted for business property relief purposes in some specific types of business.

Property Development
While dealing in land and buildings does not qualify for business property relief purposes, a property development business will qualify and the land and buildings held as trading stock by that business will be covered by business property relief.

Stately Homes
Stately homes open to the public may be covered by business property relief.

In one case, a claim for business property relief was upheld by the court when just 78% of the property was open to the public. Despite the fact that 22% of the property was closed to the public, the whole property qualified as it had to be viewed as a single asset and, furthermore, the entire exterior was important to the paying public's enjoyment of the property.

The implication here is that any building of which more than 50% is used for the public's enjoyment, as part of a commercial enterprise, might qualify for business property relief.

This would surely also extend to private museums and other similar enterprises, as long as the 'profit motive' (see Section 7.4) is present.

(All is not lost where less than 50% of the property is used for business purposes, however, as we shall see in Section 7.9.)

Bookies
The courts have held that an on-course bookmaker's pitch qualified for business property relief.

Caravan Parks
Caravan parks have occupied a lot of the courts' attention when it comes to business property relief and, to date, there have been five major cases on the subject. So far, the score is HMRC 3 – Taxpayers 2.

In essence, the taxpayers lost the cases where the majority of income came from site fees or pitch fees (which are basically a form of rent) but won the cases where the majority of income came from the provision of other services or the sale of caravans.

Most recently, the long and tortuous case of *George & Loochin (Stedman's Executors)* was eventually decided in favour of the deceased's executors when it reached the Court of Appeal. This case concerned a caravan park where a major proportion of the business income comprised site fees for the storage of caravans and mobile homes on the park. However, the saving grace for this caravan park was the fact that 72% of those fees were absorbed by overheads, mainly the upkeep of the common parts of the park.

Nevertheless, HMRC still argued that the site fees represented income from the 'exploitation of land' and that the caravan park business was thus tantamount to the mere 'holding of an investment'.

Thankfully, the judge in the Court of Appeal stated that the holding of property as an investment was only one component of the business and did not prevent it from qualifying for business property relief. He found it difficult to see why an active family business of this kind should be excluded from business property relief just because a necessary component of the business was the holding of land.

This last judgement tells us a few things:

- An 'active' business should qualify for business property relief.
- Caravan parks are very much a 'borderline' case, as they are partly concerned with the exploitation of land.
- You get a better quality of judge in the Court of Appeal.

But seriously, any business that involves some element of 'exploitation of land' runs a risk of not qualifying for business property relief.

Other Businesses & General Guidelines
As well as caravan parks, other businesses that might be classed as 'borderline' for business property relief purposes would include:

- Residential care homes
- Hostels, guest-houses or hotels with long-term residents
- Businesses providing shooting or fishing rights

The common thread in all of these businesses is the fact that providing the use of land or buildings is a vital component of the business. This is what is meant by the phrase 'exploitation of land'.

The key to obtaining business property relief in any case where the 'exploitation of land' is present is to ensure that the majority of the business income comes from the provision of services and not from the mere 'exploitation of land'.

We will look further at the question of what constitutes the majority of the business income in the next section.

Life Interests in Land
The cases where difficulty has arisen due to the 'exploitation of land' argument all involve taxpayers who actually owned that land. Naturally, this meant that their estate was extremely valuable, which is why the business property relief claim was so important.

It has been established, however, that a taxpayer who only held a 'life interest' in land could not be held to have a business that consisted of 'making or holding investments'. That taxpayer's business therefore qualified for business property relief, which was very useful since, as we shall see in Chapter 8, there are some cases where the full value of the underlying assets in which the deceased had a life interest has to be included in their estate.

This provides a potential method for ensuring that a business which could potentially fall foul of the 'exploitation of land' problem will qualify for business property relief.

The drawback, however, is that business property relief is only given at the rate of 50% where the transferor had a life interest in the property rather than absolute ownership (see Section 7.8).

Nevertheless, in some cases, business property relief may be maximised by splitting the ownership of the business from the ownership of the underlying land and placing the land in a life interest trust. This should enable the owner to claim 100% relief on the business and 50% relief on the land when there may have been no relief at all if they had owned both the business and the underlying land outright.

Example

Tom owns a caravan park in South Wales. On his death, he leaves the park business to his wife Joan and the land on which the park is set to a life interest trust with Joan as the beneficiary. Tom's nil rate band is unused and therefore transfers to Joan (see Section 6.3).

On Joan's subsequent death in March 2019, her executors claim 100% business property relief on the park business, worth £750,000, and 50% business property relief on the park land, worth £1.3m.

After business property relief, the chargeable value of the caravan park is thus reduced to £650,000 and this is covered by Joan's nil rate band plus the transferable nil rate band received from Tom: leaving no IHT to pay on the park.

If Joan owned both the park business and the park land outright, she might not have been eligible for any business property relief. The IHT arising on the park would then have been at least £560,000 (£750,000 + £1.3m - £650,000 = £1.4m x 40%).

The drawback to this technique is that it may mean that 50% relief on the value of the underlying land has been sacrificed if, in fact, the business would have qualified for business property relief anyway. A better solution may therefore be to only put the structure described above into place via a Deed of Variation after a business property relief claim on the first spouse's death has already failed. (See Section 7.32 for further details on how to safely test the position on the first spouse's death.)

Wealth Warning

The method described above is based on an old case which was only won in the Court of Appeal on a 2-1 majority. It is therefore quite possible that this decision could be overturned in a later case!

7.7 WHAT DOES 'WHOLLY OR MAINLY' MEAN IN PRACTICE?

As stated above, a business will not qualify for business property relief if it consists 'wholly or mainly' of 'dealing in securities, stocks or shares or land and buildings, or making or holding investments'.

Naturally, however, it follows that while it cannot consist 'wholly or mainly' of these activities, it can still consist 'partly' of them.

But How Much?

Quite simply, 'wholly or mainly' means 'at least 50%'. "50% of what?"; I hear you ask. Case law has sometimes, though not exclusively, interpreted the 50% test as relating to net profits. To be on the safe side, however, I would suggest trying to ensure that the business consists of qualifying activities to the extent that these account for over 50% of each of the following:

- Turnover (i.e. sales)
- Gross profit
- Net profit
- Proprietor's time
- Employees' time
- Assets employed in the business (although, as we have seen already, land employed in the business may be regarded in a number of ways)

Hybrid Businesses

It is important to remember that what is required for business property relief purposes is that the business consists 'wholly or mainly' of qualifying business activities. If the 'wholly or mainly' test is met then the whole business will qualify for business property relief, including those parts of the business which are not themselves qualifying activities.

This has important IHT planning implications as it means that business property relief may be available in respect of an investment business component which represents a minority element of a qualifying business.

Example

Ray and Dave run a property business, Kink Properties, in partnership together. Kink Properties derives around 75% of its income from property development and the remainder from property letting. Whilst HMRC would argue that part of the business amounts to the non-qualifying activity of holding investments, the main part, property development, represents a qualifying activity. Kink Properties therefore qualifies for business property relief. Furthermore, the whole of the Kink Properties business will qualify, including the investment properties.

To get relief on the whole value of the business, it is important to ensure that all of the assets held by the business are actually used in the business. A completely unrelated quoted shareholding, for example, might be regarded as a non-business asset and would thus be ineligible for relief.

116

There is an important distinction between business assets used in a non-qualifying part of the business (like Ray and Dave's investment properties), which do attract relief, and assets that are not business assets at all (like those unrelated quoted shares), which are excluded from the relief.

Assets excluded from relief are known as 'excepted assets' and we will return to this concept again in Section 7.9.

7.8   RELEVANT BUSINESS PROPERTY

The following types of property may qualify for business property relief:

Relief at 100%:

i)   An interest in a qualifying unincorporated business (i.e. a sole trade or profession, or a share in a partnership)
ii)   Unquoted shares in a company carrying on a qualifying business
iii) Unquoted securities (e.g. loan stock) in a company carrying on a qualifying business which either alone or with other unquoted shares or securities, give the transferor control of that company

Relief at 50%:

iv)   Quoted shares or securities in a company carrying on a qualifying business that, either alone or together with other quoted shares or securities, give the transferor control of that company
v)   Assets held personally by the transferor but used wholly or mainly for the purposes of a qualifying business carried on by a company under the transferor's control, or a partnership in which the transferor is a partner (or was prior to death in the case of transfers on death)
vi)   Assets held in an interest in possession trust on behalf of the transferor and used wholly or mainly for the purpose of a business under the transferor's control or a business carried on by a partnership in which the transferor was a partner. (This applies only to 'interests in possession' which are deemed to form part of the transferor's estate for IHT purposes (see Chapter 8))

Some Definitions:

Partnership
A partnership includes a Limited Liability Partnership (LLP).

> **Wealth Warning**
> Members' capital accounts in a Limited Liability Partnership carrying on a qualifying business will qualify for business property relief but members' loan accounts do not!

Unquoted

'Unquoted' means not listed on a recognised Stock Exchange. Shares that are only traded on the Alternative Investment Market (AIM) are not 'listed' and thus qualify as unquoted for business property relief purposes.

Shares traded on either tier of the American Nasdaq are regarded as quoted. In general, any stock market recognised by the laws of the country in which it is situated will usually be regarded as a 'recognised stock exchange' and shares traded there will therefore be treated as quoted.

The legislation seems to refer only to whether the shares or securities themselves are quoted. HMRC's notes, however, refer to a 'quoted company'. This will seldom make any difference but there does remain the question of how to treat unquoted classes of shares or securities issued by a company that has a stock market quotation for another class of shares or securities. On a strict interpretation of the legislation, I would argue that these continue to be 'unquoted', but it is not a point that I would like to rely on.

Control

An important point to note about headings (iii) and (iv) above is that it is only shares or securities which actually contribute to the transferor's control of the company that qualify for business property relief under these headings. For example, a shareholder who controls a quoted company by means of voting Ordinary Shares will not be entitled to business property relief on non-voting Preference Shares held in the same company. It also follows that very few securities (e.g. loan stock, etc.) will qualify for business property relief.

'Control' is generally taken to mean that the transferor is able to control over 50% of the voting powers on all questions affecting the company as a whole. A transferor holding 50% of the voting shares plus the right to a casting vote will also have 'control'. In deciding whether the transferor can control the requisite proportion of voting power, we can include:

- Shares held by their spouse.
- Shares transferred by them or their spouse to a charity, or other exempt body, after 15th April 1976 and still held by the transferee body at any time within the last five years.
- Shares that are treated as part of their estate or their spouse's estate (e.g. some types of 'interest in possession' – see Chapter 8).

Control need only exist immediately before the relevant transfer. The availability of business property relief is unaffected by whether control is lost as a result of the transfer in question (although, of course, subsequent transfers may be affected).

> **Tax Tip**
>
> When planning a transfer of shares which may result in a loss of control of the company, it may make sense to make other transfers first, such as other small share transfers or transfers of property used in the company's business falling under headings (v) or (vi) above.

7.9　WHAT IS THE VALUE OF A BUSINESS?

For business property relief purposes, the value of an unincorporated business is made up of the whole value of all of the assets of the business, including goodwill, less any business liabilities.

The assets and liabilities of the business are all those items that would need to be taken into account in order to ascertain a value for the whole business.

Business liabilities (like trade creditors, for example) will always need to be deducted from the value of the business. Loans and other liabilities will not necessarily always need to be deducted but we will look at these in more detail in Section 7.12.

Money owed to a transferor by their own business cannot be included as an additional asset in a business property relief claim.

Property on which business loans are secured cannot be included as part of the value of the business (unless, of course, the property is also used in the business).

Loans and other liabilities incurred to purchase or finance the business may need to be deducted from the value of the business when claiming business property relief. Again, we will look at these in more detail in Section 7.12.

Excepted Assets

The general rule is that business property relief is not available on the value of an asset which neither:

a) Has been used wholly or mainly for business purposes for the period of two years prior to the transfer, or the period since acquisition, if less; nor

b) Is required for the future use of the business.

In the case of property falling under heading (v) in Section 7.8, however, the above rule is revised so that, in order to qualify for business property relief, the asset in question must have either:

a) Been used for the purpose of the business of the partnership or company throughout the two years prior to the transfer, or

b) Replaced a similar previous asset (see Section 7.18) and the two assets taken together were used in the relevant business for a combined total period of at least two years within the five-year period prior to the transfer.

Remember, however, as discussed in Section 7.7, the asset only needs to be used in the business. In the case of a 'hybrid business' qualifying under the 'wholly or mainly' rule, the asset might be used in a non-qualifying component of the business and could still qualify for business property relief.

Buildings – Partial Business Use

In Section 7.6, we saw that a building used at least 50% for business purposes would qualify for business property relief as a result of the 'wholly or mainly' rule.

In many cases, however, a smaller proportion of a building may be used for business purposes.

Examples might include a dentist, doctor or vet using part of their home for an office, waiting room and surgery or a shopkeeper using the ground floor of their three-storey house as shop premises.

In cases like this, HMRC will permit a business property relief claim in respect of the business portion of the property, provided that this portion is used exclusively for business purposes. This applies to claims under headings (i), (v) or (vi) in Section 7.8.

7.10   BUSINESS PROPERTY RELIEF FOR SHARES AND SECURITIES

In Section 7.8, we examined the conditions that need to be satisfied before shares or securities may qualify for business property relief.

However, just because the shares or securities do, in principle, qualify for business property relief, this does not necessarily mean that the whole value of those shares or securities qualifies.

In order to calculate the available business property relief, it will be necessary to take into account any 'excepted assets' held by the relevant company.

The definition of 'excepted assets' for this purpose is the same as the general definition given in the previous section (not the revised one for transfers under heading (v)).

Example

Tommy owns 60% of the share capital in Pinball Limited, a trading company operating amusement arcades. The company has total assets valued at £1m, net of liabilities.

However, this includes £300,000 in cash held in a deposit account, which is surplus to the company's business requirements and not used in its trade.

The total value of Tommy's shares is £600,000. However, 30% of the company's value is attributable to a non-business asset (the surplus cash). Hence, Tommy's business property relief must be restricted to £420,000, leaving £180,000 (or 30%) chargeable to IHT.

Goodwill

In the above example, we ignored the value of goodwill. Any goodwill in the company's business would be a trading asset and would therefore increase the proportion of the shares eligible for business property relief.

For example, if Pinball Limited had trading goodwill worth £200,000, the total value of its assets would then be £1.2m. The £300,000 of surplus cash would then represent just 25% of the company's assets and Tommy's business property relief would be increased accordingly.

Valuing Shares

Valuing company shares is a highly complex subject worthy of an entire book in its own right.

When valuing company shares it is necessary to take account of goodwill and all of the company's liabilities. There is no distinction here between business liabilities and other liabilities such as loans. All of the company's tax liabilities will also need to be taken into account (this may sometimes include the potential tax arising if it were to sell its assets at their current market values: although this depends on the valuation method being used).

To establish what proportion of a company's value is based on excepted assets, however, we continue to follow the principles outlined in the previous section regarding the valuation of a business.

Cash On Deposit

Just because a company has cash on deposit, this does not necessarily make that cash an excepted asset. The question is whether that cash is surplus to the company's business requirements.

In a case like Pinball Limited, it will often be possible to argue that at least some of the cash is required for working capital. Exactly how much will depend on the circumstances of each case.

Cash that is held by a company for a specific and identifiable business purpose may be included as a business asset.

Example

Johnny owns San Quentin Limited, a company he originally formed to own and operate a nightclub, 'The Ring Of Fire'. In August 2018, San Quentin Limited sells The Ring Of Fire for £1m. The company keeps the money on deposit because Johnny is actively looking for a new nightclub that San Quentin Limited can buy. Sadly, however, Johnny dies before the company can buy the new nightclub.

Johnny leaves all of his San Quentin Limited shares to his son, Sue. Thankfully, full business property relief is available on the shares because the cash held on deposit was earmarked for a specific business purpose.

This example is based on a real case (but with different names – especially the boy named Sue), which the taxpayer's executors won.

In another case, however, a similar claim was denied when the executors claimed that surplus funds were being held pending a suitable business opportunity. The court felt this was too vague and that cash on deposit could only be counted as a business asset when it was required for a palpable business purpose.

Hence, in Johnny's case, if he had decided that he'd had enough of the nightclub business and was looking for another investment opportunity, the business property relief would have been denied.

Tax Tip

The key to maintaining full business property relief on the shares in a company holding surplus cash is to have an identifiable business requirement for that cash. This should be documented in business plans, cashflow projections, directors' board minutes, etc.

It is also worth noting that the same surplus cash would not generally qualify for business property relief when held personally. Hence, it may often make sense to retain business sale proceeds within a company when intending to reinvest them.

Other Investments

Other short-term investments held by the company might be eligible for inclusion as business assets if the same rationale as set out above regarding surplus cash can be established.

Alternatively, as we saw in Section 7.7, the company may have a 'hybrid business', and the investments might therefore be business assets in their own right.

HMRC now accepts that the holding of investments by a company may often be part of its normal business activities, although they will still attack cases where they perceive that the company is simply being used as a repository for non-business assets in order to artificially increase the amount of business property relief available.

Financing the Company

Loans and other liabilities incurred by a shareholder in order to purchase company shares, or to finance the company in some other way, may need to be deducted from the value of the borrower's shares when claiming business property relief. We will look at this issue in more detail in Section 7.13; as well as the position where a shareholder lends funds to their own company.

7.11   FINANCING A BUSINESS

As explained in Section 2.12, any liabilities incurred by the transferor to finance the acquisition, enhancement or maintenance of qualifying business property, must be taken to reduce the value attributed to that property.

Liabilities incurred prior to 6th April 2013 are exempt from this rule, but this exemption can easily be lost. We will return to this point in Section 7.15.

These rules apply equally to all forms of qualifying business property (as listed in Section 7.8). However, their most frequent application will be to unincorporated businesses (sole traders and partnerships) which we will look at in this section and the next, and to company shares, which we will look at in Section 7.13.

Nonetheless, the principles explored in this section (and in Sections 7.15 and 7.16) apply equally to all forms of qualifying business property.

Example

In June 2014, Amy (who is single) borrows £600,000 by remortgaging her house and uses the money to buy a trading business, 'The Wine House'.

In March 2019, Amy dies. She leaves her house to her sister Adele and she leaves The Wine House to her brother Pete. By this point, her house is worth £1m and The Wine House is worth £750,000.

The Wine House is eligible for business property relief, so it can be passed to Pete without any IHT liability. However, the deemed value of The Wine House for business property relief purposes is only £150,000, as Amy's mortgage must be deducted from its actual value of £750,000.

Amy's executors arrange for her house to be transferred to Adele subject to the existing mortgage (this satisfies the requirement for there to be a commercial reason for the non-repayment – see Section 2.12). Adele therefore acquires a house with equity of just £400,000 (£1m - £600,000). However, she will be liable for IHT on the full £1m value of the house less Amy's nil rate band because the mortgage has been set against the value of The Wine House.

This gives Adele an IHT liability of £270,000 (£1m - £325,000 = £675,000 x 40% = £270,000), which amounts to 67.5% of the value of her inheritance!

As we can see, these rules create an incredibly unfair result. The IHT due on Amy's house falls on Adele as a result of the general presumption that the beneficiary will bear the tax arising on a bequest of 'real property' (see Section 2.3) but she is denied any relief for the mortgage which she has taken over. She ends up facing liabilities totalling £870,000 as a result of inheriting a house worth only £1m.

Meanwhile, Pete obtains a business worth £750,000 free from any liabilities at all! It seems unlikely that this is what Amy would have intended.

Practical Pointer

Business owners who have borrowed to finance their business may wish to consider making adjustments to the legacies which they bequeath to different beneficiaries in order to prevent such unfair results from arising. For example, Amy could have left an additional sum of £240,000 to Adele and specified that this be charged against the assets of The Wine House. This would have compensated Adele for being denied any relief for the mortgage against Amy's house.

In addition to the unfairness seen above, the new rules could also lead to the collapse of many businesses.

Example

In 2014, Dusty borrows £1m by mortgaging her house and invests it in her business. Over the next few years, Dusty borrows further sums by way of personal loans, credit cards, etc, in order to fund her business.

In 2018, Dusty, who has never married, dies and leaves her entire estate to her brother Tom. At this point, her house is worth £1.2m and the other debts she has incurred to fund her business total £300,000.

Tom will be denied any relief for the mortgage over Dusty's house or the other debts she has incurred to fund her business, so he will be left with an IHT bill of £350,000 (£1.2m – £325,000 = £875,000 x 40% = £350,000).

Leaving the business to one side for the moment, Tom has inherited a house worth £1.2m but faces total debts of £1.65m, made up of:

Mortgage	*£1,000,000*
IHT	*£350,000*
Other debts	*£300,000*
Total:	*£1,650,000*

Hence, even if Tom were to sell Dusty's house, he would still face liabilities of £450,000 (more after taking sale costs into account). If Tom had no significant assets of his own, this would have to be funded from Dusty's business meaning that, in all likelihood, Tom would be unable to continue trading.

124

It is also worth noting that the amount of business property relief which Dusty receives is drastically reduced. If her business had been worth, say, £1.5m, she would have received business property relief of just £200,000 (£1.5m less £1m mortgage less £300,000 of other liabilities).

Business Property with a Lower Value than the Liabilities

In the last example, I assumed that Dusty's business continued to have a value in excess of the total liabilities she had incurred to fund it (£1.3m). However, where the total value of the qualifying business property is less than the outstanding liabilities incurred to finance it, the excess liabilities may be deducted from the remainder of the owner's estate.

Example Revisited

Let's take the same facts as above, but assume that Dusty's business is worth just £800,000 at the time of her death.

The liabilities incurred to finance her business total £1.3m, but it will now only be necessary to set £800,000 of these against the value of the business. This leaves £500,000 which can be set against the remainder of her estate.

This reduces Tom's IHT bill on Dusty's house to £150,000 (£1.2m – £500,000 – £325,000 = £375,000 x 40% = £150,000).

I have assumed throughout both versions of this example that Dusty's liabilities are eligible to be deducted from her estate (see Section 2.12).

In this revised example, Dusty effectively receives no business property relief at all: since the value of her business for this purpose is reduced to nil.

7.12 DEDUCTION OF LIABILITIES FOR UNINCORPORATED BUSINESS OWNERS

As explained in Section 7.9, business liabilities must always be deducted from the value of an unincorporated business for business property relief purposes, regardless of the date of the relevant transfer of value or the date on which the liability was incurred.

Loans and other liabilities incurred to finance the business will only need to be deducted when the transfer of value takes place after 16th July 2013 and the liability was incurred after 5th April 2013 (but see Section 7.15 for further details).

To see what this means in practice, let's look at a typical business.

Example Part 1

Duffy has her own business and has qualifying business assets with a total value of £2m.

She also has the following liabilities:

Trade creditors	*£200,000*
Business overdraft	*£20,000*
Long-term business loan	*£300,000*
Hire purchase liability on own car	*£10,000*
Hire purchase liability on employees' cars	*£25,000*
Income Tax on business profits	*£30,000*
Mortgage on her home	*£500,000*
Loan from her brother Warwick	*£250,000*

The trade creditors are a business liability and must therefore be deducted from the value of the business.

In most cases, a business overdraft is an integral part of the business meaning that it would usually need to be taken into account in order to ascertain a value for the whole business and is therefore a business liability. There will be some cases where this does not apply, but we will assume that the overdraft is a business liability in this case.

The long-term business loan is not classed as a business liability for business property relief purposes. This is because a purchaser looking to buy the business would not usually take over the loan. The loan therefore only needs to be deducted from the value of the business if it was taken out after 5th April 2013 and the transfer of value occurs after 16th July 2013. In this case, we will assume that the loan was taken out in 2012.

It is questionable whether Duffy's own car is an asset of the business. Whilst she may use it for business purposes, a purchaser looking to buy the business is unlikely to want to buy the car. Hence, as the car is not a business asset, the hire purchase liability on it does not need to be deducted from the value of the business.

The employees' cars are assets of the business: they will (most likely) transfer with the employees who are, in turn, an integral part of the business. Hence, the hire purchase liabilities on these cars are business liabilities and must be deducted from the value of the business.

Duffy's Income Tax bill is a personal liability. It does not matter that it has arisen on business profits; it will not need to be deducted from the value of her business.

Duffy's mortgage will only need to be deducted from the value of her business if:

i) It was taken out after 5th April 2013
ii) It has been used in any way, directly or indirectly, to finance her business
iii) There is a transfer of value after 16th July 2013

In this case, we will assume that the mortgage was taken out in 2008, has not been varied in any way since then, and has been used to finance Duffy's business.

Duffy borrowed the money from her brother in May 2013 and used it to purchase some business assets and reduce her business overdraft. This loan will therefore need to be deducted from the value of Duffy's business in the event of a transfer of value taking place after 16th July 2013.

Having established the status of each of Duffy's liabilities, we will now look at the position which would have arisen on a transfer of value before 17th July 2013. (This may still be relevant in some cases, such as where Duffy made a lifetime transfer before 17th July 2013.)

Example Part 2

Let us assume that Duffy transferred her business into a trust in June 2013. As the relevant transfer took place before 17th July 2013, the liabilities which need to be deducted are limited to the business liabilities only, as follows:

Trade creditors	£200,000
Business overdraft	£20,000
Hire purchase liability on employees' cars	£25,000
Total:	£245,000

Duffy will therefore be entitled to business property relief of £1.755m (£2m - £245,000). All of the other liabilities listed above are excluded and can be deducted from the general assets of her estate on her subsequent death.

We will now compare this outcome with the position arising on a transfer of value after 16th July 2013.

Example Part 3

Let us now assume that Duffy did not make the transfer described under Part 2 above, and subsequently dies in 2019. All of the facts described in Part 1 remain unaltered.

In addition to the business liabilities described above, any further liabilities incurred after 5th April 2013 which have been used, directly or indirectly, to finance the business must also now be deducted for business property relief purposes. This leads to the following deductions:

Trade creditors	£200,000
Business overdraft	£20,000
Hire purchase liability on employees' cars	£25,000
Loan from Warwick	£250,000
Total:	£495,000

Whilst they were incurred to finance her business, the long-term business loan and the mortgage on Duffy's home do not need to be deducted because they were both taken out prior to 6th April 2013.

The loan from Warwick will have to be deducted, however, as this liability was incurred after 5th April 2013.

Duffy's business property relief will therefore be reduced to £1.505m (£2m – £495,000). Her family's IHT bill will be increased by £100,000 as a result of the fact that the loan from Warwick can no longer be deducted from the general assets of her estate (£250,000 x 40% = £100,000).

The position will get even worse if Duffy subsequently refinances either her long-term business loan or her mortgage. Let's return to the example one last time to see the effect of this.

Example Part 4

In 2016, Duffy remortgaged her house for £800,000 and used the new loan to pay off both her old mortgage and her long-term business loan. All other facts outlined in Part 1 above remain the same at the time of her death in 2019.

The liabilities to be deducted from her business for business property relief purposes are now as follows:

Trade creditors	£200,000
Business overdraft	£20,000
Hire purchase liability on employees' cars	£25,000
Mortgage	£800,000
Loan from Warwick	£250,000
Total:	£1,295,000

Duffy's business property relief is reduced to just £705,000 (£2m – £1.295m). None of the liabilities listed above can be deducted from the general assets of her estate. Compared with the position before July 2013 (Part 2), this will cost her family an extra £420,000 in IHT.

See Section 7.15 for further details on the perils of varying a loan which was taken out before 6th April 2013.

7.13   DEDUCTION OF LIABILITIES FOR COMPANY OWNERS

As explained in Section 7.10, when calculating the value of shares which qualify for business property relief, all of the issuing company's liabilities need to be taken into account.

In the event of a transfer of value taking place after 16th July 2013, the owner of the shares will need to deduct any liabilities which they incurred after 5th April 2013 and have used to directly or indirectly finance their shareholding or to maintain or enhance its value.

To demonstrate these principles in practice, let's look at a similar example to the one we used in Section 7.12 but, this time, the qualifying business property is company shares.

Example Part 1

Robbie owns all of the shares in a trading company, Old Swinger Ltd. We will assume that the value of the company before taking account of any of its liabilities is £2m (in practice, valuing company shares is a more complex process than this). The company also has the following liabilities:

Trade creditors	*£200,000*
Business overdraft	*£20,000*
Long-term business loan	*£300,000*
Hire purchase liability on Robbie's car	*£10,000*
Hire purchase liability on employees' cars	*£25,000*
Corporation Tax due	*£30,000*
Loan from Robbie's brother Mark	*£250,000*
Total:	*£835,000*

All of these items are company liabilities and must therefore be taken into account in establishing the value of the company and Robbie's shares. In this case, we will assume that it is appropriate to simply deduct them from the value described above, leaving a net value for Robbie's shares of £1.165m (£2m – £835,000).

(I am assuming here that Robbie's car is a company asset: i.e. a company car. If it was his own private car then neither the car nor the hire purchase liability on it would be taken into account.)

In 2008, Robbie mortgaged his house for £500,000 in order to buy his shares in Old Swinger Ltd. As this liability was incurred before 6th April 2013, it does not need to be taken into account for business property relief purposes.

Hence, as things stand, the value of Robbie's shares for business property relief purposes is the same (£1.165m) in the case of a transfer of value either before or after 16th July 2013.

It can readily be seen from the above example that the rules applying to transfers of value after 16th July 2013 will generally have less impact on company owners than on other business owners.

However, company owners still remain vulnerable to the perils of varying existing loans taken out before 6th April 2013 (see Section 7.15).

Example Part 2

In 2016, Robbie remortgaged his house for £800,000 and used the new loan to both pay off his old mortgage and to lend £300,000 to Old Swinger Ltd to enable the company to pay off its long-term business loan. All other facts, as outlined in Part 1 above, remain the same at the time of his death in 2019.

The value of Robbie's shares in Old Swinger Ltd remains unaltered (£1.165m). The company has paid off its long-term loan but has simply replaced this liability with another: the debt due to Robbie.

However, Robbie's estate now includes the £300,000 debt due to him from Old Swinger Ltd as an additional asset. This asset is not eligible for business property relief (see further below).

Robbie's new mortgage was taken out after 5th April 2013, so any part that has been used, directly or indirectly, to finance the purchase of his shares, or to enhance their value, must be deducted for business property relief purposes and cannot be deducted from the general assets of his estate.

The £500,000 which was used to repay the original mortgage has been used indirectly to finance Robbie's shares and is thus caught by these rules. This sum must therefore be deducted from the value of Robbie's shares, thus reducing his business property relief to £665,000 (£1.165m – £500,000).

As explained above, the £300,000 which Robbie loaned to the company did not enhance the value of his shares, which was the same before and after he made the loan. Hence this part of his new mortgage can still be deducted from the general assets of his estate.

On the other hand, the loan has become an additional chargeable asset in its own right, so there is no overall IHT saving.

The change in Robbie's position caused by the remortgaging can be illustrated as follows:

	Before	After
Chargeable Assets:		
Shares in Old Swinger Ltd	£1,165,000	£665,000
Loan to Old Swinger Ltd	-	£300,000
	£1,165,000	£965,000
Less Deductions:		
Business property relief	£1,165,000	£665,000
Mortgage	£500,000	£300,000
Net*	(£500,000)	Nil

* - the net sum available to be deducted from the general assets of Robbie's estate

As we can see, the remortgaging will cost Robbie's family an additional £200,000 (£500,000 x 40%) in IHT.

Loans to Your Own Company

In Part 2 of the above example, we saw the impact of lending money to your own company.

From the company's perspective, the borrowed funds will enhance its value but this will be matched by the liability which is due to you. Hence, there is no overall impact on the company's value.

You will have a new asset: the debt due to you from the company. This will need to be included in your estate.

A debt due to you from your own company is a separate asset in its own right and is highly unlikely to attract business property relief. As explained in Section 7.8, it is only debts in the form of securities which actually contribute to your control of the company that qualify for business property relief.

In summary, lending money to your own company will not generally provide you with any additional business property relief and will not immediately save any IHT.

Naturally, however, there are many other good reasons why you might lend money to your company and we will revisit this topic in Section 7.14.

Rights Issues

In Section 7.22, we will look at the potential benefits of rights issues for increasing the amount of business property relief available to a company owner. In that section, it is assumed that the company owner has substantial private wealth available to fund the rights issue.

Funding the rights issue by way of borrowings taken out after 5th April 2013 will not work so well, however.

Example Part 3

The facts are the same as in Part 2 above except that, instead of lending £300,000 to the company, Robbie subscribes for additional shares by way of a rights issue.

The value of the company has now increased to £1.465m (£1.165m + £300,000) because there is no debt due to Robbie to match the liability which has been paid off.

Robbie will not have acquired any additional asset: he will only have enhanced the value of his existing shareholding.

As a result of this, however, the entire £800,000 of Robbie's new mortgage must now be deducted from the value of his shares for business property relief purposes because it has all been used, directly or indirectly, to finance the purchase of his shares, or to enhance their value.

The end result is as follows:

Chargeable Assets:
Shares in Old Swinger Ltd   £665,000 (£1,465,000 – £800,000)

Less Deductions:
Business property relief   £665,000
Mortgage   Nil
Net   Nil

As we can see, the overall position remains the same as in Part 2 and, once again, the remortgaging will have cost Robbie's family an additional £200,000 in IHT.

7.14 BORROWING TO INVEST IN YOUR BUSINESS

The examples in Sections 7.11 to 7.13 demonstrate the fact that borrowing after 5th April 2013 in order to finance your business, by any means, will not give rise to any immediate IHT savings.

Refinancing or varying earlier borrowings which have been used to finance your business will often lead to additional IHT costs and should be avoided wherever possible.

Naturally, however, financing your business will usually have other benefits and it is hoped that the value of your business will increase as a result. This may lead to some indirect IHT savings as the future growth in your business's value will be sheltered by business property relief whereas future growth in funds or investments held privately outside the business would be fully exposed to IHT.

In other words, the real benefit lies in making sensible commercial investments through the medium of a qualifying trading business and thus increasing your business property relief as you grow your business (provided such investments do not endanger the business's trading status – see Section 7.7).

7.15 LIABILITIES INCURRED BEFORE 6 APRIL 2013

As explained in Sections 2.12 and 7.11, liabilities incurred before 6th April 2013 are exempt from the new rules which we have been looking at over the last few sections.

However, any variation in the terms of such a liability after 5th April 2013 will make it a new liability for these purposes and will mean that it must be deducted from the value of the relevant qualifying business property.

We have seen the disastrous consequences of this in several examples already, but it is vital to understand that, in addition to a complete refinancing of those existing liabilities, those same consequences may arise in the event of other, less significant, variations in the terms of the liability, such as:

- Changes to the term (period) of a loan
- Changes in the security for a loan
- A change from fixed interest to variable interest, or vice versa (unless such a change is already part of the existing terms)
- Additional advances on the same loan account

The last point is not entirely certain but it would be far safer to arrange for any additional advances to be treated as a separate loan account.

The additional advances will still be subject to the new rules, but the exempt status of the existing balance should be protected.

Simple changes in the interest rate on a loan should not cause any problems: provided that such changes are within the original terms of the loan.

An important issue which is as yet unresolved is whether a change in the lender which is beyond the borrower's control (e.g. where one bank takes over another's mortgage book) will lead to the loan being treated as a 'new liability' for these purposes.

7.16   MULTIPLE TRANSFERS

Over the past few sections, we have seen how liabilities incurred after 5th April 2013 to finance qualifying business property must be deducted from the value of that business property in the event of any transfer of value taking place after 16th July 2013.

This applies to any chargeable transfer, including:

- Transfers on death
- Chargeable lifetime transfers (see Section 4.2)
- Potentially exempt transfers becoming chargeable on the transferor's death within seven years (see Section 4.5)
- Trust anniversary and exit charges (see Sections 8.18 and 8.19)

Once a liability has been taken into account on one chargeable transfer, it cannot be taken into account again on another transfer made by the same transferor (except where the earlier 'transfer' was a trust anniversary charge). Remember, however, that a potentially exempt transfer only becomes a chargeable transfer if the transferor dies within seven years.

Example

In 2014, Woody mortgaged his house for £1m and used the money to purchase shares in a trading company, Movenelo Ltd. In 2018, Woody gives his shares in Movenelo Ltd to his elder son, Bev. This is a potentially exempt transfer.

In 2025, Woody dies, leaving his remaining estate to his younger son, Kelly.

If Woody died within seven years of his gift to Bev, that gift will have become a chargeable transfer and his mortgage will have to be taken into account for business property relief purposes. Kelly will then be denied any relief for the mortgage.

If, on the other hand, Woody was still alive on the seventh anniversary of his gift to Bev, that gift will have become fully exempt. Kelly will then be entitled to claim a deduction in respect of Woody's mortgage, thus saving him £400,000 (£1m x 40%) in IHT.

I have assumed in this example that Woody's mortgage will meet the necessary conditions for a deduction, as explained in Section 2.12.

7.17 THE MINIMUM HOLDING PERIOD

To qualify for business property relief, the relevant property must have been owned by the transferor for a minimum of two years prior to the transfer.

There is an exception to this requirement where the property had replaced other qualifying property (see Section 7.18) and both assets taken together had been owned by the transferor for at least two years out of the five-year period preceding the transfer. This effectively provides a form of rollover relief for business assets for IHT purposes.

When a widow or widower inherits business property, the ownership period for this purpose includes the ownership period of their deceased spouse.

> **Wealth Warning**
> A transferor spouse's previous ownership period is **not** included in the case of a lifetime transfer of business assets.

Additionally, the minimum ownership period requirement is ignored when two successive transfers of the same property take place within two years and:

i)   the earlier transfer qualified for business property relief,
ii) the second transfer would otherwise qualify for business property relief, and
iii) at least one of the two transfers occurred on death

7.18 REPLACEMENT BUSINESS PROPERTY

The replacement of relevant business property by other relevant business property has been referred to a few times in the preceding sections.

Broadly, this means that on a disposal of the original business property, the same value was reinvested in new qualifying business property.

The replacement business property does not need to be in the same kind of business as the original business property, nor does it need to be the same type of property.

Hence, for example, an individual could sell an unquoted manufacturing company and reinvest the proceeds in a partnership share in a hotel business.

Provided that all of the other necessary rules are met, business property relief may still be available even when more than one replacement has taken place. Hence, in the preceding sections, where we refer to 'the two assets taken together', this could also apply to three or more assets, each of which replaced their predecessor.

Where a taxpayer relies on a replacement in order to qualify for business property relief, the amount of business property relief available is generally restricted to the amount that would have been available had the replacement not taken place.

For the specific purposes of this rule, however, the following changes are disregarded:

- The formation, alteration or dissolution of a partnership
- The acquisition of a business by a company controlled by the former owner of that business (a.k.a. an 'incorporation')

7.19   EXTRA RULES FOR LIFETIME TRANSFERS

Where business property relief applied at the time of a lifetime transfer and the transferor then dies within seven years, there are some extra conditions that must be satisfied for business property relief to also then apply at the time of the transferor's death.

The conditions are:

i)   The transferee must continue to own the original transferred assets throughout the period from the date of the original transfer to the date of the transferor's death or, if earlier, the date of the transferee's own death

ii)   The original transferred assets must continue to be relevant business property for business property relief purposes at the end of the period in condition (i) above

It is therefore generally necessary for the assets to be qualifying business property in the transferee's hands at the time of the earlier of the transferor or transferee's death.

This does not apply, however, if the original assets were shares or securities that were either quoted at the time of the original transfer, or unquoted throughout the period in condition (i).

Wealth Warning

Where a transferee holds a minority holding of unquoted shares, these will cease to be relevant business property if the company obtains a quotation. This could result in a 40% IHT bill if the transferor dies within seven years of the original transfer.

Where the transferee retains part of the original asset transferred at the end of the period covered by condition (i) then business property relief continues to apply to that part, as long as condition (ii) is also satisfied.

135

Furthermore, the transferee may retain their business property relief entitlement if they dispose of the original assets and acquire replacement assets (as defined in Section 7.18).

The following further conditions must be met in order for the transferee to retain business property relief entitlement in these circumstances:

a) The replacement assets must be acquired within three years of the transferee's disposal of the original assets
b) Both the transferee's sale of the original assets and their acquisition of the replacement assets must take place on 'arm's length' terms (see Section 2.1)
c) The whole consideration received on the sale of the original transferred assets must be expended in acquiring the replacement assets
d) The transferee must own the replacement assets at the time of their own death if they predecease the transferor. In other cases, they must generally own the replacement assets at the time of the transferor's death but this rule does not apply where the transferor's death occurs within the 'allowed period' – see below
e) Apart from the 'allowed period', either the original transferred assets or the replacement assets must be owned by the transferee throughout the period from the original transfer to the date of the transferor's death or, if earlier, the date of the transferee's death
f) The replacement assets must be relevant business property in the transferee's hands at the date of the transferor's death or, if earlier, the date of the transferee's death (except as noted below)

The Allowed Period

The three-year period under condition (a) above begins when the transferee enters a binding contract to sell the original transferred assets. Fortunately, it is also only necessary for them to enter, but not necessarily complete, a binding contract to acquire the replacement assets within the requisite period. (There's more on binding contracts coming up in Section 7.21)

This three-year period, which is known as the 'allowed period', can also extend after the transferor's death, so that the replacement may take place after the transferor dies.

For these purposes, condition (f) above is amended so that the replacement assets need to be relevant business property in the transferee's hands at the time that the transferee acquires them.

The wording of the legislation governing condition (d) seems to suggest that only one replacement is allowed under these circumstances, unlike other 'replacements', as considered in Section 7.18.

Tax Tip

What all this means is that, if you receive qualifying business property in a gift from someone else, you may find yourself with an IHT bill if you sell that property within seven years.

However, if you can wait at least four years before selling the gifted property, you will have the opportunity to restore your business property relief by acquiring replacement business property if your benefactor should pass away unexpectedly.

One last point on replacement assets following a lifetime transfer – an acquisition of qualifying agricultural property (see Section 7.30) will qualify as a replacement asset for these purposes.

Finally, it is important to remember that a lifetime transfer of qualifying business property could still be a 'Gift with Reservation of Benefit' (see Section 4.9). This would mean that the property effectively remained in the transferor's estate and IHT would be payable if the property did not still qualify for business property relief at the time of their death.

In particular, any excessive salary payments to the transferor could make the transfer a 'Gift with Reservation'. (I.e. excessive salary paid to the transferor following the transfer of a business, partnership share or shares or securities in a company.) The same would apply to any other benefits provided in excess of a normal commercial level, including excessive pension contributions.

7.20 LIFETIME TRANSFERS OF BUSINESS PROPERTY BECOMING CHARGEABLE ON DEATH

If the transferee loses the business property relief on a transferred asset then IHT will become payable if the transferor should die within seven years of the original transfer.

Additional IHT may also be payable on a transferor's death when the transferred asset only qualifies for business property relief at 50%.

In both cases, any other available reliefs, such as the annual exemption, may of course be taken into account.

Where the original transfer was a chargeable lifetime transfer (e.g. to a trust), only that transferee will be affected by any loss of business property relief.

However, where the original transfer was a potentially exempt transfer, the loss of business property relief will mean that the whole of the transferor's estate must be recalculated on the basis set out in Section 4.5, but without the business property relief originally claimed on the transfer.

Example

Brian uses his annual IHT exemption every year but, prior to June 2018, he had made no other transfers of value for over seven years.

Brian owns an unquoted trading company, Satisfaction Limited. In June 2018, he gives shares in the company worth £1m to the Wyman Discretionary Trust. Whilst this is a chargeable lifetime transfer, it is covered by business property relief, meaning that no IHT is payable at this stage.

In February 2019, Brian gives another £1m worth of shares to his son Mick and in March 2019, he gives £100,000 in cash to his nephew Keith. In May 2019, Satisfaction Limited is floated on the stock exchange and becomes Satisfaction Holdings PLC. Sadly, the ensuing celebrations take their toll on Brian and he is found dead the next morning.

Brian's lifetime transfers to the Wyman Discretionary Trust, Mick and Keith must now all be brought into account for IHT purposes and business property relief is no longer available on the transfers to the Wyman Discretionary Trust and Mick.

The £1m transfer to the Wyman Discretionary Trust is now fully chargeable. After deducting Brian's nil rate band of £325,000, the remaining £675,000 is chargeable at 40%, giving the trust an IHT bill of £270,000.

However, for the purposes of working out any IHT on other transfers made by Brian in the last seven years, the chargeable lifetime transfer to the Wyman Discretionary Trust is deemed to still be at its original value after business property relief, i.e. Nil.

Hence, Brian's nil rate band is still available in computing the IHT on the £1m gift to Mick, which now also becomes chargeable. Mick's IHT bill is therefore also £270,000. Mick's gift, however, does exhaust Brian's nil rate band, so the whole £100,000 of the gift to Keith is chargeable to IHT at 40%, giving him a bill of £40,000.

Poor Keith never even got any Satisfaction Limited shares and yet the simple fact that the company was floated on the Stock Exchange has cost him £40,000!

This example shows what a dangerous combination gifts of shares and company flotations present. Not only did the flotation lead to an IHT cost for the transferees holding shares, it also had an adverse effect on another transferee.

Wealth Warning

Transferees receiving gifts from a transferor who has also made gifts of relevant business property are in an extremely vulnerable position. It may make sense to take out some life insurance on the transferor in these circumstances.

Things could have been worse. If Brian had made his gift to Mick before his gift to the Wyman Discretionary Trust, the trust's IHT bill would have been £400,000. As things stand, at least Brian's nil rate band has effectively been used twice.

138

Tax Tip

In view of the danger that business property relief might be lost following a lifetime transfer, it is better to make chargeable transfers of qualifying business property first before potentially exempt transfers.

7.21 HOW TO PRESERVE BUSINESS PROPERTY RELIEF

For anyone with a qualifying business, business property relief is an incredibly valuable relief.

The trouble is that you still need to qualify for the relief at the moment at which a transfer takes place. That moment may be death in many cases and this carries some inherent problems.

Firstly, it is generally pretty unpredictable when this will be. Secondly, it may be some time after you cease to be interested in running a business. Most people will want to retire at some point and, unfortunately, this will often result in the loss of their business property relief.

Selling Up

As soon as you have a binding contract for sale, you are, for IHT purposes, no longer regarded as owning the asset being sold. Instead, you are regarded as owning a right to the sale proceeds. That right is generally not a qualifying asset for business property relief purposes. Hence, at one stroke of a pen, you can lose your business property relief and substantially increase your family's IHT bill in the event of your death.

Example

Eddie owns an unquoted trading company, Cochran Limited. The company is Eddie's only asset so, as things stand, Eddie has no need to worry about IHT.

Eddie gets a great offer from a French company, Aznavour S.A., to buy Cochran Limited for £10.325m. He decides to accept the offer, so he flies to Paris, takes the Metro to Aznavour S.A.'s offices and signs a binding contract to sell his company.

Leaving the office, Eddie looks the wrong way crossing the street and steps in front of a bus. IHT bill: £4m!

This example is based on a true story and readily demonstrates the ease with which business property relief can be lost and the dire consequences that may result. An entrepreneur like Eddie might well have been intending to reinvest his sale proceeds in a new business venture and hence might have regained the protection of business property relief within a few weeks by virtue of the 'replacement property' rules which we examined in Section 7.18. Perhaps Eddie should have considered taking out some insurance to cover the IHT risk during this short interval!

When an individual who has sold a qualifying business within the last three years gets a little more warning of their demise, the 'replacement property' rules might provide an answer.

> **Tax Tip**
> The protection of business property relief can generally be maintained if the taxpayer reinvests all of the sale proceeds from qualifying business property into new qualifying business property within three years.

Exceptions to the Loss of Business Property Relief on Sale

A binding contract for sale will not result in a loss of business property relief if the contract is:

a) For the sale of an unincorporated business to a company that is to carry on that business where the purchase consideration is wholly or mainly shares or securities in that company.

b) For the sale of shares or securities in a company for the purposes of reconstruction or amalgamation.

Liquidation and Winding Up

Business property relief is lost on a company's shares if the company is in liquidation or in the process of being wound up. There is an exception to this, however, if the winding up is being carried out as part of a scheme of corporate reconstruction or amalgamation (e.g. a company reorganisation or a merger of two companies).

Retirement

Business property relief is lost as soon as a partner retires from a qualifying partnership business. Any capital the retired partner leaves in the business is simply regarded as a loan and is ineligible for business property relief.

One way to avoid this problem is for the partner to continue in partnership, but with a very small profit share. (Remaining in partnership does, of course, have commercial implications, which should also be considered.)

When a sole trader retires there is no business so there can be no business property relief. The answer here may be to take on a partner and then, at a later date, to 'semi-retire' – i.e. reduce to a very small profit share in the same manner as described above.

A taxpayer owning qualifying shares or securities in a trading company can happily retire without any loss of business property relief as their position depends on their shareholding and not on whether they actually participate in the company's business.

Tax Tip
Incorporating the business prior to retirement may sometimes be a good way to preserve business property relief.

Buy-Out Clauses On Death: A BIG NO-NO!

It is common business practice for business partners to enter into an agreement whereby their executors will sell their partnership share to the surviving partners in the event of their death.

Similar agreements are also often used by shareholder/directors of unquoted companies whereby their executors sell their shares back to the company, or to their fellow directors, in the event of their death.

Whilst these agreements make a good deal of commercial sense, from a business property relief perspective, they represent a disaster waiting to happen. This is because, at the moment of death, a binding sale contract will come into force and the estate will not hold relevant business property but, as we saw above, will instead hold a non-qualifying right to sale proceeds.

To avoid this problem, it is essential to avoid any form of agreement that may form a binding contract on the death of a partner or director.

Cross Options

A far better alternative is to use non-coterminous cross options.

In other words, the business partners should enter into an agreement whereby, in the event of a partner's death, their executors will have an option to sell the deceased's partnership share and the surviving partners will have an option to buy it.

Similarly, private company directors would enter into an agreement whereby, in the event of a director's death, their executors will have an option to sell the deceased's shares or securities in the company and either the company itself or the surviving directors will have an option to buy them.

To be on the safe side, it is wise to ensure that the options are 'non-coterminous'. Broadly, this means that the option to purchase and the option to sell may only be exercised at different times. (E.g. the deceased's executors must exercise the option to sell within six weeks of the deceased's death and the surviving business partners, or directors, must exercise the option to purchase more than six but less than twelve weeks after the deceased's death.)

HMRC has specifically confirmed that this approach is acceptable in the case of a business partnership and there is no reason to suppose the same principles would not be equally valid in the case of unquoted company shares or securities.

Using cross options will therefore preserve any business property relief entitlement while also satisfying the original commercial objective of allowing the deceased's share of a business to be 'bought out'.

Other Approaches for Partnerships

HMRC has also confirmed that the following other methods for dealing with a deceased partner's share of a business will preserve any business property relief entitlement available:

- Partnership ceases on death, partnership assets to be realised and deceased partner's estate receives appropriate share of proceeds

- Partnership continues and deceased's estate represents the deceased

- Partnership share falls into deceased's estate with surviving partners having an option to purchase at either a valuation or an agreed formula-based price

- The deceased's partnership share accrues to the surviving partners but the deceased's estate is entitled to payment at either a valuation or an agreed formula-based price

- Cross options (as explained above), which must be exercised within a set period following the partner's death

7.22   MAXIMISING BUSINESS PROPERTY RELIEF

Where an individual owns and controls a qualifying trading company, the whole value of that company could effectively be exempt from IHT. As that individual nears the end of their life, therefore, it would make sense to ensure that the value of the company is maximised.

Furthermore, any assets held personally by the individual and used in the company's business would only qualify for 50% business property relief. Again, it might make sense to ensure that these were held in the company.

The potential savings that could be achieved can be illustrated by way of an example.

Example

Madge is a very wealthy old woman. Among her many assets is her unquoted trading company, Ciccone Ltd. She also owns a CD pressing plant worth £10m, which is used by the company.

Ciccone Ltd is currently worth £4m. This value takes account of the fact that the company owes £2m for the purchase of new equipment and also has a bank overdraft of £1.5m.

If Madge were to die with things as they stand, her personal representatives would be able to claim business property relief as follows:

	£
Ciccone Ltd: £4m @ 100%	*4,000,000*
Pressing Plant: £10m @ 50%	*5,000,000*
TOTAL	*9,000,000*

Realising that she isn't immortal after all, Madge decides to undertake some IHT planning. First, she transfers the pressing plant into the company. She is able to avoid CGT on this transfer by using a 'holdover relief' election. SDLT is, however, payable on the market value of the property. In this case, the SDLT amounts to £489,500.

Madge then uses £4m out of her substantial private wealth to subscribe for further new shares in Ciccone Ltd. This enables the company to pay off the bank overdraft, the debt for the new equipment and the SDLT on the property transfer.

Ciccone Ltd will now be worth £17.5m and, after just two years, the whole of this value will be covered by 100% business property relief.

The overall value of Madge's estate will be virtually unchanged except for the £489,500 paid in SDLT. However, this simple piece of planning will save her family £3.6m in IHT!

Note that it will take two years for Madge's new shares in Ciccone Limited to qualify for business property relief. The transfer of the pressing plant, however, will provide an immediate saving.

Tax Tip
New shares issued by way of a rights issue are treated as part of the original shareholding for the purposes of business property relief. Hence, a new investment into an existing qualifying trading company which is structured as a rights issue may be eligible for full business property relief immediately.

Practical Pointer
Although the transfer of the pressing plant in the above example can be carried out free of CGT, there may be other important tax consequences if the company subsequently sells the property.

The potential advantages or disadvantages of holding property through a company are covered in depth in the Taxcafe.co.uk guide *'Using a Property Company to Save Tax'*.

Wealth Warning

The IHT planning undertaken by Madge worked because her company was in debt and was using the pressing plant in its business. If, on the other hand, she had injected so much capital into the company that it had a surplus in excess of its usual trading requirements, there would have been a restriction on her business property relief under the 'excepted assets' rules (see Section 7.10).

The restriction would have operated by reference to the amount of the 'non-trading' surplus as a proportion of the company's total net assets. If the surplus were large enough, the company might even have failed the 'wholly or mainly' test (see Section 7.7) and thus ceased to qualify for business property relief altogether!

7.23   SHELTERING INVESTMENTS WITH BUSINESS PROPERTY RELIEF

Business property relief on company shares may be reduced, or possibly lost altogether, if a non-trading asset, such as an investment property or quoted share portfolio, were transferred into the company. (Such a transfer may also give rise to CGT liabilities – plus SDLT in the case of a property.)

However, as we have already seen, there would nevertheless remain the possibility of arguing that a 'hybrid business', qualifying under the 'wholly or mainly' principle (see Section 7.7) existed, so that the investment property or quoted share portfolio might be sheltered from IHT within the trading company.

But how far can we push this?

If investments are simply being dumped into a trading company, HMRC is unlikely to accept the 'hybrid business' argument and, as we saw in Section 7.7, may argue that the company is simply being used as a repository for non-business assets.

The important distinction to remember is that investments can only be sheltered within a trading company qualifying for business property relief if they form a part of the company's business.

A random cobbled together collection of non-trading investments will not be good enough.

The best way to make use of the trading company 'shelter' would therefore be to build an investment 'arm' to the company's business over a number of years.

It would be vital to ensure that this part of the business remained comfortably less than 50% of the company's overall business, bearing in mind the various possible tests set out in Section 7.7.

To maintain full business property relief on the company's shares, its investment business 'arm' would need to be an integral part of the company's overall business and it is important to reflect this in the company's records, including management accounts, directors' board minutes, cashflow projections, etc.

Example

After making the transfer of the pressing plant and subscribing for new shares, which we saw in Section 7.22, Madge begins to make some quoted investments within Ciccone Limited. She runs the entire enterprise as a single business, ensuring that management accounts, directors' board minutes and other company documentation all record the fact that the investment arm is an integral part of Ciccone Limited's business.

A few years later, the total value of the company is £35m, including £10m worth of investments and trading assets worth £25m.

By building the investment portfolio within Ciccone Limited instead of privately, Madge has reduced her IHT exposure by another £4m.

A similar approach could also be taken to shelter investments from IHT within a trading partnership.

It would be difficult for a sole trader to achieve the same result, however, as HMRC would probably view them as having two businesses: one qualifying for business property relief and one not. Nevertheless, this problem might perhaps be overcome if the 'investments' were an integral part of the same business.

Tax Tip
One good way to argue that investments are an integral part of any business is to make investments in companies operating in the same industry. These investments will provide the investor with valuable information on their competitors, including access to their competitors' shareholders' meetings, and there is therefore a strong argument that this can be regarded as an integral part of the business.

Wealth Warning 1
Under the 'wholly or mainly' test for business property relief purposes, a company could still qualify with just under 50% of its activities being non-trading activities.

However, for the purposes of a number of CGT reliefs, including entrepreneurs' relief and holdover relief on a gift of shares, the company may lose its trading status if just 20% of its activities are non-trading activities.

This may have significantly adverse consequences for the company's shareholders. The criteria to be used for this 20% test would broadly follow the same headings examined in Section 7.7 and are thus potentially extremely wide.

The loss of entrepreneurs' relief could result in extra CGT liabilities of up to £1m for each shareholder on a sale of shares in the company. We will look at the importance of holdover relief in Chapter 11.

Wealth Warning 2
If making investments via a trading company, it is important to ensure the company's Memorandum and Articles of Association permit this activity. Any activity not so permitted is strictly illegal and thus cannot be regarded as part of the company's business.

7.24   MONEY BOX COMPANIES

In one IHT case, a company with a business consisting of lending money to other associated companies was held to be carrying on a qualifying business for business property relief purposes. It seems, therefore, that money lending can be a qualifying business.

However, an important factor in this particular case was the fact that the loans were unsecured and repayable on demand. This meant that the company's business comprised a business of 'making loans' rather than one of 'investing in loans' and this was enough to enable the company's owner to obtain business property relief. The fact that the loans were made to associated companies did not seem to affect the business property relief position. This is good news since it is doubtful whether many people will wish to make unsecured loans to non-associated companies.

This decision opens up some interesting planning possibilities. A person with a non-qualifying company, such as a property investment company, for example, could set up a money-lending company to make loans to the non-qualifying company.

The loans would need to be unsecured and repayable on demand and the volume of activity carried on by the money-lending company would need to be sufficient to make it a business (see Section 7.4). The money-lending company would also need to charge interest in order to provide the necessary 'profit motive'.

Under these circumstances, it would be possible to reduce the value of the non-qualifying company while the value of the money-lending company may be eligible for business property relief, thus saving IHT on the death of the owner of both companies.

The non-qualifying business probably needs to be in a company in order to get the necessary reduction in value that saves the IHT. (See Section 10.20 for some further benefits of putting non-qualifying businesses into a company).

7.25   CHANGING THE BUSINESS TO SAVE INHERITANCE TAX

It is worth bearing in mind that a business only needs to qualify for business property relief throughout the two-year period prior to the transfer. Hence, the business owner could build up a valuable non-qualifying business over many years and then eventually change it into a qualifying business at a later stage. If the owner survives for at least two years after making the change, they can avoid IHT on the business.

Example

Steve has built up an unquoted property investment company, Tyler Properties Ltd, over many years. He is now 70 years old and wishes to retire.

In April 2018, Steve retires and his daughter Liv takes over the running of the company. Steve continues to own the company and Liv is paid a salary for running it.

Liv immediately begins to change the company's business to one of property development. This process is completed by March 2019.

Sadly, in May 2021, Steve dies and leaves Tyler Properties Ltd to Liv. As the company had carried on a qualifying trading activity for the previous two years, the shares left to Liv are fully covered by business property relief and no IHT is due.

The change in the company's business activity may give rise to some additional Corporation Tax costs. However, where the change takes place gradually, over a number of years, these should not be too severe.

Remember also that the change in activity does not need to be absolute, as it is only necessary for the company to pass the 'wholly or mainly' test (see Section 7.7) during the last two years prior to the transfer.

For IHT purposes, Steve would also have been able to claim business property relief on a lifetime transfer of his Tyler Properties Ltd shares at any time after the company had been carrying on a qualifying business for at least two years.

However, this would mean that Liv would need to continue the qualifying business for up to another seven years in order to retain business property relief (see Section 7.19). This could also lead to a CGT liability for Steve on the share transfer if the company still held any investment assets at that time.

7.26   BUSINESS SUCCESSION PLANNING

From a tax perspective, the last thing a dying person should do is to sell a business that qualifies for business property relief!

The day before the sale, the business would have been completely covered by business property relief and available to be passed on to their family free of IHT.

The day after the sale, the sale proceeds would be completely exposed to IHT, resulting in the loss of up to 40% in IHT.

This is on top of any CGT that arose on the sale. As we shall see in Chapter 11, CGT could also generally be avoided if the family sold the business shortly after the original owner's death.

In practice, unfortunately, and much to HMRC's delight, it will often be necessary to sell the business before the owner's death. Very often, a large proportion of a business's value can be lost when its proprietor dies. After all, it is better to let HMRC take 40% of a great deal than to deny them their share of very little.

Ideally, business succession planning is something that should be looked at much earlier on, when the original proprietor is still hale and hearty and looking forward to a well-deserved retirement. We will return to some of the relevant practical issues involved in passing on a business in Section 10.19.

If a 'deathbed sale' situation does arise, however, one way to avoid the pitfalls described above would be to sell the business in exchange for unquoted shares in a trading company. Full business property relief would then be preserved and CGT can also generally be avoided.

7.27   BUSINESS PROPERTY RELIEF FOR SMALLER SHAREHOLDINGS

Any shareholding in an unquoted trading company qualifies for 100% business property relief. This includes shares in AIM companies.

The problem is that when one considers the generally volatile nature of unquoted shares, combined with the minimum two-year holding period for business property relief, putting your wealth into these types of assets just to save IHT is a pretty risky business.

Nevertheless, under the right circumstances, it is certainly something to consider. Let's look at an example.

Example

Noel wins a substantial sum on the National Lottery. "Great," his brother Liam says, "how 'bout helpin' me out with me business then?". Noel agrees to give Liam £100,000 to help get his new business started. However, if Noel simply gives Liam the money, this will be a potentially exempt transfer and if Noel dies within seven years, it will have to be brought back into his estate.

So, what Noel does instead is to subscribe for shares in Liam's company, Wonderwall Ltd. After just two years, the Wonderwall Ltd shares will qualify for business property relief and Noel can then give them to Liam free from IHT (subject to the points set out in Section 7.19).

7.28 THE AIM EXEMPTION

I have said it enough times but I know you think it's too good to be true, so here it is again:

Shares traded on the alternative investment market (AIM) are eligible for 100% business property relief. In other words, IHT really is still voluntary and here's how to avoid volunteering in five easy steps:

i)   Sell everything you've got unless it already qualifies for business property relief or agricultural property relief at 100%
ii) Put £325,000 on deposit
iii) Buy an annuity to give yourself sufficient guaranteed income to get by on (this step is optional but probably sensible)
iv) Put everything else into a portfolio of AIM shares
v)   Survive two years

Too drastic for you? Perhaps, but the key point to remember is that, although AIM shares are classed as 'unquoted' for most tax purposes, including business property relief, they are still traded on the London Stock Exchange and are thus effectively liquid assets (albeit that, due to the relatively low level of trading, it can sometimes be difficult to sell AIM shares at a fair price).

Are they risky? Well, yes, all investments are risky, but AIM shares have often outperformed the FTSE. By 2017 there were approximately 950 companies quoted on AIM with a combined market value of over £100 billion.

Furthermore, the risk is substantially reduced if you invest in a portfolio of shares and there are financial products available to enable you to do this with professional fund managers choosing your AIM investments for you.

The fund managers will monitor the performance of your investments and will make changes to the portfolio to protect your investment and your business property relief. Such changes can usually be made without any loss of business property relief due to the replacement property rules (see Section 7.18).

And you can afford a bit of risk anyway can't you? Think about it – if you lose, say, 20% of your investment, but save 40% in IHT, your family are still better off aren't they?

Better still, you can even eliminate the risk altogether by investing in a protected IHT service with a built-in life assurance policy. If your investment has fallen in value when you die, the life policy will pay out the shortfall. The life policy itself can be made tax-efficient by being written into trust (see Section 10.15).

All you need to do is to survive for the requisite two-year period. You can then leave your family up to 67% better off, even if your AIM portfolio has performed badly!

Naturally, a scheme like this does not come cheap and the fund managers' charges can be quite expensive. Furthermore, the life assurance premiums will typically absorb any income from the investment: and you will still have to pay Income Tax on any dividends paid by the AIM companies in your portfolio which total more than your 'dividend allowance' (see Appendix H).

However, under the right circumstances, it could be well worth bearing these costs for the sake of the ultimate 40% tax saving. For an elderly person with surplus funds, the potential to avoid IHT after surviving just two years represents a huge incentive.

Furthermore, anyone investing the proceeds from the sale of other qualifying business property within the last three years could obtain business property relief immediately, thus exempting their entire investment from IHT even if they die shortly afterwards.

And it's worth remembering that an investment in AIM shares is not locked away permanently. If your circumstances change and you need to realise some of those funds, which are no longer 'surplus' to requirements after all, you can simply sell some or all of your AIM portfolio. This makes an AIM portfolio very attractive to anyone who wishes to save IHT without actually giving any of their money away. The portfolio provides a means to protect some of your wealth from IHT when you are unsure whether you can genuinely afford to live without it.

On the other hand, in view of the costs inherent in a protected AIM portfolio investment, a wealthy person with funds that are quite definitely surplus to requirements and a life expectancy of well over seven years might do better to simply give that surplus away and take out term life insurance to cover the risk of a premature death within seven years.

Nevertheless, while the full five-step plan outlined above may not be for you, there could still be a place for some AIM shares in your IHT planning strategy.

Wealth Warning 1
Whilst AIM shares are eligible for business property relief in principle, it remains important that the companies in which you invest are themselves carrying on qualifying businesses. This will, however, include AIM companies with a 'hybrid business' that passes the 'wholly or mainly' test (see Section 7.7).

Wealth Warning 2
If your AIM shares get a full listing, your business property relief will be lost (unless you control the company). Having said that, if this does happen, you will probably have made a nice profit on the deal, so it wouldn't be all bad would it?

Wealth Warning 3
Capital gains on sales of AIM shares and dividends received on AIM shares are subject to CGT and Income Tax respectively in the normal way. There are no special reliefs applying to AIM shares for these taxes.

7.29   AIMING TOO HIGH

As with any other form of qualifying business property, any liabilities incurred after 5th April 2013 and used, directly or indirectly, to purchase qualifying AIM shares must be deducted from the value of those shares for business property relief purposes in the event of any transfer of value taking place after 16th July 2013.

This means that it is no longer possible to obtain additional business property relief by borrowing against other assets in order to purchase AIM shares.

In this context, it is also important to bear in mind that HMRC takes a very broad view of what is meant by 'indirectly'.

Example

Ella owns a house worth £1.5m and has savings and investments totalling £1.2m. In 2018, she sells off all of her investments and invests the proceeds, together with all of her savings, into qualifying AIM shares. (I have ignored CGT on the sale of her investments for the sake of illustration, but this needs to be taken into account.)

A short time later, Ella mortgages her house for £1m. She gives £600,000 to her grandchildren and uses the remaining £400,000 to replace some of her savings: to assist in funding her mortgage and to provide her with a bit of a 'cushion'.

According to HMRC's guidance, Ella should be treated as having used £400,000 of her mortgage to indirectly finance the purchase of her AIM shares, restricting her business property relief to £800,000 (£1.2m – £400,000).

Their logic is that Ella could have achieved substantially the same result by investing just £800,000 of her savings in AIM shares and taking out a mortgage of just £600,000 to provide funds to give to her grandchildren.

As always, HMRC's guidance is not actually the law, but it can often be persuasive and, until the matter is actually tested in court, it would be wise to operate on the basis that their interpretation is correct.

In other words, it would appear sensible for someone in Ella's position to restrict their AIM investment to the amount that they can actually afford without taking on any additional borrowing.

7.30   AGRICULTURAL PROPERTY RELIEF

Agricultural property relief applies in a broadly similar way to business property relief. The following types of property may be covered:

   i)   Agricultural land or pasture
   ii)   Buildings used for the intensive rearing of livestock or fish
   iii) Stud farms
   iv)   Farmhouses, cottages and other farm buildings
   v)   Woodlands

Property under (iv) or (v) must generally be occupied on a basis ancillary to property also occupied under (i), (ii) or (iii); although buildings used to grow indoor crops, such as mushrooms, may qualify in their own right without the need for any additional agricultural land.

The relief applies to agricultural land anywhere in the European Economic Area (Appendix G), the Channel Islands or the Isle of Man.

To qualify for agricultural property relief, the land or buildings must either have been:

a)   Occupied (i.e. used) by the transferor for agricultural purposes for a period of at least two years prior to the date of transfer, or

b)   Owned by the transferor and used for agricultural purposes (by anyone) for a period of at least seven years prior to the date of transfer

Occupation by a company controlled by the transferor is treated as occupation by the transferor for the purposes of (a) above. Occupation by a partnership is treated as occupation by the partners.

Agricultural property relief is given at rates of 50% or 100%, depending on the exact circumstances of the transfer and subject to the usual raft of provisions designed to prevent abuse. It is essential that agricultural activities are being carried out on the land at the time of the transfer. Furthermore, the relief is restricted to the 'agricultural value' of the land or property. This is the value of the land or property if transferred subject to a condition that it must remain in agricultural use permanently.

Any excess value may be eligible for business property relief in some cases. Where the transferor is actively farming the land themselves, this will usually qualify as a trading activity for business property relief purposes.

Farming syndicate arrangements are available to provide IHT shelters for investments of £200,000 or more.

A separate IHT deferral relief is available for woodlands in the European Economic Area that do not qualify for agricultural property relief.

Agricultural Liabilities

The rules set out in Sections 7.11 to 7.16 apply equally to liabilities incurred to finance agricultural property, woodlands, or (where appropriate) shares and securities in companies carrying on these activities.

7.31   FARMHOUSES

If you ever discuss IHT in your local pub or golf club, some bright spark is bound to tell you they have avoided IHT by buying a farm.

For a start, the mere fact that they are around to make this bar room boast means they have not actually avoided IHT yet. More specifically, though, the problem with a lot of so-called 'farmhouses' is that they are really just a country house with some farmland nearby. This alone is not enough to secure agricultural property relief.

A normal size farmhouse occupied by a working farmer is indeed eligible for agricultural property relief but it is essential that the house is 'of an appropriate character' and is occupied for the purposes of farming throughout the two years prior to the relevant transfer (or seven years where occupied by someone other than the owner).

To be occupied for the purposes of farming, the house must be occupied by the person with day-to-day responsibility for running the farm (e.g. a farm manager). A farm owner who has only limited involvement in the day-to-day running of the farm does not occupy their home for the purposes of farming.

So, simply buying an old farmhouse isn't necessarily enough to enable you to claim agricultural property relief. The fact that the farmhouse does not qualify does not necessarily preclude the rest of the farm from qualifying for relief, so our bar room braggart is not entirely wrong, although this may only be a small comfort as very often the majority of the value will be in the house.

Even when a farmhouse does qualify for agricultural property relief, the relief is restricted to its 'agricultural value': the value it would have if sold subject to a covenant requiring it to remain in agricultural use. In some cases, there will be a substantial difference between this and the house's open market value and the excess will not be eligible for agricultural property relief. Whether any of the excess value is eligible for business property relief will depend on the exact circumstances of the case.

The major problem for genuine farmers is the fact that the house must be occupied for the purposes of farming throughout the two years prior to the relevant transfer (or seven years where occupied by someone other than the owner).

Elderly farmers who are seeking to retire should therefore consider passing the farmhouse to their children whilst it still qualifies for relief.

7.32   THE SAFETY NET

Given the numerous and highly complex conditions that must be satisfied to obtain business property relief or agricultural property relief, the matter will often be in doubt when the business owner dies.

If the owner simply leaves the business or agricultural property to their surviving spouse, the matter will still not be resolved as this transfer will usually be exempt anyway. However, if the deceased left the property to a discretionary trust in their Will, HMRC would need to examine the case and, hopefully, the matter will soon be resolved.

How does this help?

If business or agricultural property relief is denied, there should be time to appoint the assets to the surviving spouse free from IHT (see Section 16.3).

The tax is at least deferred and the executors will know where they stand. Furthermore, the surviving spouse may even have time to correct whatever defects there were in the property so that there is a better chance of claiming relief successfully on their subsequent death.

If it turns out that full business property relief or agricultural property relief is available, there is a chance to do some further planning, as outlined in the next two sections.

7.33   THE DOUBLE DIP

Where full business property relief or agricultural property relief is available, the relevant property can safely be left to a discretionary trust free from IHT. The deceased's spouse (or unmarried partner) can then buy the relevant property from the discretionary trust for full market value.

> **Wealth Warning**
> Due to the rules on deduction of liabilities used to acquire relievable property (see Sections 2.12 and 7.11), the purchase will need to be funded from other existing assets and not by way of borrowing.

On the survivor's death, the chargeable value of their estate will effectively be reduced twice:

i)   Through business property relief or agricultural property relief on the qualifying property
ii)   By using other chargeable assets or funds for the purchase

This provides the effective 'double dip', illustrated by the following example.

Example

On his death, Damon leaves the family business to the Parklife Discretionary Trust and leaves the remainder of his estate to his widow Justine. Justine then buys the business from the trust for £1m, its current market value, using some of the funds inherited from Damon.

On Justine's death, her estate comprises the family business, worth £1.2m, and other assets worth £650,000. Her IHT calculation is therefore as follows:

Total estate value	*£1,850,000*
Less:	
Business property relief	*£1,200,000*

Chargeable estate	*£650,000*
	========

Justine's chargeable estate is covered by her nil rate band of £325,000 plus her transferable nil rate band received from Damon, leaving her executors with no IHT to pay.

If Damon had left the business to Justine rather than the trust, she would not have used £1m of other funds to purchase it. Those funds would then have been in her estate on her death, thus giving rise to an IHT bill of £400,000.

Hence, as we can see from the example, this technique effectively enables a surviving spouse or partner to benefit from a double deduction in respect of any qualifying business or agricultural property.

The purchase of the business shortly after the original owner's death should give rise to little or no CGT due to the 'uplift on death' (see Section 11.2).

The same would apply to any inherited assets which are sold in order to fund the purchase of the business.

However, the major drawback which exists after the changes introduced from 17th July 2013 (see Section 7.11) is that the purchase of the business must be funded from other existing assets: either assets already held by the surviving spouse or partner, or other assets inherited from the deceased spouse or partner. Funding the purchase through borrowing will no longer be effective.

This restriction severely limits the usefulness of this technique, although it will still be possible to use it in some cases.

There are also a few other little 'flies in the ointment' here:

i)   Stamp Duty or SDLT will be payable on the surviving partner's purchase of the business.
ii)   Although any inherited assets will benefit from the 'uplift on death', the surviving spouse or partner may still suffer some CGT liabilities if they have to sell any of their own existing assets to fund the purchase of the business.
iii) The discretionary trust will be subject to higher rates of Income Tax on income from the funds it holds; although the effects of this can be mitigated by paying income out to beneficiaries (see Section 8.22 for more details).
iv)   The discretionary trust will be subject to anniversary and exit charges (see Chapter 8) if it holds assets with a value in excess of the nil rate band.

Having said all that, it is worth bearing in mind that the technique allows funds with a value equal to the market value of the deceased's business to be put into a discretionary trust with no 'entry charge', so it is a very efficient way to set up a trust. We will look at the potential savings which a trust may yield in Chapter 9.

7.34   MAKE HAY WHILE THE SUN SHINES

If a person dies leaving property which is fully exempt under business property relief or agricultural property relief, there is a strong argument to suggest that it would be wise to pass this property directly to the deceased's children rather than risk any possibility that the relevant relief may be lost before the deceased's surviving spouse or partner also dies.

Business property relief or agricultural property relief could be lost during the surviving spouse or partner's lifetime due to either a change in legislation or a change in the nature of the business.

In many cases, the fear of losing the relief may place unwelcome constraints on the business. By passing the business directly to the next generation, such constraints are effectively removed (although the problem will of course eventually return).

This approach will not suit every family, of course, and most people will want to be sure that their spouse or partner is financially secure before they are happy to pass the family business straight to their children.

For those who literally are 'making hay', i.e. running the family farm, it is often a good idea to pass the farmhouse directly to the children on the first spouse's death since agricultural property relief may subsequently be lost if the surviving spouse is unable to run the farm on their own.

Chapter 8

IHT Planning With Trusts

8.1 WHAT IS A TRUST?

In its simplest form, a 'trust' is basically an arrangement under which someone is given the legal title to an asset and is 'trusted' to hold that asset on behalf of one or more beneficiaries.

Trusts have a long and honourable history as a well-established mechanism for protecting the vulnerable, such as widows, orphans or disabled people. They originated in the 12th Century when crusaders would entrust their assets to another person before setting off to fight in the Holy Land.

Some definitions:

'Trustee' - The person trusted to hold the asset
'Beneficiary' - The person on whose behalf the asset is held
'Settlor' - The person who transferred the asset into the trust
'Absolutely' - When assets finally leave the trust and become the property of the ultimate beneficiary we say that the beneficiary now holds those assets 'absolutely'
'Testator' - A deceased person who left a valid Will (which may sometimes have been used to set up a trust)

Very often, the settlor will also be a trustee. Legally, there is nothing to prevent the settlor from also being a beneficiary, although this usually renders the trust ineffective for IHT planning purposes and can also give rise to some unwanted CGT liabilities on the transfers.

Settlements and Settled Property

In legal parlance (and within tax legislation), the act of putting assets or funds into a trust is generally referred to as a 'settlement'. When a trust is created, this is also referred to as a 'settlement'.

The assets held within the trust are known as 'settled property'. Every time new assets or funds are put into the trust a new item of 'settled property' is created. Each item of 'settled property' has its own separate identity for IHT purposes and this is especially important when there are changes to the IHT treatment of trusts.

Example

On 20th March 2006, Marc set up the Jeepster Discretionary Trust and transferred £1m into it. On 25th March 2006, Marc transferred another £1m into the trust. Although there is only one formally constituted trust, it contains two distinct items of 'settled property', one settled on 20th March 2006 and one settled on 25th March 2006.

It is important to remember that IHT law applies not only to a trust in its entirety, but also to each individual item of settled property within that trust. In our example, the Jeepster Discretionary Trust is one settlement containing two items of settled property.

A single trust may hold settled property subject to an interest in possession whilst other property is held on discretionary trust. For IHT purposes, each item of settled property is treated according to the relevant rules relating to that particular item of property.

A trust may therefore be regarded as an envelope, which may contain any number of different items of settled property of differing types.

In most cases, for the sake of simplicity, we will generally assume throughout this guide that each trust has only one type of settled property within it. Remember always, however, that IHT law applies to each item of settled property in its own right.

Fundamental changes were made to the IHT treatment of trusts with effect from 22nd March 2006. These changes have far-reaching consequences and it will therefore often make a critical difference whether property was 'settled' before or after that date.

Naturally, when planning for the future, we will only be concerned with the current regime and any potential future changes. Nonetheless, as we shall see later in this chapter, many people will also still be affected by the earlier rules.

Before we move on to look at some of the useful IHT planning techniques which trusts provide, we need to understand a bit more about trusts and how they are treated for tax purposes.

8.2   WHAT TYPES OF TRUST ARE THERE?

In essence, there are really only two kinds of trust: an 'interest in possession trust' and a 'discretionary trust'.

The distinction between these two main types of trust revolves entirely around whether any beneficiary is entitled to enjoy an 'interest in possession' in any of the settled property within the trust. We will look further at what constitutes an 'interest in possession' in Section 8.3. We will also look at what constitutes a discretionary trust in Section 8.4.

For IHT purposes, however, it is necessary for us to further sub-divide the two main types into a number of other categories. Following the changes made in 2006, these categories may be listed as follows:

- Bare Trusts
- Charitable Trusts
- Bereaved Minors' Trusts
- Pre-22/3/2006 Interest In Possession Trusts

- Disabled Trusts
- Immediate Post-Death Interests
- Transitional Serial Interests
- 18 to 25 Trusts
- Post-22/3/2006 Interest In Possession Trusts
- Discretionary Trusts

Whilst, as explained above, there are only two fundamental types of trust, each of the ten different categories listed above is subject to different rules for IHT purposes.

The question of whether there is an 'interest in possession' in trust property nevertheless remains a crucial factor in determining how the trust will be treated for IHT purposes. Every item of settled property will either be subject to an 'interest in possession' or will be held on discretionary trust.

Various other factors will then need to be considered in order to determine which of the ten categories listed above each item of settled property will fall into.

As explained in Section 8.1, a single trust may hold items of settled property that fall into two or more different categories. Hence, we may sometimes get a sort of 'hybrid' trust that is subject to different rules on its different parts.

Prior to April 2008, there was another category of trust, known as an 'accumulation and maintenance trust', which was exempt from the 'relevant property' regime. Such trusts had until 5th April 2008 to convert to a different type of trust, failing which they became a relevant property trust (see Section 8.15).

8.3   WHAT IS AN INTEREST IN POSSESSION?

Whenever a specific individual is beneficially entitled, for a specified period, to the income from, or to otherwise enjoy, an asset within a trust, that person has an 'interest in possession'.

Where more than one person is to share the income or enjoyment of the assets for a specified period, this is also an interest in possession.

In such cases, the income may be shared in any proportion specified in the Trust Deed.

If, however, the trustees have discretion over the income paid to the beneficiaries, this would make the trust a discretionary trust.

Example

Nicole transfers a number of investment properties into the All Saints Trust. Under the terms of the trust, each year's rental profits must be paid to the beneficiaries as follows:

- *Half to Nicole's sister, Natalie*
- *The first £10,000 of the remainder to her friend, Melanie*
- *The remaining balance to her niece, Shaznay*

Each beneficiary's interest is an interest in possession because each of them receives a specific defined amount under the terms of the Trust Deed which is not dependent on the discretion of the trustees.

Life Interests

Where a beneficiary is entitled to an interest in possession for the remainder of their life, we refer to this as a 'life interest' (sometimes also known as a 'liferent'). A trust that is subject to a life interest is often referred to as a 'Life Interest Trust'.

Generally speaking, therefore, the IHT treatment of a life interest trust is exactly the same as any other interest in possession trust.

The Remainder

'The remainder' is a term that is often used to describe the right to assets, which comes into force after an interest in possession ends.

The most common example would be when a person leaves a life interest in property to their spouse with the remainder to their children. This would mean that, on the spouse's death, the property passes absolutely to the children.

Reversion to Settlor

It is worth noting that it is possible to create an interest in possession trust where the remainder interest reverts to the original settlor. This, in itself, does not invoke the 'Gift with Reservation' rules (see Section 4.9), as long as the settlor and their spouse are excluded from any benefit during the period that the interest in possession exists.

Income Tax Treatment

All other things being equal, an interest in possession trust is generally to be preferred whenever possible as it enjoys a more beneficial Income Tax regime than a discretionary trust. See Section 8.22 for further details.

8.4   DISCRETIONARY TRUSTS

A discretionary trust is basically any trust, or part thereof, where no person is entitled to an interest in possession. The trustees therefore have the discretion to decide who to allow to have the enjoyment of the trust's assets, who to pay the income of the trust to, and how much.

There is usually a defined class of beneficiaries from whom the trustees can choose, such as "all my grandchildren", for example.

It is possible for a discretionary trust to have just one beneficiary as long as there is some theoretical possibility of there being at least one other additional beneficiary at some time and the trustees have discretion over whether, and when, to pay out income.

The assets of a discretionary trust will always be treated as 'relevant property' (see Section 8.17) unless the trust qualifies as:

- A bereaved minor's trust (Section 8.9)
- An 18 to 25 trust (Section 8.14)
- A disabled trust (Section 8.11) or
- A charitable trust (Section 3.5)

8.5   INHERITANCE TAX REGIMES FOR TRUSTS: AN OVERVIEW

In essence, there are three IHT regimes for settled property held within trusts, as follows:

- The relevant property regime,
- Trust property included in the beneficiary's estate, and
- Exempt trusts

Where settled property falls into the relevant property regime, it is subject to IHT charges in its own right, as detailed in Sections 8.17 to 8.21. Such settled property is referred to as 'relevant property' for IHT purposes.

Most other categories of settled property are treated as if they belong absolutely to the beneficiary and are included in the beneficiary's estate for IHT purposes, as explained in Section 2.9.

The scope of the third regime, 'exempt trusts', was severely curtailed by the changes made by Gordon Brown in 2006 but, as the name implies, it provides complete exemption from IHT for certain types of trust.

The various categories of trust fall into these three regimes, as follows:

Relevant Property:
    Discretionary Trusts
    Post-22/3/2006 Interest in Possession Trusts (Note 1)
    18 to 25 Trusts (Note 2)

In Beneficiary's Estate:
> Pre-22/3/2006 Interest in Possession Trusts
> Disabled Trusts
> Immediate Post-Death Interests
> Transitional Serial Interests
> Bare Trusts

Exempt:
> Bereaved Minors' Trusts
> 18 to 25 Trusts (Note 2)
> Charitable Trusts

This table is naturally a simplification of the position, but hopefully a useful one.

Notes
1. A new interest in possession created on or after 22nd March 2006 that does not qualify under any other category of trust will fall into the relevant property regime. Typically, this will occur in the case of most lifetime transfers into trust after 22nd March 2006 or new interests in possession coming into force on the termination of a previous interest in possession after 5th October 2008.
2. 18 to 25 trusts are effectively exempt until the beneficiary attains the age of 18 and then fall into the relevant property regime thereafter.

8.6   TRANSFERS INTO TRUST

On Death

Transfers into trust made on the occasion of the transferor's death are generally chargeable to IHT in the same way whatever type of trust is involved.

The regimes described in the previous section determine the way in which the settled property is treated later; they do not usually alter the amount of IHT arising on the transferor's death.

The only exceptions to this rule are charitable trusts and the fact that the spouse exemption applies to an immediate post-death interest for a surviving spouse (see Section 8.12).

In all other cases, transfers into trust arising on death form part of the estate in the normal way and will be subject to IHT as usual.

Transfers on Death and the Residence Nil Rate Band

Transfers of qualifying property, on death, into a trust for the benefit of one or more of the deceased's direct descendents, will qualify for the residence nil rate band, where available, provided that one of the following types of trust are used:

- Bare Trust
- Bereaved Minors' Trust
- Disabled Trust
- Immediate Post-Death Interest
- 18 to 25 Trust

Lifetime Transfers

As we saw in Section 4.2, most lifetime transfers into trust are now chargeable lifetime transfers. Lifetime transfers to disabled trusts or bare trusts are, however, potentially exempt transfers and transfers to charity are exempt.

8.7   THE TRUST HIERARCHY

All trusts must take their place in what I call the 'Trust Hierarchy'.

Every trust will be categorised as the highest type of trust within the hierarchy for which it qualifies. For example, a trust that qualifies as an Immediate Post Death Interest (ranked sixth in the hierarchy) cannot be an 18 to 25 Trust (ranked eighth) even if it would otherwise qualify.

The trust hierarchy is as follows:

1. **Charitable Trusts**
2. **Bare Trusts**
3. **Bereaved Minors' Trusts**
4. **Pre-22/3/2006 Interest in Possession Trusts**
5. **Disabled Trusts**
6. **Immediate Post-Death Interests**
7. **Transitional Serial Interests**
8. **18 to 25 Trusts**
9. **Relevant Property Trusts**

Readers will note that two of our categories from Section 8.2 are absent here. Discretionary trusts and post-22/3/2006 interest in possession trusts (not falling into any other category) will both be relevant property trusts.

The first step in our trust hierarchy deals with Charitable Trusts, which have exempt status.

We will now proceed to examine each of the remaining steps of our trust hierarchy in turn. Remember throughout this process that any trust that qualifies at one point in the hierarchy cannot also qualify lower down the hierarchy.

Tax Tip

As we shall see in the sections that follow, several of the above categories of trust must be created immediately on the settlor's death. However, in Chapter 16, we will see that both Deeds of Variation and distributions from most trusts made within two years of the settlor's death will be treated as if they had occurred immediately on death. Hence, in practice, most of the trusts, which in theory need to be set up immediately on death, can often actually be set up at any time within two years after death.

8.8   BARE TRUSTS

Assets that are simply held in someone else's name are held on 'bare trust', sometimes also known as an 'absolute trust'. A bare trust only exists where the beneficiary has full beneficial ownership of the trust assets and has an immediate and absolute right to both capital and income.

Most commonly, a bare trust exists when an adult holds property on behalf of a minor who will become absolutely entitled to the asset on reaching the age of 18 (sometimes 16 in Scotland). Bare trusts for minors occur frequently because persons under the age of 18 cannot take legal title to property in England or Wales. The position in Scotland is slightly different and legal title is sometimes possible at 16. Bare trusts may sometimes continue beyond this point until the beneficiary calls for the trust assets to be transferred to them.

Assets held on bare trust are not regarded as 'settled property' for IHT purposes and are simply treated as belonging to the beneficiary. We will see some useful consequences of this in the next chapter.

8.9   BEREAVED MINORS' TRUSTS

The 'trust for a bereaved minor', to give it its proper name, is a very restrictive class of trust. Where the appropriate rules are met, trust property will be exempt from IHT and there will be no charges if a beneficiary dies or assets are transferred out of the trust. The basic conditions are:

i)   The beneficiary of the trust must be under 18 years of age
ii)   At least one of the beneficiary's parents is dead
iii)   The trust was set up under:
    a.   Intestacy,
    b.   The criminal injuries compensation scheme, or
    c.   The Will of a deceased parent
iv)   The beneficiary must be absolutely entitled to the trust assets by the age of 18 at the latest
v)   Trust assets may only be applied for the benefit of the minor until he or she reaches the age of 18
vi)   Trust income may either be applied for the benefit of the minor or given directly to them. (The minor may have an interest in possession, if the settlor so desires.)

For the purposes of these rules, a 'parent' includes a natural parent, a step-parent, an adopted parent and any other person with 'parental responsibility' (e.g. a legal guardian).

Whilst the above rules are clearly designed for a single beneficiary, a trust may still qualify with two or more beneficiaries, as long as each of them obtains absolute entitlement to their own share of the trust assets at the age of 18.

The major problem with this type of trust is that the beneficiary must gain absolute possession of the trust assets at the age of 18. Many people are horrified at the prospect of the entire family fortune suddenly being at the whim of someone so young. The risk of them frittering everything away before they have the wisdom to look out for their own future is all too obvious.

Thankfully, these concerns were at least partly recognised when the concept of the '18 to 25 Trust' was introduced. We will come on to these trusts in Section 8.14, but it is worth noting that a bereaved minor's trust can be converted to an '18 to 25 Trust' without charge.

Small Payments for Non-Qualifying Purposes

Small payments which do not qualify under points (v) or (vi) above are permitted. These are limited to the lower of the following amounts each year:

- £3,000
- 3% of the total value of settled property in the trust

8.10 PRE-22/3/2006 INTEREST IN POSSESSION TRUSTS

Prior to 22nd March 2006, whenever a beneficiary had an interest in possession they were treated, for IHT purposes, as if they owned the asset outright. Subject to certain exceptions, the termination of their interest, on death or otherwise, represented the transfer of the underlying asset for IHT purposes.

Interests in possession already in existence on 21st March 2006 continue to be treated as part of the beneficiary's estate for IHT purposes.

Wealth Warning

Note that the old rules only apply to **'settled property'** transferred into trust before 22nd March 2006. Any new lifetime transfers of assets into an existing trust will constitute new settled property and will be subject to the new rules.

The consequences arising when an interest in possession already in existence on 21st March 2006 comes to an end differ according to whether this occurred before or after 6th October 2008 and are dealt with in Sections 8.13 and 8.16.

Changes to Terms

Where the terms of a pre-22/3/2006 interest in possession trust are altered after 5th October 2008, including a change to the period of the interest, this will result in the settled property subject to that interest in possession becoming 'relevant property'.

The trust would then be subject to the IHT charges explained in Sections 8.18 and 8.19. However, where there is no change to the actual beneficiary, there would not be a chargeable lifetime transfer and hence no 'entry charge'.

Extended 'Old' Interest in Possession Trusts

During the transitional period which ended on 5th October 2008, it remained possible to extend the life of the trust by altering the terms applying to the existing beneficiary or by transferring the interest to a beneficiary with a longer life expectancy. See Section 8.13 for further details.

8.11 DISABLED TRUSTS

Assets within a trust set up for the benefit of a qualifying disabled person are exempt from the 'relevant property' provisions and are instead treated as being part of the beneficiary's estate.

Self-settlement by a person with a condition expected to lead to a qualifying disability is permitted. This extension only applies to self-settlements; other settlors must wait until the beneficiary's condition deteriorates enough for them to qualify under the general rules.

A disabled trust may be either a discretionary trust or an interest in possession trust. Further rules apply to the use of funds held by a discretionary trust.

The rules governing disabled trusts are mainly designed to cover beneficiaries with a mental disability but will often also cover a person with a terminal illness.

Practical Pointer

This provides the opportunity for the settlor to put property into trust during their terminal illness. While this will not save any IHT, it will enable the trustees to manage all or part of the estate following the settlor's death without having to wait for the grant of probate or confirmation.

8.12 IMMEDIATE POST-DEATH INTERESTS

An interest in possession created immediately on death, either by Will or intestacy, is termed an 'Immediate Post-Death Interest' and forms part of the beneficiary's estate for IHT purposes.

The settled property subject to the immediate post-death interest will therefore be included in the beneficiary's own IHT calculation if they should die whilst still entitled to the interest in possession or within seven years of the termination of that interest.

Most importantly, however, this means that the spouse exemption is available on the creation of an immediate post-death interest.

A transferable nil rate band may also be set against the value of an immediate post-death interest brought into the spouse's estate on their death.

Furthermore, where an immediate post-death interest ends during the beneficiary's lifetime and property passes to a Bereaved Minor's Trust under the terms of the original settlor's Will, this will be a potentially exempt transfer.

Combining this with the spouse exemption provides a potential opportunity to pass assets tax free to minor children.

Example

James wishes to leave his estate to his five-year-old daughter Beatrice. If he left the estate directly to Beatrice or to a trust for her benefit, the IHT arising would be colossal.

Instead, therefore, James leaves just £325,000 (his nil rate band) to a bereaved minor's trust for Beatrice and everything else to an immediate post-death interest trust in favour of his estranged wife, Heather. Heather's immediate post-death interest lasts for a fixed period of three years, after which the estate passes into Beatrice's bereaved minor's trust.

The bulk of James's estate initially passes into Heather's immediate post-death interest tax free under the spouse exemption and, three years later, it passes into the trust for Beatrice as a potentially exempt transfer.

As long as Heather outlives James by at least ten years, his entire estate can pass to Beatrice tax free.

Technically, taking the strict letter of the legislation, Heather's interest would only need to last two years and a day, rather than three years, as described above. However, HMRC frequently challenges life interests of only just over two years under the associated operations rules (see Section 10.21). The legacy to Heather could then be ignored and James's entire estate could be subject to IHT (except his nil rate band).

Whether three years is even long enough is not clear as any fixed period for Heather's interest may make the transfer into Beatrice's trust a bit too much of a certainty for HMRC's liking. Clearly though, the longer Heather's interest lasts, the more robust the arrangement will be (but bear in mind that the transfer into Beatrice's trust needs to take place before she is 18).

Nonetheless, the associated operations rules are usually only used in blatant cases of tax avoidance, so a more subtle version of this approach is more likely to work, especially where the couple are still living together immediately before the transferor's death.

Immediate post-death interest trusts in favour of a surviving spouse that terminate on their remarriage are commonplace and would not generally be challenged.

Other conditions that might terminate the spouse's interest, such as emigration or bankruptcy, for example, might also be acceptable.

The difficulty in a case like James's above, is that he will want some certainty that the estate will pass to the child reasonably soon.

A clause terminating the surviving spouse's interest when the child reaches a certain age might, perhaps, be subtle enough for the scheme to work.

Nevertheless, there will always need to be some risk that the spouse's interest in possession will last for a few years in order for this strategy to be effective. This could mean the loss of several years' income for the ultimate beneficiary in some cases, but if this saves them from losing 40% of the capital, it could be worth it.

The surviving spouse may sometimes be prepared to give up their interest voluntarily. This would not create a bereaved minor's trust, but could result in a bare trust in favour of the child with similarly beneficial results. The implications of such a voluntary transfer were discussed in Section 6.15.

A similar strategy could be used to pass assets tax free to adult children but, in this case, the assets must pass to the children absolutely after the spouse's interest in possession terminates. An '18 to 25 trust' cannot be used in the same way, as the transfer from the immediate post-death interest would then be a chargeable lifetime transfer.

For example, the deceased might leave an interest in possession to their surviving spouse, which terminates on their child's 21st birthday when the assets pass absolutely to the child.

As long as the deceased's spouse survives until the child's 28th birthday (i.e. seven years later), the whole process should take place free from IHT.

As this is a more 'common-sense' approach than passing assets to a minor, there is probably less risk of an attack under the associated operations rules.

An immediate post-death interest may also be set up so that the settled property transfers to a bereaved minor's trust or '18 to 25 trust' for the benefit of the original testator's children on the death of the original beneficiary. (IHT is still payable on the original beneficiary's death in the normal way.)

When a testator adds new settled property to an existing interest in possession trust this will also be treated as an immediate post-death interest.

8.13 TRANSITIONAL SERIAL INTERESTS

Where an interest in possession in a settlement made before 22nd March 2006 came to an end before 6th October 2008 and was replaced by a new interest in possession in the same settled property within the same trust, the old rules will continue to apply to that new interest in possession.

The new replacement interest in possession is termed a 'Transitional Serial Interest' and will continue to form part of the beneficiary's estate for IHT purposes. (Unless the new interest in possession qualifies under a higher category in the trust hierarchy, such as a Bereaved Minors' Trust, for example.)

Example

Maurice died on 10th December 2005 and left a life interest in all of his assets to his brother, Robin. Under the terms of Maurice's Will, on Robin's death, the assets are to remain in trust for the benefit of Maurice's nephew, Andy. Robin died on 30th September 2008, so the old rules continue to apply to Andy's interest in possession.

Alternatively, Robin might have chosen to renounce his life interest in favour of Andy. If Robin had done this before 6th October 2008, this would have represented a potentially exempt transfer (as the old rules still applied) and the trust assets would form part of Andy's estate.

Changes to Terms

Where the terms of a pre-22/3/2006 interest in possession trust were altered before 6th October 2008, including a change to the period of the interest, this will also constitute a Transitional Serial Interest.

No Second Chances!

When a transitional serial interest comes to an end itself and is replaced by a new interest in possession, the new interest will be relevant property and will be taxed as set out in Sections 8.17 to 8.19.

This will include cases where changes are made to the terms of the transitional serial interest, including the period of the interest.

Further details of the consequences arising on the termination of a transitional serial interest are set out in Section 8.16.

Spouses and Civil Partners

Where a pre-22/3/2006 interest in possession comes to an end on the beneficiary's death and a new interest in possession in favour of the deceased's spouse comes into being, this new interest will also be a transitional serial interest.

This means that the spouse exemption will apply to the settled property that falls into the deceased's estate under these circumstances.

This continues to apply to pre-22/3/2006 interests in possession transferring to a spouse on the death of a beneficiary after 5th October 2008.

The same treatment does not, however, apply when a transitional serial interest comes to an end on a beneficiary's death and the spouse exemption would not then be available to a new interest in possession arising at that time.

8.14 18 TO 25 TRUSTS

To meet the justifiable concerns raised by many bodies in the wake of the original Budget 2006 announcements, a further new category of trust was created: the '18 to 25 Trust'.

The '18 to 25 Trust' is essentially the same as a Bereaved Minors' Trust (Section 8.9) in all respects except that the beneficiary must become absolutely entitled to the trust property by the age of 25 at the latest, rather than by 18.

Between the ages of 18 and 25, the beneficiary must either be entitled to an interest in possession or else the trust funds must be accumulated for their benefit (subject to the exception for small non-qualifying payments described in Section 8.9).

An '18 to 25 Trust' only retains its IHT exempt status until the beneficiary reaches the age of 18. Thereafter, the trust assets effectively become 'relevant property'.

There is no IHT charge when the trust assets become 'relevant property' on the beneficiary's 18th birthday, but the exit charges explained in Section 8.20 will then apply as if the trust had been set up on this date.

This means that there will be a maximum exit charge of 4.2% if the trust assets pass to the beneficiary at the age of 25 (in addition to the IHT already paid on the parent's death – making a total charge of up to 44.2%!).

More details of the exit charges applying to '18 to 25 Trusts' are given in Section 8.20. Exit charges also apply in the same way if the beneficiary of an '18 to 25 Trust' dies after the age of 18.

An '18 to 25 Trust' cannot arise if an immediate post-death interest is created instead, as this takes precedence under the trust hierarchy. An immediate post-death interest will often be preferable anyway, as this avoids the exit charge that would apply to an '18 to 25 Trust'.

8.15 RELEVANT PROPERTY TRUSTS

Before March 2006, only discretionary trusts were subject to the 'relevant property' regime, which we will examine in detail in Sections 8.17 to 8.21. For this reason, that regime was sometimes referred to as 'the discretionary trust regime'.

Now, however, any trust not falling under any other category in the trust hierarchy will be subject to the relevant property regime.

This will include most lifetime settlements made after 21st March 2006, even those conferring interests in possession on the settlor themselves (known as 'self-settlements'), or on their spouse, and any new 'reverter to settlor' trusts (see Section 8.3).

Discretionary trusts also generally continue to fall within the relevant property regime unless they qualify under one of the other trust categories set out in Section 8.7.

When settled property falls within the relevant property regime, IHT charges may arise when the settlement is made, when assets come out of the trust, and every ten years while they're in it.

Remember, as explained previously, this may apply to any new settlement, not just a newly constituted trust. There is, however, a partial exception to this rule for life policies held in trust and we will return to this in Section 10.14.

Transfers on Death

Most interests in possession created on death will qualify as 'immediate post-death interests', as explained in Section 8.12, and should therefore escape the relevant property regime. Dangers arise, however, where the interest in possession does not arise immediately on death. In particular, a new interest in possession which replaces an 'immediate post-death interest' may fall within the relevant property regime (unless, as always, it qualifies under a higher category in the trust hierarchy).

8.16 END OF TRUST INTERESTS WITHIN BENEFICIARY'S ESTATE

As we saw in Section 8.5, there are five types of trust that are regarded as forming part of the beneficiary's estate.

Property within these trusts is subject to IHT at 40% when the beneficiary's interest comes to an end by reason of their death (subject to the exemptions explained in Chapter 3 and the 'reverter to settlor' exemption explained below).

Under certain circumstances, property within a pre-22/3/2006 interest in possession trust may be eligible to pass into an immediate post-death interest trust, a bereaved minor's trust or an '18 to 25 Trust' on the original beneficiary's death.

Interests Ending During the Life of the Beneficiary

If the beneficiary becomes absolutely entitled to the trust property, this will be a non-event for IHT purposes, as the property remains within the same estate.

If the original settlor or the beneficiary's spouse becomes absolutely entitled to the property, or it goes to charity, the transfer will be exempt.

In other cases, when the beneficiary's interest ends during their lifetime, a potentially exempt transfer will take place if:

- One or more individuals become absolutely entitled to the trust property
- Property transfers to a bare trust
- Property transfers to a disabled trust
- Property subject to an immediate post-death interest transfers to a bereaved minors' trust

All other transfers on termination of a beneficiary's interest during their lifetime will now be chargeable lifetime transfers and the transferred property will fall into the relevant property regime.

If the original beneficiary retains an interest in former trust property, this may constitute a 'Gift with Reservation'. See Section 4.9 for further details.

Reverter To Settlor Trusts

When property reverts to the original settlor on the termination of a pre-22/3/2006 interest in possession trust, the resultant transfer of value is exempt from IHT. This exemption only applies when the property passes back to the settlor absolutely.

8.17   THE RELEVANT PROPERTY REGIME

To make life easier, for the rest of this guide I will refer to any trust that falls into the relevant property regime as a 'relevant property trust'.

A relevant property trust is treated as a separate and distinct person in its own right for IHT purposes. This has the following major consequences:

- Lifetime transfers into a relevant property trust are chargeable transfers, not potentially exempt transfers
- Transfers into a relevant property trust will generally be ineligible for the spouse exemption
- Assets within a relevant property trust are not generally included in a beneficiary's estate for IHT purposes
- No charges arise on the death of a beneficiary or termination of their interest in the trust's assets, but
- A charge may arise when assets leave the trust (see Section 8.19)
- There is no 'revert to settlor' exemption (see Section 8.16)
- Ten-year anniversary charges apply (see Section 8.18)

In essence, therefore, IHT may arise when assets go into a relevant property trust, when they come out of it, and every ten years while they're in it.

Nevertheless, a relevant property trust's 'separate life' does give rise to some very useful tax-planning opportunities, which we will consider further in Chapters 9 and 12.

8.18 TEN-YEAR ANNIVERSARY CHARGES

Unfortunately, to counter the possible advantages of a relevant property trust's 'separate life', these trusts are subject to an IHT charge on every tenth anniversary of their creation. We will now examine how this charge is calculated. It gets rather complex but we will work through a practical example at the end to illustrate the main points.

The anniversary charge is calculated as follows:

i)   Take the total value of all the relevant property in the trust on the anniversary date.

ii) Add any settlements made into other trusts (except charitable trusts or an immediate post-death interest for the settlor's spouse) by the same settlor on the same date as any settlements into this trust where that date is either the date on which the trust was first set up, or a date falling after 9th December 2014.

iii) Calculate the amount of IHT payable on a hypothetical chargeable lifetime transfer of a sum equal to the total of (i) and (ii) on the anniversary date, taking account of:
   a. The nil rate band, but not any other exemptions, and
   b. Any chargeable transfers made by the settlor in the seven years prior to setting up this trust (including any potentially exempt transfers becoming chargeable on the settlor's death).

iv) Using the amount derived at step (iii), the 'Effective Rate' of IHT on the hypothetical lifetime transfer is calculated.

v) The 'Effective Rate' is multiplied by 3/10ths and then applied to any amounts in (i) above derived from assets that have been held by the trust throughout the ten-year period.

vi) For any amounts within (i) which are derived from assets held for less than ten years, the charge is reduced by one fortieth for every complete calendar quarter that those assets were not held as relevant assets of the Trust.

vii) The rate applying to any charges under (vi) may be increased to take account of further chargeable lifetime transfers made by the settlor (other than to the trust itself), including any potentially exempt transfers becoming chargeable on the settlor's death.

For charges arising before 10th December 2014, only settlements made into other trusts on the same day as the trust was first set up needed to be included in step (ii). This treatment continues in respect of trusts set up under Wills executed before 10th December 2014 where the testator died before 6th April 2017.

For charges arising before 18th November 2015, the value of any other 'non-relevant' property in the trust on the day that it entered the trust or, if later, the date that it ceased to be relevant property, also had to be included in the hypothetical chargeable lifetime transfer at step (iii).

Now *that* calls for an example!

As usual, all exemptions and reliefs other than the nil rate band will be ignored, for the sake of simplicity.

Example

On 1st April 2009, Mel set up the Spice Discretionary Trust for the benefit of her granddaughters, Emma and Melanie. She immediately transferred various assets worth a total of £80,000 into the trust. No IHT was payable at that time as the amount transferred was below the nil rate band.

On the same day, Mel also transferred £50,000 into an interest in possession trust for her niece, Victoria.

Previously, on 26th November 2008, Mel had given her sister Geri £135,000.

Sadly, Mel passed away in January 2015. (Fortunately, the nil rate band covered all of her lifetime transfers within the previous seven years.)

On 1st April 2019, the assets in the Spice Discretionary Trust are worth £330,000. The anniversary charge is calculated as follows:

	£
Value of relevant property on anniversary date:	330,000
Other settlement made on the same day:	50,000
Previous chargeable transfers:	135,000
(i.e. the potentially exempt transfer to Geri,	
which became chargeable on Mel's death)	
Cumulative total for hypothetical transfer:	**515,000**
Less nil rate band	325,000
Gives:	190,000
IHT at lifetime rate (20%)	**£38,000**
'Effective Rate' of IHT on the	
hypothetical transfer:	
(£38,000 divided by £330,000 PLUS £50,000)	10%
Rate for anniversary charge:	
3/10ths of 10%	3%
IHT Payable:	
3% x £330,000	**£9,900**

The result of this rather tortuous calculation is that IHT of only £9,900 is payable on the assets in the Spice Discretionary Trust. Remember that, had these assets still been in Mel's estate at the time of her death, IHT of up to £132,000 would have been payable on them.

The Impact of 'Same Day Settlements'

The position in our example would have been better if Mel had waited until the next day to make the gift into Victoria's interest in possession trust. In fact, the ten-year anniversary charge applying to the Spice Discretionary Trust would then have been just £8,400.

As explained above, the 'Effective Rate' applying to each trust is increased as a consequence of both chargeable transfers in the previous seven years and other settlements into trust made on the same day.

Naturally, it is fairly easy to avoid making a lifetime settlement on the same day as a settlement into another trust, but it is difficult to avoid this happening where settlements are made on death and this was the reason for the changes introduced in December 2014 which have now effectively blocked a well-known planning strategy known as 'pilot trusts'. In short, 'pilot trusts' no longer work!

Undistributed Versus Accumulated Income

Trust income that has simply not yet been distributed to beneficiaries at the anniversary date is not included in 'relevant property' for the purposes of the ten-year anniversary charge. (Nor for any 'exit charges' – see Section 8.19.) However, once the trustees have 'accumulated' that income, it does become part of the relevant property of the trust. Broadly, it is then treated like a new transfer of value made on the date of the 'accumulation'.

Where the trustees have a duty to accumulate the trust income, it is treated as being accumulated as soon as it is received. Where the trustees have no power to accumulate trust income (e.g. in the case of an interest in possession trust) it will not usually be treated as accumulated at any time (but see further below).

In all other cases (e.g. most discretionary trusts), the general rule is that income is 'accumulated' when the trustees decide not to distribute it to the trust's beneficiaries.

In addition, any income which has not been distributed or formally accumulated after five years is deemed to have been accumulated for IHT purposes.

Unconverted Accumulation and Maintenance Trusts

Where an old accumulation and maintenance trust falls into the relevant property regime from 6th April 2008 (see Section 8.2), its first anniversary charge thereafter will be restricted.

Example
Thom set up the Yorke Family Accumulation and Maintenance Trust on 6th January 1998. Thom had made no chargeable transfers within the previous seven years. The trust became a relevant property trust on 6th April 2008. On the twentieth anniversary of Thom's original settlement, 6th January 2018, the trust assets are worth £1m. The trust is subject to an anniversary charge as follows:

	£
Value of relevant property on anniversary date:	*1,000,000*
Cumulative total for hypothetical transfer:	*1,000,000*
Less nil rate band	*325,000*
Gives:	*675,000*
IHT at lifetime rate (20%)	***£135,000***
'Effective Rate' of IHT on the	
hypothetical transfer:	*13.5%*
Rate for anniversary charge:	
13.5% x 3/10 x 39/40	*3.94875%*
IHT Payable:	
3.94875% x £1,000,000	***£39,488***

The charge is reduced by a factor of 39/40ths because the property within the trust only became relevant property on 6th April 2008, so that only 39 calendar quarters had expired by the anniversary date on 6th January 2018.

A similar result arises when an interest in possession has emerged from an accumulation and maintenance trust between 22nd March 2006 and 5th April 2008. In this case, however, the charge runs from the date that the interest in possession arose. The anniversary dates continue to be based on the date of the original settlement.

8.19   EXIT CHARGES

Transfers of assets out of a relevant property trust may also give rise to IHT charges. These 'Exit Charges' are based on broadly similar principles to the ten-year anniversary charge. The 'Effective Rate' arrived at in each case is multiplied by three-tenths, and then also multiplied by one-fortieth for every complete calendar quarter expiring since the most recent ten-year anniversary, or since the creation of the trust in the case of transfers taking place within the first ten years.

For an Exit Charge arising in the first ten-year period, the hypothetical lifetime transfer used to derive the Effective Rate is based on the value of the assets in the trust at its commencement, plus any further settlements made into the trust between then and the date of the transfer.

Example

Let's assume the same facts as in the first example in Section 8.18 above, except that:
  i)   *In 2014 Mel transferred a further £30,000 into the Spice Discretionary Trust, and*
  ii) *On 29th June 2018, the trustees gave £20,000 to Emma out of capital.*

The exit charge on Emma's gift is calculated as follows:

	£
Value of property settled on 1st April 2009:	*80,000*
Other settlement made on the same day:	*50,000*
Previous chargeable transfers:	*135,000*
Value of property settled in 2014:	*30,000*
Cumulative total for hypothetical transfer:	***295,000***
Nil rate band	*325,000*
IHT Payable:	***NIL***

Tax Tip
As this example demonstrates, IHT can often be avoided when the trust's assets are distributed to beneficiaries before the first ten-year anniversary of the trust. We will look at the opportunities this provides in more detail in Chapter 9.

To continue our look at exit charges, however, let's make a slight revision to our example.

Example Revised

Let's now assume that the gift to Geri which became chargeable on Mel's death was actually £235,000. What does this do to Emma's exit charge?

The cumulative total for the hypothetical transfer is now £395,000.

Deducting the nil rate band of £325,000 leaves:	*£70,000*
IHT at lifetime rate (20%)	*£14,000*
'Effective Rate' of IHT on the hypothetical transfer: (£14,000 divided by £160,000*) (* £80,000 + £50,000 + £30,000)	*8.75%*
Rate for exit charge: 8.75% x 3/10 x 36/40	*2.3625%*
IHT Payable: 2.3625% x £20,000	***£473***

Points To Note

i) If Emma bears the tax, the exit charge will be £473, as above. However, if the trust were to bear the tax, 'grossing up' would apply. The 'grossing up' rate in this case would be 2.3625/97.6375 (100 – 2.3625), giving rise to a 'grossed up' charge of £484.

ii) Only 36 calendar quarters are counted here. The 37th quarter does not end until 30th June 2018 and, as the transfer to Emma took place before that date, this quarter had not yet expired. If the transfer had been made two days later, we would have needed to include the 37th quarter.

Later Exit Charges are based on the Effective Rate applying at the previous ten-year anniversary, as adjusted for any further settlements into the trust since then.

Distributions of income out of the trust do not give rise to Exit Charges. Care must be taken, however, that the income is not allowed to 'accumulate' first before distribution.

8.20   EXIT CHARGES: SPECIAL CASES

There are a number of cases where Exit Charges may apply at a reduced rate.

The Exit Charge applying to an unconverted accumulation and maintenance trust will be based on the number of complete calendar quarters that have expired since the later of 5th April 2008 and the trust's most recent ten-year anniversary date.

Similarly, the Exit Charge for an interest in possession which emerged from an accumulation and maintenance trust between 22nd March 2006 and 5th April 2008 will be based on the number of complete calendar quarters that have expired since the interest emerged.

The Exit Charge applying to an '18 to 25 Trust' (see Section 8.14) is based on the number of complete calendar quarters that have expired since the later of:

    i)   The date of the settlor's death, and
    ii) The beneficiary's 18th birthday

Example

Luther died on 14th February 2015 and left his entire estate, worth £10.325m, to an 18 to 25 trust for the benefit of his two children equally. Luther's son Michael was born on 8th May 1995 and his daughter Janet was born on 1st April 1998. Under the terms of Luther's trust, both children will gain absolute entitlement to their share of the trust assets on Janet's 21st birthday, 1st April 2019. The exit charges applying on that date may be calculated as follows:

	£
Value of property settled on 14th February 2015:	10,325,000
Less:	
Nil rate band for 2018/19	325,000

	10,000,000
IHT at lifetime rate (20%)	**2,000,000**
'Effective Rate' of IHT on the	
hypothetical transfer:	19.37046%

Exit Charges

Michael -
Rate applying: 19.37046% x 3/10 x 16/40 =   2.3244552%
IHT Payable:
2.3244552% x £10,325,000 x ½ =   **£120,000**

Janet -
Rate applying: 19.37046% x 3/10 x 12/40 =   1.7433414%
IHT Payable:
1.7433414% x £10,325,000 x ½ =   **£90,000**

There are several important points to note about this example:

- The value of Luther's estate given in this example is its net value after accounting for the IHT arising on Luther's death.
- To keep things simple, I have made these calculations based on a single settlement of £10,325,000. In fact, Luther actually settled half of this amount on each of his children. The 'same day settlements' rule (see Section 8.18) operates to produce the same result however.
- I have assumed that Luther did not make any non-exempt transfers of value in the last seven years of his life.
- Michael was already over 18 on the date of his father's death, so his exit charge runs from that date. There are 16 complete calendar quarters between 14th February 2015 and 1st April 2019, so a factor of 16/40ths is applied.
- Janet was under 18 when her father died, so her exit charge runs from her 18th birthday. There are 12 complete calendar quarters in the three-year period between her 18th and 21st birthdays, so a factor of 12/40ths is applied (but see the 'Tax Tip' below).
- Not only does poor Michael have to wait longer to receive his inheritance, but he is also more highly taxed!
- Both exit charges have been calculated on the basis that the beneficiary settles the tax arising.

Tax Tip

Janet's exit charge would have been at a lower rate if she had become absolutely entitled to her share of the settled property two days before her 21st birthday. Only 11 complete calendar quarters would then have expired, the tax rate applying would have been reduced to 1.598% and Janet would have saved £7,500!

In general, therefore, when setting up an '18 to 25 Trust', it will make sense to allow the beneficiaries to become absolutely entitled to their inheritance two days before one of their birthdays (somewhere between their 19th and 25th birthday, as desired).

By following this advice, the maximum charge of 4.2% should never arise!

Penal Exit Charges

Bereaved minors' trusts and '18 to 25 Trusts' are both subject to a penal exit charge regime which, broadly speaking, will apply if trust assets are not distributed to the beneficiary by the age of 18 or 25 respectively. The maximum potential charge under this regime is 21%.

The penal exit charge does not apply to distributions of trust assets arising due to the death of the beneficiary before attaining the relevant age (i.e. 18 or 25), or to the conversion of a bereaved minors' trust to an '18 to 25 Trust' (or vice versa).

8.21 DEATH OF SETTLOR

When a settlor dies, potentially exempt transfers made within the last seven years of their life become chargeable transfers. This may lead to retrospective increases to the amount of any exit charges or ten-year anniversary charges where the settlor has also made transfers of value into a relevant property trust within that same seven-year period.

8.22 INCOME TAX AND TRUSTS

As I said in Section 8.3, interest in possession trusts generally have a better Income Tax position than discretionary trusts.

Discretionary trusts pay Income Tax at the 'trust rate' (currently 45%) on all trust income in excess of a small basic rate band of just £1,000 (except for dividend income which has its own 'dividend trust rate', currently 38.1%).

In other words, after the first £1,000 of trust income, a discretionary trust is taxed as if it were an individual with income in excess of £150,000.

Some of the Income Tax paid by the trust can be recovered by the beneficiaries when income is paid out to them. However, at best, there remains a significant cashflow disadvantage and, at worst, the trust's Income Tax burden effectively becomes permanent when income is retained in the trust.

An interest in possession trust, on the other hand, is generally taxed at basic rate only. The beneficiary entitled to the income then includes that income in their own tax calculation and pays any higher rate Income Tax due.

Looked at another way, an interest in possession trust is given the 'benefit of the doubt' and taxed at basic rate, with any extra tax due paid by the beneficiary. A discretionary trust is treated as a 'worst case scenario' and, apart from the first £1,000, taxed as if it were a wealthy individual, with the resultant excess tax then being reclaimed by the beneficiary.

There is an exception for 'trusts for vulnerable individuals' under which a discretionary trust can be taxed as if its income belonged directly to the 'vulnerable' beneficiary. This will generally only apply to disabled trusts, trusts for bereaved minors and a few other trusts where the beneficiary is aged under 18.

See Section 10.18, however, regarding lifetime settlements made for the benefit of your own minor children.

Charitable trusts are generally exempt from Income Tax unless they undertake trading activities.

Chapter 9

More Advanced Planning With Trusts

9.1   THE RELEVANT PROPERTY TRUST SHELTER

Because relevant property trusts are effectively treated as separate persons for IHT purposes, they provide an opportunity to shelter assets in a vehicle which exists outside of any individual person's estate. (Subject, of course, to the anniversary and exit charges explained in Chapter 8.)

In Section 8.15, we saw that relevant property trusts may now be created through most lifetime transfers into trust (but see Section 9.8 below). To create a relevant property trust on death will usually still require a discretionary trust.

In effect, and subject to any other transfers that you may be making, there is the opportunity to transfer assets equal in value to the nil rate band into relevant property trusts every seven years free from IHT.

In fact, taking the annual exemption and the fact that the nil rate band will hopefully begin to increase again after 2021 into account, it should be possible to accumulate a considerable amount of value within the relevant property trust.

Let's look at an example with a wealthy couple starting their IHT planning this year.

Example

Salvatore and Cherilyn are a wealthy married couple with adult children. Neither of them has made any transfer of value prior to 6th April 2018. On that date they set up the Caesar & Cleo Family Trust with their children as the beneficiaries and each transfer £331,000 into it. The first £6,000 of each person's transfer is covered by their annual exemptions for 2018/19 and 2017/18 (see Section 5.2) and the remaining £325,000 by their nil rate band.

Hence, while there is a chargeable lifetime transfer, no IHT is payable at this stage. A total of £662,000 is now 'sheltered' in the trust.

On 6th April 2019, Salvatore and Cherilyn are each able to put a further £3,000 into the trust. Each transfer is covered by the annual exemption for 2019/20 so a total of £668,000 has now been transferred to the trust free from IHT.

The couple again make transfers equal to the annual exemption on 6th April 2020. By this point, they have transferred a total of £674,000 into the trust free from IHT.

From 2021/22 onwards, the Government starts to increase the nil rate band in line with inflation once more. Based on an annual inflation rate, per the CPI (see Section 3.2), of 2.5%, this will start with an increase to £334,000 for the 2021/22 tax year. [NOTE: this is purely an assumption made for the sake of illustration.]

On 6th April 2021, Salvatore and Cherilyn are therefore each able to put a further £12,000 into the trust. £3,000 of each transfer is covered by the annual exemption, leaving a chargeable lifetime transfer of £9,000. This brings each person's cumulative chargeable transfers up to £334,000 (£325,000 plus £9,000), which is covered by the nil rate band for 2021/22. A total of £698,000 has now been transferred to the trust free from IHT.

The couple follow the same principle in each of the following three years, bringing the total cumulative amount transferred into the trust free from IHT as at 6th April 2024 up to £770,000. (Assuming the same annual inflation rate as before – 2.5%)

After 6th April 2025, however, the first transfers made by the couple on 6th April 2018 will no longer need to be counted when calculating their cumulative chargeable transfers.

On 7th April 2025, Salvatore and Cherilyn will therefore each be able to transfer £338,000 into the Caesar & Cleo Family Trust free from IHT. This is because, at this point, each person's cumulative chargeable lifetime transfers in the last seven years are just £36,000.

The projected nil rate band at this point (following the principles explained above and assuming 2.5% annual inflation) is £371,000, meaning that each of them can make a new chargeable transfer of £335,000 without giving rise to any IHT. Adding the annual exemption gives a total tax-free transfer of £338,000 each. These latest transfers bring the total value transferred into the trust to date up to £1.446m.

Following the same principles for the next two years produces the following results:

Date	Transfer (Each)	Total Value Transferred To Date (Both)
7th April 2026	£13,000	£1,472,000
7th April 2027	£13,000	£1,498,000

Great – almost £1.5m has now been 'sheltered'. However, on 6th April 2028, our 'shelter' springs a bit of a leak – the ten-year anniversary charge hits. To calculate this charge, let's assume that all of the trust's income has been distributed to the beneficiaries each year, but that the assets within the trust have grown in value at the rate of 10% per annum (compound). This produces a total value for the trust assets at 6th April 2028 of £2,866,960.

The transfers made by each of the two settlors will be treated separately, so that each has their own nil rate band (which is now £401,000 per our projections).

The 'Effective Rate' is derived by taking 20% of the value of trust assets in excess of two nil rate bands as a percentage of the value of those assets. In this case, the 'Effective Rate' is 14.4052% (£2,866,960 – 2 x £401,000 = £2,064,960 x 20% = £412,992, which, divided by £2,866,960, produces a rate of 14.4052%).

This rate is then multiplied by 3/10ths and then one-fortieth of this result is deducted for each calendar quarter that the relevant assets were not in the trust. The assets in the trust from the outset are therefore subject to a charge of 4.3216%. The assets that have been in the trust for nine years suffer a charge of 3.8894%, those held for eight years suffer 3.4573%, and so on.

In total, the anniversary charge amounts to £91,219. This represents just 3.18% of the value of the assets in the trust. If Salvatore and Cherilyn still held those assets personally, they would be exposed to potential IHT charges of 40%, or £1,146,784. The potential saving is therefore huge.

Note that I have made a fairly conservative assumption regarding future increases to the nil rate band: namely that it will merely rise in line with the CPI after the expiry of the current twelve year 'freeze' on 5th April 2021.

However, it is possible that the nil rate band may be subject to more significant increases after 2021. If so, the value of the planning technique described in the example above will be substantially enhanced.

9.2   SERIAL TRUSTS

There is one major drawback to the method used by Salvatore and Cherilyn in the previous section. By using just one trust, they had access to just one extra nil rate band each. It would be better to set up a new trust every seven years and thus continually increase the number of nil rate bands available.

Hence, what Salvatore and Cherilyn should have done is to set up the Caesar and Cleo No. 2 Family Trust on 7th April 2025 and make their next seven years' worth of transfers into that trust. Then, on 8th April 2032, they could set up the Caesar and Cleo No. 3 Family Trust, and so on, for as long as they are able. For a start, this more sophisticated approach would have reduced the charge arising on 6th April 2028 to £63,686.

The longer-term calculations for this planning technique get quite horrendous but, if Salvatore and Cherilyn are lucky enough to survive until 8th April 2038, then, on the basis of our projection methodology set out in Section 9.1 above, they would then have the following assets in trust:

Caesar and Cleo Family Trust:	£4,556,968
Caesar and Cleo No. 2 Family Trust:	£2,804,637
Caesar and Cleo No. 3 Family Trust:	£1,719,108
Total:	£9,080,713

The above figures take account of anniversary charges of £63,686 in 2028, £71,912 in 2035 and £224,487 in 2038. The total Inheritance Tax paid so far is thus £360,085. This compares with the potential Inheritance Tax of £3,632,285 had these assets still been held by Salvatore and Cherilyn personally.

9.3 HOW USEFUL IS THE RELEVANT PROPERTY TRUST SHELTER?

You don't need to be in a couple to use the technique described in Sections 9.1 and 9.2. It works just as well for an individual: you just have to halve all the numbers. It must be admitted, however, that there are some restrictions to this technique and we will examine these in Section 9.8.

You may also wonder whether using relevant property trusts to shelter assets is really effective in view of the anniversary and exit charges. It is worth bearing in mind, however, that the tenth anniversary charges arising under the method given in Section 9.2 generally only work out at around 3.5%.

Twentieth anniversary charges (if the assets are still in trust at that time) will tend to be higher, say around 4.5% to 5%, and, if you get to a thirtieth anniversary, we can expect charges of around 5.5%.

In general, however, the anniversary charges within the trusts are likely to work out at less than 0.55% per annum on average. This effectively means you would need to live more than 70 years after setting up the trust before the anniversary charges began to exceed the tax saved on your death.

Following the method (and assumptions) set out in Sections 9.1 and 9.2, I have been able to calculate the projected IHT savings for a couple based on the number of years they survive after starting the plan:

Years Survived	Total Net Assets In Trust	Total Net Assets In Estate	Saving
1	£733,699	£700,520	£33,179
2	£811,679	£748,172	£63,507
3	£914,616	£818,589	£96,027
4	£1,026,907	£895,328	£131,579
5	£1,149,416	£979,021	£170,395
6	£1,283,081	£1,070,363	£212,718
7	£2,081,489	£1,562,119	£519,369
8	£2,308,143	£1,712,251	£595,892
9	£2,555,330	£1,876,596	£678,734
10	£2,842,707	£2,067,376	£775,331
11	£3,162,108	£2,278,434	£883,675
12	£3,510,789	£2,509,717	£1,001,072
13	£3,891,434	£2,763,249	£1,128,185
14	£4,959,811	£3,432,454	£1,527,357
15	£5,483,392	£3,779,699	£1,703,693
20	£9,021,205	£6,155,660	£2,865,545
25	£15,628,527	£10,597,384	£5,031,143
30	£25,934,655	£17,703,857	£8,230,798

Notes

i) In compiling the above figures, it is assumed that the trusts are wound up at the time of the couple's death. This does not necessarily need to happen, but I have done so here in order to make the comparison fair. The 'Total Net Assets In Trust' are the remaining funds distributed to beneficiaries less the IHT charges suffered at this time.

ii) 'Total Net Assets In Estate' is the total net sum left in the estate after IHT from the same assets if these had been retained personally. To create a fair 'like with like' comparison, it is assumed that the deceased's nil rate band is used against these assets.

iii) 'Saving' is, broadly speaking, the overall net tax saving. To be more accurate though, it is actually the additional net amount left to the beneficiaries after IHT.

iv) It is assumed that neither member of the couple makes any other transfers of value outside the relevant property trust plan.

v) The above table takes the simplistic view that both members of the couple die at the same time. In reality this is unlikely to be the case, but the table still serves as a fair illustration of the savings that might be achieved.

vi) A single individual following the same technique would produce savings equal to half of those shown above.

vii) As explained in Section 9.1, the savings could be far greater if there are more substantial increases in the nil rate band after 2021.

viii) The savings shown above are based on using 'serial trusts', as outlined in Section 9.2.

It is interesting to note that the projected savings start almost immediately, with over £33,000 saved even if the couple die after just one year. This arises because, once the assets are in the trust, any capital growth is immediately safeguarded from inclusion in your estate.

The savings steadily increase over time but there are significant additional increments in the total saving at each seventh anniversary, as a new nil rate band effectively becomes available.

This table is a perfect illustration of the benefit of starting IHT planning as early as possible. The table above is not given in tax terms due to the cashflow impact of ten-year anniversary charges which render a direct 'tax paid' comparison slightly unfair after the first ten years. Nevertheless, it does ably demonstrate that an excessive concern over anniversary and exit charges is generally unwarranted!

9.4   HOW TO AVOID ANNIVERSARY AND EXIT CHARGES

Anniversary and exit charges can easily be avoided by:

a) Distributing all trust assets to the beneficiaries before the tenth anniversary of the trust's creation, and

b) Ensuring that the cumulative value of 'relevant transfers' does not exceed the nil rate band when the assets are distributed

Remember that the value of 'relevant transfers' for this purpose includes:

i) All transfers of relevant property into the trust
ii) Accumulated income within the trust (see Section 8.18)
iii) Chargeable transfers made in the seven years before setting up the trust (including potentially exempt transfers becoming chargeable on death)
iv) Other settlements of relevant property made on:
    a. the day the trust was set up, or
    b. the same day as any settlement into this trust after 9th December 2014

We will see a simple example of how anniversary and exit charges may be avoided in Section 9.6.

Even when following the above strategy, up to ten years of 'capital growth' in the value of the trust assets can be accumulated free from IHT.

However, in order to achieve the significant longer-term benefits outlined in Section 9.3, or to maintain some of the practical advantages discussed in Section 9.5, it may actually be preferable, in the long run, to suffer ten-year anniversary charges.

9.5 WHY NOT JUST GIVE ASSETS TO THE BENEFICIARIES?

As we know from Chapter 4, assets can be passed directly to other individuals as potentially exempt transfers and all that is required is then to survive seven years to ensure that no IHT is payable. In the right circumstances, this is naturally a much simpler way to avoid IHT.

However, using a relevant property trust will often have significant practical advantages over giving assets directly to your ultimate beneficiaries, including:

- Control: Although you cannot benefit from the gifted assets (see Section 9.8), you will be able to retain control over them.
- Assets in the relevant property trust are outside any person's estate. This will avoid the danger of unexpected IHT liabilities arising if your beneficiaries should pre-decease you.
- Relevant property trusts can be used as a vehicle to 'skip a generation' (or even two) and pass family wealth directly to grandchildren or great-grandchildren, while still providing the settlor's children with income during their lifetime.
- The income from, or enjoyment of, assets can be given to your beneficiaries at an early age without exposing them to the risk of losing the underlying capital due to their own inexperience, a bad marriage, or some other misfortune.

On top of all these practical issues there is also the fact that assets can be transferred into a relevant property trust free from CGT and we will look at this in the next section.

9.6   HOW TO AVOID INHERITANCE TAX AND CAPITAL GAINS TAX AT THE SAME TIME

As explained in Section 4.10, the transfer of any assets other than cash will generally be treated as a sale of those assets at market value for CGT purposes.

However, because a transfer to a relevant property trust is a chargeable transfer for IHT purposes, the transferor is given the ability to 'hold over' any capital gains arising on the assets transferred.

What this means is that no CGT is payable on the transfer and the trust is treated, for CGT purposes, as having acquired the asset at the same price as that originally paid by the transferor.

Furthermore, when, at a later date, the trust then transfers the asset to the ultimate beneficiary, the trustees and the beneficiary may, once again, claim that the capital gain should be 'held over'.

Hence, by this method, appreciating assets may be passed on free of both IHT and CGT.

Example

Eric has an investment property worth £325,000, which he wishes to pass to his partner Patty. They are not married and Eric is concerned that he will have a substantial CGT bill if he gives the property directly to Patty.

Instead, therefore, Eric sets up the Slowhand Trust with Patty as the beneficiary. Eric then transfers the property to the trust and elects to hold over the capital gain arising. Eric has made no previous transfers of value, so his chargeable transfer of £325,000 is covered by his nil rate band.

A couple of years later, the trust transfers the property, now worth £375,000, to Patty. Patty and the trustees of the Slowhand Trust jointly elect to hold over the capital gain arising, with the result that Patty is deemed to have acquired the property for the price that Eric originally paid for it.

There is no exit charge on the transfer to Patty as the nil rate band covers the £325,000 that the property was worth when Eric put it into the trust. The fact that the property is now worth £375,000 is irrelevant.

Points to Note

i)   Only the transferor needs to elect to hold over the gain going into the trust, whereas the trustees and the beneficiary must jointly elect to hold over the gain when the asset is transferred out of the trust.

ii)   Increases in the value of trust assets after transfer into the trust will not give rise to any additional charges as long as those assets are distributed to beneficiaries within ten years of the trust's formation.

Wealth Warning

Where gains have been held over in this manner on the transfer of residential property, neither the trust nor the beneficiary will be entitled to any principal private residence relief on the property for CGT purposes.

See also the comments in the next section regarding SDLT where there is a mortgage on the property.

9.7 INVESTMENT PROPERTY TRUSTS

The technique described in the previous section, which allows assets to be passed on free from both IHT and CGT, is well suited to an investment property business.

The CGT holdover relief described above functions just as well when the trust is used to pass property to the transferor's adult child and, in the case of investment properties, the restriction on the main residence exemption will generally be irrelevant. A simple interest in possession trust for the benefit of the adult child will suffice for this purpose.

Where two settlors jointly transfer property into the trust, two nil rate bands will be available. A couple could therefore use this technique to transfer up to £650,000 worth of rental property to their adult child free of both CGT and IHT. All they need to do then is to survive the requisite seven years.

After seven years, the couple will each have a new nil rate band available and could therefore do it all over again. A couple with a life expectancy of over 21 years could conservatively expect to be able to pass over £3m worth of rental property to their adult children free from tax!

The Impact of Mortgages

When undertaking this planning technique, it is important to take any outstanding loans or mortgages secured against the property into account. Such loans are a useful means to provide greater flexibility for IHT planning but represent a potential hazard for CGT purposes and a major drawback as far as SDLT is concerned.

For IHT purposes, when a property is transferred subject to a mortgage, the value of the transfer is only the net equity in the property. This provides a useful mechanism to 'tweak' the transfer value if required.

Conversely, however, any mortgage or other loan assigned to the trust or to the beneficiary will be deemed to represent consideration paid for the property transferred. For CGT purposes, it is not possible to hold over any part of the gain that would have arisen on a sale of the property for the amount of this deemed consideration.

Furthermore, where the deemed consideration is £40,000 or more (or more than £150,000 for a commercial property) SDLT will generally be payable.

Example

Paul and Linda jointly own a residential investment property worth £800,000 and wish to pass it to their adult daughter, Stella. They bought the property for just £200,000 and it currently has no outstanding loans against it.

A direct transfer of the property to Stella would give Paul and Linda a total CGT bill of up to £168,000 (£600,000 x 28%). Fortunately, neither Paul nor Linda has made any other transfers in the last seven years. The couple therefore decide to transfer the property into an interest in possession trust for Stella's benefit in March 2019 and to elect to hold over the gain arising for CGT purposes. As things stand, however, this would give rise to an immediate IHT charge at 20% on the excess of the property's value over £662,000 (see Section 9.1), i.e. £27,600.

Paul and Linda therefore decide to mortgage the property prior to the transfer and assign the loan to the trust. This will reduce the property's net equity value at the time of the transfer and thus reduce or eliminate the IHT charge.

CGT should not present a problem unless Paul and Linda take out a loan of more than their original purchase price of £200,000. However, if they take out a loan of £40,000 or more, SDLT will be payable on the transfer. The loan required to eliminate any IHT charge on the initial transfer is £138,000 (£800,000 - £662,000). The loan required to be sure of also avoiding any exit charge when the property is ultimately passed to Stella is £150,000 (£800,000 - £650,000). The required loan would therefore produce a SDLT charge of £4,400 or £5,000 (see the Taxcafe.co.uk guide 'How to Save Property Tax' for SDLT rates).

On the other hand, restricting the loan to just £39,999 to avoid SDLT would still leave an IHT charge of £19,600 on the initial transfer (£800,000 - £39,999 - £662,000 = £98,001 x 20%) plus an additional small exit charge (up to £660 for each year the property is in the trust) when the property passes to Stella absolutely.

Paul and Linda therefore decide to take out a loan of £138,000 and the trust pays SDLT of £4,400 on the transfer.

Two years later, the trust transfers the property to Stella and she and the trustees jointly elect to hold over the gain arising. Most of the property's equity value on the original transfer (£662,000) is covered by Paul and Linda's nil rate bands, leaving just £12,000 exposed to an exit charge at 1.2% (two years represents eight calendar quarters so the charge works out at 20% x 3/10 x 8/40 = 1.2%). Stella therefore pays an exit charge of £144.

Stella will have to pay a further £4,400 in SDLT, due to the outstanding mortgage, bringing the total tax cost of the whole exercise up to £8,944 (£4,400 x 2 + £144).

I have assumed in this example that Stella already owns another residential property, so that the additional 3% SDLT charge applies on both property transfers (see the Taxcafe.co.uk guide 'How to Save Property Tax').

Despite the drawback of SDLT, the example nevertheless demonstrates the huge tax-saving potential of using trusts to pass investment property to adult children or other beneficiaries. In this case, the couple faced an unpleasant choice between an immediate CGT charge of £168,000 and an eventual IHT bill of at least £320,000.

By using a trust, they were able to pass a valuable investment property to their daughter almost tax free. In many cases, the same result can be achieved completely tax free.

9.8   LIMITATIONS TO PLANNING WITH RELEVANT PROPERTY TRUSTS

When using relevant property trusts as IHT shelters, it is vital to ensure that it is impossible for the transferor to benefit from the trust. Otherwise, the 'Gift with Reservation' rules (see Section 4.9) apply, rendering the trust ineffective for IHT purposes.

In theory, it is permissible for the transferor's spouse to benefit from the trust. However, in practice, it would generally be very difficult to ensure that the transferor did not benefit without also excluding their spouse from any benefit. Hence, for lifetime IHT planning with relevant property trusts, it generally makes sense to ensure that the transferor's spouse is also unable to benefit from the trust.

Furthermore, CGT holdover relief is not available for gifts into a trust where the settlor, their spouse or a dependent minor child of the settlor is able to benefit in any way from the recipient trust. Gifts to such trusts (known as 'settlor-interested trusts') give rise to an immediate CGT charge in many cases.

9.9   DISCOUNTED GIFT TRUSTS

A very useful type of trust that has been used in IHT planning over many years is the 'Discounted Gift Trust' or 'Reversionary Interest Trust'. These trusts are usually provided by life insurance companies and different companies tend to give their trusts their own different names but the basic principles employed are broadly similar.

A discounted gift trust is actually not a single trust, but a series of mini-trusts. The transferor gives a substantial sum to the discounted gift trust, which is then divided up among the mini-trusts which carry the following rights:

Mini-Trust 1: income accumulated for one year, after which the original funds in the Trust are returned to the transferor.
Mini-Trust 2: income accumulated for two years, after which the original funds in the Trust are returned to the transferor.
Mini-Trust 3: income accumulated for three years, after which the original funds in the Trust are returned to the transferor.

And so on ...

The accumulated income in the trusts is held for the benefit of the transferor's eventual beneficiaries. The effect of this is that the transferor continues to receive an 'income' stream from their investment, despite the fact that much of it is no longer in their estate for IHT purposes.

The statistical value of the reversionary interests in the mini-trusts does still have to be included in the transferor's estate, but this is less than the amount of the original investment and steadily reduces as time passes.

Actually, what the transferor is receiving is not, strictly speaking, income at all, but a return of capital. This has the added advantage of being free from Income Tax too!

The insurance companies providing these investments were quick to adapt to the changes made in 2006 and continue to provide discounted gift trust schemes using absolute trusts. This reduces the flexibility of the scheme but prevents a chargeable lifetime transfer from arising on the initial investment.

Another form of discounted gift trust using relevant property trusts can also be set up but this will give rise to a chargeable lifetime transfer when the initial investment is made. Nevertheless, the structure may still sometimes work satisfactorily for investments that do not exceed the nil rate band.

9.10   LOAN TRUSTS

Another popular scheme provided by many life insurance companies is the 'Loan Trust'. In essence, the transferor does not make any transfer of value to the trust but simply lends funds to it. As there is no transfer of value, there can be no IHT charge.

Funds invested within the trust will (one hopes) experience capital growth, but the beauty of this scheme is that the capital growth is outside the original transferor's estate. All that the original transferor is due is a repayment of the original loan and hence this is the only value remaining in their estate.

The loan can be interest-free if desired (see Section 2.12) and the transferor may progressively withdraw their original loan capital. This capital can be spent on the transferor's own living expenses, thus gradually removing its value from their estate. Alternatively, the transferor could gift the benefit of the loan to another individual as a potentially exempt transfer (Section 4.3).

Meanwhile, the capital growth and accumulated income within the trust belongs to the beneficiaries and is thus also kept out of the transferor's estate.

A loan trust may be set up as an absolute trust in order to avoid any danger of becoming a relevant property trust. An absolute loan trust would be exempt from any anniversary or exit charges. Otherwise, as a relevant property trust, there would be some risk of anniversary and exit charges, but these could generally be avoided by ensuring that the trust assets are distributed before the trust's net value exceeds the nil rate band (but see Section 9.4 for further advice on avoiding anniversary and exit charges).

9.11 EXCLUDED PROPERTY TRUSTS

Those who did not have a UK 'Domicile of Origin' (see Section 14.2) but who have subsequently acquired actual or deemed UK domicile, or who have elected to 'opt-in' for IHT purposes (see Section 6.19), may generally exclude non-UK assets transferred into a trust for their benefit before they acquired UK domicile, or deemed UK domicile, or opted in.

Where such assets are still held in the trust at the relevant time, they may be excluded from the value of the beneficiary's estate for IHT purposes. Property held in such trusts is known as 'excluded property'.

This treatment even extends to property transferred into the trust by the beneficiary themselves: since the 'excluded property' rules take precedence over the 'Gifts with Reservation' provisions (see Section 4.9).

Hence, any person who is shortly about to become UK domiciled or deemed UK domiciled (see Section 2.2), or who is planning to 'opt-in' (see Section 6.19), could transfer any non-UK assets into a trust for their own benefit before this occurs and thus prevent those assets from becoming subject to UK IHT.

An excluded property trust can also be used to shelter non-UK assets inherited from a non-UK domiciled person and may be put in place via a deed of variation where appropriate.

As explained in Section 2.12, any liabilities incurred, directly or indirectly, to finance excluded property must be deducted from the value of that property and cannot be deducted from other chargeable assets.

See also Section 2.2 regarding indirect holdings of UK residential property.

9.12 OLDER BENEFICIARIES

Imagine you've decided to buy your mother a house. Very kind of you and there's nothing wrong with that. The trouble is that, by making this generous gift, you may push your mother's estate over the nil rate band threshold and thus create an IHT charge on her death. It may therefore be better to set up a relevant property trust and buy your mother's house through that. The property will not then fall into her estate and you can even give her the security of a life interest.

This approach will always be worth considering when making gifts of less than the nil rate band to any beneficiary with a significantly shorter life expectancy than the donor.

Chapter 10

Practical Aspects of IHT Planning

10.1   THE BIGGER PICTURE

I don't do IHT planning; I do 'Estate Preservation'. What is important is not just saving IHT but preserving family wealth for the benefit of the next generation. Saving IHT is just one part of preserving wealth and it is important never to lose sight of this bigger picture.

When we come to the bigger issue of estate preservation, there are many other factors to be taken into account. In this chapter we will look at some of these other factors, as well as some practical aspects of IHT planning itself.

10.2   COMMERCIAL ISSUES

From early on in my career I was taught 'never to let the tax tail wag the commercial dog'. In other words, it is almost always more important to get the commercial aspects right before letting tax planning dictate your actions.

For example, putting all of your savings into a share of *'Dave's Dodgy Autos'* might be a great way to avoid IHT, but what's the use of that if Dave runs off to South America with all your money? After all, when all is said and done, Theresa May and Philip Hammond will only take 40%, so they are (just slightly) better than Dodgy Dave.

On the other hand, as we saw in Section 7.28, saving 40% may still be beneficial overall, even in some slightly uncommercial situations. It's a question of getting the right balance and is best expressed as follows:

> **Bayley's Law**
>
> *"The truly wise taxpayer does not seek merely to minimise the amount of tax paid but rather to maximise the amount of wealth remaining after all taxes have been accounted for."*

10.3   INTERACTION WITH OTHER TAXES

After commercial issues, the next most important issues to watch out for in IHT planning are often caused by other taxes. When undertaking any tax planning, it is essential to consider all taxes, not just the one that you are trying to save. A saving of 3% SDLT at the expense of 20% in VAT, for example, is of little benefit!

IHT planning will often involve transferring assets and this can have important implications for:

- CGT
- Income Tax
- Corporation Tax
- Stamp Duty (on shares and securities)
- SDLT (on land and buildings)
- VAT

The pre-owned assets regime creates a complex area of interaction between IHT planning and Income Tax and we will look at this in Chapter 13. However, the other tax which interacts most frequently and most dramatically with IHT must surely be CGT and we will look at that particular 'clash of the titans' in Chapter 11.

10.4   VALUATIONS

Valuation is a key part of IHT. We are frequently concerned with the value of land, buildings, unquoted shares or unincorporated businesses.

Very often, the value of an asset owned by an individual is dependent on the proportion of a larger asset that they own. We saw a simple example of this with Bjorn's chairs in Section 2.1.

In practice, the most significant examples of this are in the case of unquoted shares. A controlling (i.e. over 50%) shareholding in a private company might be worth £5,000 per share, for example, while a small minority holding in the same company might be worth just £600 per share.

These changes in proportionate value can have major implications for any transfers of value that result in the transferor's shareholding falling into a lower value category.

Example

The 10,000 issued shares in Fleetwood Limited are held as follows:

The Peter Green Charitable Trust:	*3,000*
Mick:	*1,000*
John:	*1,500*
Christine:	*500*
Lindsay:	*2,000*
Stevie:	*2,000*

It has been established that shares in the company can be valued as follows:

Holdings of 50% or more:	*£5,000 per share*
Holdings of 25% to 49.9%:	*£3,000 per share*
Holdings of 10% to 24.9%:	*£2,000 per share*
Holdings of less than 10%:	*£600 per share*

Hence, in the absence of any further information, it appears that the shareholdings should be valued as follows:

The Peter Green Charitable Trust:	*3,000 x £3,000 = £9m*
Mick:	*1,000 x £2,000 = £2m*
John:	*1,500 x £2,000 = £3m*
Christine:	*500 x £600 = £0.3m*
Lindsay:	*2,000 x £2,000 = £4m*
Stevie:	*2,000 x £2,000 = £4m*

Mick decides to give one share to his daughter Nikki. This reduces the value of his remaining holding of 999 shares to £599,400 (999 x £600). The gift to Nikki is therefore treated as a transfer of value of £1.4006m (£2m - £599,400) despite the fact that her share is worth just £600.

This preposterous result could be absolutely disastrous for Nikki. If Mick should die within three years of making this gift, Nikki could face an IHT bill of up to £560,240. All for a share worth just £600!

Let's hope that business property relief is available on these shares and that Nikki does nothing to mess it up. She certainly needs to hope that Fleetwood Limited isn't floated in the next seven years.

With numbers like this, there are clearly times when a gift should not be accepted!

10.5   RELATED PROPERTY

When valuing assets for IHT purposes, each person's own assets are usually valued simply on the basis of what they personally own.

However, we sometimes need to take account of the 'related property' provisions.

In valuing a person's assets for IHT purposes, those assets are treated as if they are part of a larger holding of assets made up of all the assets:

- Held by the person themselves,
- Held by their spouse, and
- Which have been held by a charity or similar exempt body within the last five years and which were originally transferred to that body by the person or their spouse after 15th April 1976

Let's now return to our previous example to see the effect of these provisions in practice.

Example

Lindsay and Stevie are married. Hence, the shares held by each of them must be valued as part of a hypothetical holding of 4,000 shares.

John and Christine are also married. Furthermore, Christine gave the 3,000 shares to the Peter Green Charitable Trust in 1977.

The shares held by John, Christine and the Peter Green Charitable Trust must therefore all be valued as part of a hypothetical holding of 5,000 shares.

The various shareholdings must therefore now be valued as follows for IHT purposes:

The Peter Green Charitable Trust:	*3,000 x £5,000 = £15m*
Mick:	*1,000 x £2,000 = £2m*
John:	*1,500 x £5,000 = £7.5m*
Christine:	*500 x £5,000 = £2.5m*
Lindsay:	*2,000 x £3,000 = £6m*
Stevie:	*2,000 x £3,000 = £6m*

Now let us suppose that Christine gives one share to her son Mac. That share, we know, is only worth £600. However, the transfer results in Christine's remaining holding being part of a hypothetical holding of 4,999 shares. This will be worth £3,000 per share, meaning that Christine's remaining 499 shares are deemed to be worth £1.497m for IHT purposes.

The transfer of value on Christine's gift to Mac is thus £1.003m (£2.5m - £1.497m), which is actually more than £700,000 greater than Christine's entire shareholding is worth (but see the 'Tax Tip' below), not to mention almost 1,700 times the value of Mac's single share.

If Christine should die within three years, Mac could face an IHT bill of up to £401,200!

As we can see from this example, the 'related property' provisions can cause further and perhaps unexpected problems with small gifts being given massive hypothetical values for IHT purposes.

The most disappointing aspect of this situation is probably the fact that giving assets to charity can result in unexpected IHT consequences at any time in the future. There is no seven year time limit here; the impact of the charity's shareholding on your future IHT bill is permanent!

Tax Tip

In a recent case, the deceased's executors argued successfully that, due to a little known provision within the IHT laws, the value of any item of 'related property' could not be taken to be more than the total value of the property owned by the transferor.

The impact of the 'related property' rules can be reduced if transfers are timed carefully. This is particularly relevant to unquoted shareholdings held by married couples where business property relief may not be available.

Example

Jack and Diane are a married couple and both own shares in Mellencamp Limited, an unquoted investment company.

Jack owns 2% of the company and his shares are worth just £2,000.
Diane owns 49% of the company and her shares are worth £245,000.

Under the related property rules, however, their shares must be valued as part of a combined shareholding of 51%. This shareholding, being enough to provide control of the company, is worth £510,000.

The couple now wish to give their son John a 25% share in the company.

Jack transfers his 2% stake to John first. This represents a transfer of value of £20,000 (2/51 x £510,000). [Subject to the point set out in the 'Tax Tip' above, which we will ignore for the purposes of this example.]

Diane then transfers a further 23% to John. This represents a transfer of value of £115,000 (23/49 x £245,000), bringing the total to £135,000.

If Diane had made her transfer first, this would have been a transfer of value of £230,000 (23/51 x £510,000). Jack's subsequent transfer would then have been a transfer of value equal to 2/28ths of the value of a 28% shareholding, let's say £10,000 for the sake of argument.

Hence, by making the smaller share transfer first, the couple have reduced the effective transfer of value by £105,000, providing a potential IHT saving of up to £42,000 (at 40%).

10.6   JOINTLY HELD PROPERTY

Any form of property can be held jointly, including bank accounts, shares and securities or land and buildings.

The key point to note about jointly held property is that, on a joint owner's death, their share may sometimes pass by survivorship and not by intestacy or under the deceased's Will. This has major implications for IHT planning, as you may not be free to transfer your share of jointly held property in the most tax-efficient manner.

After the joint bank account, the next most common form of jointly held property in the UK is land and buildings, sometimes referred to as 'real property'. In fact, most couples in the UK now own their home jointly.

In England and Wales, there are two different legal forms for jointly held property, 'Joint Tenants' or 'Tenants in Common'.

Joint Tenants

In a joint tenancy the ownership of each joint owner's share passes automatically on death to the other joint owner (or joint owners). This is what is meant by 'survivorship'. Furthermore, neither joint owner is normally able to sell their share of the property without the consent of the other.

This may restrict the scope for IHT planning with the property and joint tenancies are therefore generally less desirable than tenancies in common purely from a tax planning perspective.

Having said that, however, the security provided by the right of 'survivorship' will often be of more value to many couples.

Tenants in Common

Under a tenancy in common, the joint owners are generally each free to do as they wish with their own share of the property and there is no right of survivorship. The joint owners' shares in the property need not be equal.

A tenancy in common therefore opens up a wide range of IHT planning opportunities which may not always be available under a joint tenancy.

Practical Implications

As explained above, each person's share in a joint tenancy will usually pass to the other joint owner by survivorship. In the case of the family home, the surviving joint owner will usually be the widow or widower of the deceased. Following the introduction of the transferable nil rate band (see Chapter 6), this will usually be the best result anyway.

Nevertheless, for the reasons explained in Section 6.8, this may sometimes still be bad IHT planning.

It is, however, possible to 'break' a joint tenancy via a deed of variation (see Section 16.1) executed within two years after a joint owner dies.

Alternatively, it may be preferable to sever the joint tenancy during both owners' lifetimes as this provides more certainty to the intended IHT planning. It is not always wise to rely on being able to use a deed of variation to rectify the situation!

Once a joint tenancy has been severed or broken, whether during the owner's lifetime or via a deed of variation, it becomes a tenancy in common.

A share in property held under a tenancy in common may be passed to anyone, under the terms of the deceased's Will, or possibly via a deed of variation, as explained in Section 16.1.

Hence, whenever undertaking any IHT planning on the family home in England or Wales which involves passing a share of the property to anyone other than the surviving spouse, it may be wise to first ensure that the property is held under a tenancy in common and not a joint tenancy.

Breaking a joint tenancy to create a tenancy in common can be achieved at a reasonably modest cost and should, in itself, be tax free, as it is not treated as a disposal for CGT purposes, nor an acquisition for SDLT purposes.

> **Wealth Warning**
> If you change your property to a tenancy in common and then draw up your Wills to put the appropriate IHT planning measures in place, remember to make sure that you also buy any new property as tenants in common if you move house!

Scotland

In Scotland, joint ownership of real property mainly comes in a form known as 'Pro Indivisio' ownership which operates in a broadly similar manner to a tenancy in common.

A form of beneficial joint tenancy is also available in Scotland using a 'survivorship destination'. This cannot be severed unilaterally, which can sometimes lead to some practical difficulties if one joint owner decides that they wish to pass their share to someone other than the other joint owner.

A 'survivorship destination' can, however, be broken by a deed of variation where the surviving joint owner is prepared to co-operate.

Nonetheless, relying on using a deed of variation when the time comes may not always be wise so, once again, it may make more sense to break the 'survivorship destination' during both owners' lifetimes in order to better facilitate any IHT planning which involves passing a share of the property to someone other than the surviving joint owner.

And be careful when you move house too!

10.7   VALUING JOINTLY HELD PROPERTY

A useful benefit of jointly held property is the fact that a discount often applies to the value of a joint owner's share of the property.

Example

Two sisters, Mel and Kim, live together in Appleby Manor, which they own jointly. Sadly, Kim dies on 1st September 2018, when Appleby Manor is worth £1.5m.

Kim's half share in Appleby Manor is not valued at £750,000, as one might expect, but at a discount of 15%, i.e. at £637,500. This discount produces an effective IHT saving of £45,000.

The discount applies to reflect the practical difficulty in selling a joint owner's part share of a property. The discount also reflects the fact that the other joint owner has a right to occupy the property and is therefore akin to a 'sitting tenant', thus further reducing the value of a joint share in the property.

The 15% discount used in the example above was established by an IHT case back in 1982. In a more recent case, it was suggested that a discount of just 10% might now be more appropriate, especially where the surviving joint owner is not likely to remain in occupation of the property.

Nevertheless, conventional wisdom seems to be that a 15% discount is still appropriate in the case of residential property occupied by the surviving joint owner. A lower rate of discount may be appropriate in other cases but it is certainly still worth claiming.

HMRC takes the view that the related property rules (see Section 10.5) prevent any discount from applying where a property is held jointly by spouses. This view has recently been challenged on the basis that the related property rules should not apply to jointly held property and the correct position is currently uncertain.

Unfortunately, due to the different nature of joint property titles in Scotland, the usual discount does not generally apply to property in Scotland.

10.8   OTHER JOINTLY HELD ASSETS

A jointly held bank or building society account in England or Wales passes in its entirety to the surviving joint account holder on the other joint account holder's death.

In Scotland, a joint account holder's share of a joint account usually falls into their general estate to be dealt with according to the terms of their Will or under the laws of intestacy (see Section 10.11).

In either case, the deceased's share of the joint account is included in their estate for IHT purposes (although it will usually be exempt if it passes to their spouse). The deceased's share will generally be taken to be half of the account balance and no discount can apply.

Other jointly held property, such as paintings, antiques and personal effects may be subject to a substantial discount due to the fact that a joint owner is generally unable to sell such property.

Tax Tip

Unmarried couples can save substantial amounts of IHT by jointly holding tangible moveable property (such as antiques) and separately passing each joint share to their intended beneficiaries (but not each other). At present it is unclear whether a similar approach might work for married couples.

10.9 MORTGAGES

It is important to be aware that any transfer of property which is still subject to a mortgage will require the lender's consent. If the transferee takes over the mortgage, the outstanding borrowings will be deemed to constitute purchase consideration and may give rise to a SDLT charge if they are £40,000 or more; or more than £150,000 in the case of commercial property.

10.10 RESIDENTIAL CARE FEES

Whilst IHT is a major worry, many people are far more concerned about losing their property to the local authority in order to pay nursing home or residential care fees in their old age. In some cases, the local authority may even be able to force a sale of a property which has previously been given away if they can show that this was done to avoid payment of the fees.

In some instances, however, it has been accepted that, where a property has been given away for IHT planning purposes, the local authority were unable to claim that the taxpayer's motive was to avoid the care fees.

Nevertheless, this approach is not entirely reliable, as many families have found to their cost (see further in Section 11.8).

A better approach is often to take out long term care insurance or even emergency care assurance. The latter approach generally requires the payment of a single lump sum premium in exchange for an annuity covering the residential care fees. The amount of the premium is generally equal to around two to three years' worth of the care fees.

Emergency care assurance is a useful strategy employed by many families who wish to have certainty about the cost of looking after their elderly relative.

If necessary, the premium can be funded by way of a loan secured against the relative's former home, thus enabling the family to keep the property and perhaps even benefit from the CGT uplift on death (see Section 11.2).

10.11 WILLS AND INTESTACY

Most people are pretty relaxed about dying intestate (without a Will) until they realise what would actually happen. Most of us know we should make a Will, but a great many of us put it off until it's too late.

Quite apart from any IHT planning, a Will is sensible as, without a valid Will, your assets will be divided up according to the ancient laws of intestacy and this may well be very different to what you would have liked. More importantly, a Will is essential for nominating the future guardians of your children if, as Oscar Wilde would have put it, they are careless enough to lose both parents.

In the tables which follow, 'Issue' generally means your children but, if your children pre-decease you, their children will take their place. For example, if you have three children and one of them pre-deceases you, leaving two children of their own, the share going to 'your children' will be divided so that one third of that share goes to each of your surviving children and one sixth goes to each of your grandchildren by your deceased child.

Dying Without a Will: England and Wales

If you are domiciled in England and Wales, and die without a Will, your estate will be divided up as follows:

1. If you leave a spouse and issue

The first £250,000 and all personal possessions go to your spouse. 50% of the balance is divided equally between your children. The remaining 50% is held on trust, with your spouse having a life interest and the remainder going to your children.

2. If you leave a spouse but no issue

If you have no surviving parents, siblings, nephews or nieces, your entire estate goes to your spouse.

Otherwise, your spouse's share is restricted to £450,000 plus all personal possessions and 50% of the remaining balance.

The other 50% of the balance goes to your parents if they survive you, to your siblings if both of your parents pre-decease you, or to your nephews and nieces if your siblings also pre-decease you.

3. If you leave issue but no spouse

Your estate is divided equally between your children.

4. If you leave no spouse or issue

Your estate goes to the nearest relatives to survive you, based on the following order of priorities:

    i)   Your parents
    ii)   Your siblings, or their issue (i.e. your nieces and nephews)
    iii) Your grandparents
    iv) Your aunts and uncles

5. If no near-relatives survive you

Your entire estate goes to the Crown!

Dying Without a Will: Scotland

There are current proposals for major reforms to the laws of succession in Scotland, although it is uncertain whether these will be adopted. At present, if you are domiciled in Scotland, and die without a Will, your estate will be divided up as follows:

1. If you leave a spouse and issue

Your spouse gets:

- i) Your interest in any dwelling (i.e. the family home) up to a value of £300,000. If the family home's value exceeds this amount, the spouse's entitlement is limited to the right to receive the sum of £300,000.
- ii) Personal possessions up to the value of £24,000.
- iii) The first £42,000 of the remaining estate.
- iv) One third of any other moveable property (i.e. anything other than land and buildings).

Your children then get the remainder of your estate.

2. If you leave a spouse but no issue

Your spouse gets your interest in any dwelling and personal possessions as per (i) and (ii) above, plus:

- i) The first £75,000 of the remaining estate.
- ii) One half of any other moveable property (i.e. anything other than land and buildings).

The rest of your estate falls into your 'free estate' and is dealt with below. If you have no surviving parents, siblings or issue of your siblings, your spouse will effectively receive your entire estate.

3. If you leave issue but no spouse

Your estate is divided equally between your children.

4. If you leave no spouse or issue

Your entire estate will be dealt with under the rules for a 'free estate'.

Free Estate

In dealing with your free estate, any claimant's children or remoter issue may take the place of a claimant who has pre-deceased you, except where the deceased claimant was your spouse or parent. If you are survived by at least one parent and at least one sibling (or their issue), 50% of your free estate goes to your parents and 50% to your siblings or their issue.

In any other case, the free estate goes to the nearest relatives to survive you, based on the following order of priorities:

i)   Your siblings
ii) Your parents
iii) Your surviving spouse (for cases under (2) above)
iv) Uncles and aunts
v)   Grandparents
vi) Grandparents' siblings
vii) Great-grandparents, etc.

If you have no relatives, as set out above; yes, you've guessed it, everything goes to the Crown.

So, as you can see, whether you live in Swansea, Penzance or Aberdeen (and probably Belfast too, although I don't have those rules available), you really shouldn't be relaxed about dying without a Will.

It is not unknown for widows to be forced to sell the family home due to the operation of the above rules and, without proper provision, children could end up being taken into care.

The statutory rules set out above take no account of common-law partners, step-children or many other important personal relationships. A remote cousin could get everything in priority to a fondly loved step-child!

The Crown could even get your house in priority to a common-law partner you've lived with for decades. And you thought IHT was bad enough!

OK, sermon over.

10.12 STATUTORY RIGHTS

In England, Wales or Northern Ireland, you may generally distribute your entire estate as you wish under the terms of your Will. Surviving spouses may, however, apply to the courts for an increased share of the estate where the amount already provided to them in the Will does not represent adequate financial provision for their care and maintenance. In essence, this is something akin to posthumous divorce proceedings.

Similar applications may be made on behalf of dependent minor children of the deceased.

A different system operates in Scotland where 'legal rights' take priority over the terms of the deceased's Will unless waived by the beneficiaries concerned. Legal rights for beneficiaries of a deceased domiciled in Scotland are:

Surviving spouse: Where there are no issue of the deceased, one half of the deceased's moveable property, otherwise one third.
Surviving issue: Where there is no surviving spouse of the deceased, one half of the deceased's moveable property, otherwise one third.

Remember, the question of whether you are domiciled in Scotland is the same as any other domicile issue (see Chapter 14). Hence, you may have lived in London for many decades, but, if you or your parents were born in Scotland, you could still be domiciled in Scotland and your spouse and children will still have 'legal rights' as set out above.

Current proposals for the reform of the laws of succession in Scotland include a proposal to abolish legal rights for adult children. Again, however, it is uncertain whether this proposal will be adopted.

10.13   LIFE INSURANCE

One simple way to prevent your estate from being excessively inflated on your death is to ensure that all forms of life insurance cover which you have are written in favour of other family members. Such policies are effectively held on bare trust (see Section 8.8).

In that way, the proceeds of the policies will never fall into your estate but will go, instead, to your intended beneficiaries free of IHT.

This should also extend to the 'Death Benefit' under any pension schemes where possible (see Section 10.16).

Ideally, if they can afford to do without it, your spouse should not be the beneficiary under any of your life policies. In practice, this suggestion may sometimes be somewhat impractical, especially when you have a young family, but it is worth reviewing the position as you get older.

Payments of regular insurance premiums will usually be covered by the annual exemption or the exemption for normal expenditure out of income (see Section 5.8), so these do not usually present a problem.

Depending on the exact circumstances, and for the reasons outlined in Section 4.4, a large lump-sum premium paid on a policy written in favour of another individual may represent a potentially exempt transfer, a chargeable lifetime transfer, or a mixture of both.

10.14   LIFE POLICIES WRITTEN IN TRUST

By writing a life policy 'into trust', you will be using a form of interest in possession trust rather than a bare trust. This retains the advantage of keeping the proceeds of the policy out of your estate but also means you can vary the intended beneficiaries over the course of your lifetime. Furthermore, this also ensures that no IHT arises if any of those beneficiaries should pre-decease you.

For these reasons, it generally made sense to write life policies 'into trust' before March 2006.

For many policies written into trust before 22nd March 2006, it is 'business as usual' and their beneficial treatment still continues. HMRC has even confirmed that the payment of a regular premium on a policy already held by a pre-22/3/2006 interest in possession trust will generally continue to be classed as a potentially exempt transfer if not already exempted under some other provision.

One change of beneficiary between 22nd March 2006 and 5th October 2008 will have turned the trust into a transitional serial interest (see Section 8.13) and it will effectively retain its beneficial treatment.

Any other changes of beneficiary, however, will bring it into the relevant property trust regime (see Sections 8.17 to 8.19).

New life policies written into trust will generally fall into the relevant property trust regime. This also applies where changes are made to existing policies and those changes were not already permitted under the terms of the policy on 22nd March 2006.

Where any life policy falls into the relevant property trust regime, it may potentially be subject to entry, exit and anniversary charges.

Payments of regular premiums will usually be covered by the annual exemption or the exemption for normal expenditure out of income (see Section 5.8), so these do not usually present a problem in themselves.

Any large lump-sum premium payments, however, will be chargeable lifetime transfers and will give rise to immediate IHT liabilities where the policyholder's nil rate band has been exhausted.

Ten-yearly anniversary charges will be applied to the policy (see Section 8.18). Generally, the policy's value for this purpose will be taken to be the cumulative amount of premiums paid to date, although in cases where the policyholder is in poor health at the anniversary date, it is feared that HMRC may argue that a greater value should be used to reflect the likelihood of the policy's imminent maturity. (An image of a vulture has suddenly jumped into my mind!)

Worst of all, of course, an exit charge of up to 6% (see Section 8.19) will apply when the policyholder dies. That's still a lot better than 40% though!

10.15 INSURING FOR INHERITANCE TAX LIABILITIES

Much of the IHT planning discussed elsewhere in this guide depends on the transferor surviving for a certain period after a transfer, or some other transaction, has been made. Often the period concerned will be seven years, but survival to other anniversaries can often also be critical. When death occurs before the expiry of the critical period, unexpected tax bills can arrive as a nasty surprise. It is often a good idea, therefore, to take out some term life insurance on the transferor to guard against this possibility.

Wealth Warning

Make sure that the transferor themselves is not the beneficiary of the term insurance as this will inflate the value of their estate and lead to an effective 'grossing up' of IHT liabilities.

10.16 PENSIONS

A special regime applies to funds remaining in a pension scheme after the death of a scheme member. The key features are as follows:

i)   Death benefits paid out when a member dies before the age of 75 without having taken a pension are tax free (subject to point (v) below)

ii) Other death benefits paid out when the scheme member dies are subject to a charge of 55%

iii) No charge applies to funds remaining within a registered pension scheme following the death of a scheme member (e.g. funds retained in the scheme to provide a pension to the deceased's spouse or another dependant)

iv) Unused funds of a member dying with no living dependants may be donated to charity tax free

v)   Where the pension scheme trustees have no discretion over the payment of lump sums on a members' death and the relevant funds must therefore be paid into the deceased's estate, IHT will be chargeable on those funds in the normal way

The charge under point (ii) is not actually IHT as such (although it arises on death) and must be paid by the scheme administrator before payment of the death benefit.

The combination of points (ii) and (v) means that a maximum total charge of 73% (55% + 40% of the remaining 45%) may arise in some cases. This is easily avoided by ensuring that the scheme trustees have the discretion to pay death benefits directly to the deceased's beneficiaries instead.

Taking points (i) and (iii), however, it will now often be possible to pass on the value of a pension fund tax free: either by way of a lump sum paid directly to the beneficiary (where the scheme member dies before the age of 75 and has not yet taken a pension), or by using the remaining scheme funds to provide the beneficiary with a pension.

Unregistered Schemes

Lump sum death benefits paid out by a pension scheme which is neither a registered pension scheme nor a 'qualifying non-UK pension' are subject to IHT in the normal way.

10.17   LOTTERY SYNDICATES

Lottery, pools and other gambling syndicates are 'breeding grounds' for potential IHT problems. Just imagine this:

Example

Donny wins £15m on the National Lottery. It's in all the newspapers, so you can bet that HMRC knows about it. He gives £3m to each of his brothers, Wayne, Merrill, Jay and Jimmy. Tragically, just a few weeks later, Donny is killed whilst water skiing in Utah.

HMRC demands almost £6m in IHT from Donny's family as the transfers to his brothers were made only weeks before his death.

"But we were in a syndicate" protest the brothers. "Prove it!" replies HMRC.

The simple answer to this problem, of course, is to make sure that you have documentary evidence of any syndicate arrangements.

We can also take the principle of the lottery syndicate one step further. A few years ago, I heard on the radio that an 84 year-old lottery winner had given away his entire £13m win to a combination of charities and family and friends.

Like most other people (I suspect), my first thought was "what a nice chap", but then the cynic in me took over and I began to wonder if there was perhaps an IHT planning motive present here.

But, at 84, our lottery winner's life expectancy was around five and a half years. Hence, whilst his charitable transferees are in the clear, his family and friends would be well advised to keep 40% of their gifts to one side in case their benefactor doesn't last too long.

Our winner could, however, have planned things better.

Let's suppose that he had previously drawn up a lottery syndicate agreement with his family and friends and agreed to share any winnings with them. Naturally, his family and friends would also agree to contribute to the weekly lottery stake. However, in practice, the transferor would then pay the weekly stake himself.

The transferor's payment of the weekly stake would represent a transfer of value, but it should be sufficiently small to be exempt as 'normal expenditure out of income', or else to be covered by the annual exemption.

I would suggest that this course of action would make sense for any elderly person playing the lottery (or 'doing the pools', etc.).

10.18 MINOR PROBLEMS

You may have noticed that I tend to base most of my examples around gifts to adult children. This is because making transfers of value to minor children carries a few extra complications.

Gifts to Minors by Parents

Any gift from a parent to their own minor child is subject to the Income Tax 'settlements' legislation, even if made to the child on bare trust (see Section 8.8). This means that the parent is subject to tax on any income or capital gains derived from the gifted assets (subject to a general exemption for income not exceeding £100 per annum and the further exemptions for Child Trust Funds and Junior ISAs explained below).

As we saw in Section 9.8, CGT holdover relief is not available on a gift into a trust for the benefit of the settlor's minor child.

Theoretically, the 'Gift with Reservation' rules (see Section 4.9) do not necessarily apply to a gift to a minor child but, in practice, it is often very difficult for the transferor not to benefit in any way from a gift to their own minor child.

The best way for a parent to make large IHT effective gifts to minor children is probably to use relevant property trusts (see Sections 9.1 to 9.3). Given the inability to hold over any capital gains, it will generally make sense to make cash settlements into the trust.

For smaller gifts, either a Child Trust Fund or a Junior ISA may be the best vehicle to use (see further below).

Grandparents

Grandparents may generally make gifts to minor grandchildren without facing the problems set out above.

There is therefore some scope for parents to make potentially exempt transfers to grandparents who might some time later make gifts to their grandchildren. There are a few hurdles to jump here though.

Firstly, the associated operations rules (see Section 10.21) would apply if there were any connection between the potentially exempt transfer to the grandparent and their later gift to the grandchild.

Secondly, the gift from the grandparent to the grandchild would also be a potentially exempt transfer and would become chargeable in the event of the grandparent's death within seven years. Hence, there is a strong chance of actually making matters worse unless the grandparent has very little wealth of their own.

Trusts for Minors

HMRC appears to take the view that a minor cannot have an immediate post-death interest (see Section 8.12), as the Trustee Act 1925 would make such a trust discretionary in nature. Anyone intending to leave assets to trust for the benefit of a minor should therefore consider using a bereaved minor's trust, an '18 to 25 Trust', or even just a bare trust.

A bare trust carries some advantages for Income Tax and CGT purposes, as the minor's own allowances could be set against income and capital gains. (A similar result may be obtained for some other trusts by way of the 'trusts for vulnerable individuals' exception which we looked at in Section 8.22, but this carries a few formalities and limitations which will not always be desirable.)

Child Trust Funds and Junior ISAs

Every child born in the UK between 1st September 2002 and 2nd January 2011 should have a Child Trust Fund. Junior ISAs are available to all UK resident minors who were not eligible for a Child Trust Fund.

Parents, family and friends of minor children may put up to £4,260 in total into the child's Child Trust Fund or Junior ISA in 2018/19 (similar amounts apply each year). Monies will be invested in a long-term investment account to grow free from Income Tax or CGT, like a normal cash ISA.

On maturity, funds within a Child Trust Fund may be transferred to an ISA in the child's name. Junior ISAs automatically convert into a normal ISA when the child reaches 18. No withdrawals are permitted before this time.

> **Wealth Warning**
> Like normal ISAs, Child Trust Funds and Junior ISAs are not exempt from IHT.

In principle, payments into Child Trust Funds or Junior ISAs will be potentially exempt transfers although, in most cases, they will probably be covered by the annual exemption or the exemption for normal expenditure out of income.

10.19 INCOME, CAPITAL AND CONTROL

One of the major practical problems which stands in the way of effective IHT planning is the fact that the prospective transferor usually wishes to shed capital (in order to save IHT), but needs to retain income (in order to survive!)

On top of this, the prospective transferor will very often wish to retain control of the underlying investments.

In Chapter 9 we saw how relevant property trusts could be used as a means to retain control. We also saw how discounted gift trusts and loan trusts provided effective means to retain an 'income' stream. However, the 'Gift with Reservation' rules (see Section 4.9) generally make it very difficult to retain both income and control whilst still giving away capital effectively.

Where business property relief is available (see Chapter 7), the taxpayer is in the happy position that retaining control of their capital and keeping their income will not give rise to an IHT liability.

For investments or businesses which do not qualify for business property relief, possible methods to get around this fundamental dilemma include:

- Holding property through a company with a share structure which separates rights to income and capital and voting rights
- Holding property through a partnership or Limited Liability Partnership
- Family debt schemes (see Section 6.16)

Each of these methods also provides opportunities to pass on capital in small parcels, thus making effective use of the IHT and CGT annual exemptions (but see Section 10.21).

Another problem, of course, is that elderly people sometimes hang on to control for too long. We will look at some possible solutions to this situation in Section 15.13.

10.20   CORPORATE DEBT

As we saw in Section 7.13, liabilities owed by a company reduce the value of that company and hence also the value of the shares in it.

When a person dies owning shares in a company, it is the value of those shares that is brought into their estate and there is no need to claim a separate deduction for the company's liabilities. Hence, there is also no need to meet the rules described in Section 2.12 regarding the payment of a liability out of the assets of the deceased's estate.

In some cases, it may therefore make sense to ensure that borrowings to finance investments which do not qualify for any form of relief are made through a company.

Example

Phil has offered to lend his brother Don £500,000 to help him start a property investment business. The loan will be unsecured and interest-free.

If Don borrowed the money personally and later died still owing this money to Phil, his executors would need to repay Phil out of the assets of Don's estate in order to be able to claim a deduction for this loan for IHT purposes (see Section 2.12).

Instead, however, Don sets up a company, Ever Lee Investments Ltd. He then gets Phil to lend the money to the company.

The debt to Phil will now automatically reduce the value of Don's shares in Ever Lee Investments Ltd for IHT purposes without having to worry about meeting the rules in Section 2.12.

This technique solves the problem of having to repay a loan on the borrower's death but if such a loan was used to indirectly finance relievable property or excluded property, the other rules described in Section 2.12 would then apply.

10.21 ASSOCIATED OPERATIONS

Where there are two or more transfers of the same property, or two or more transactions which affect the same property, HMRC may invoke the associated operations rules.

Broadly speaking, where these rules are applied, the transfers or transactions are treated as if just one transfer from the original transferor to the ultimate recipient had taken place, thus undoing any tax planning which the intermediate steps tried to achieve.

HMRC's powers under the associated operations rules are extremely wide-ranging and, as we have seen several times throughout this guide, there are many IHT planning techniques which might potentially be caught. Nevertheless, where there are sufficiently good non-tax reasons for carrying out the transactions involved, the application of the associated operations rules may still be avoided.

Time is a good defence against the associated operations rules: the longer the gap between one transaction and the next, the less likely the planning measures are to be attacked. Uncertainty is also important. Where subsequent transfers are uncertain of being carried out at the time of an earlier transfer, they are far less likely to be deemed to be associated operations.

10.22 THE GENERAL ANTI-ABUSE RULE

A general anti-abuse rule (or 'GAAR' for short) was introduced in 2013. The GAAR is intended to be targeted at 'artificial' and 'abusive' or 'aggressive' tax avoidance schemes which go beyond the scope of normal tax planning and which use loopholes in the tax legislation in a way that was not intended by Parliament. We are being told that 'normal' tax planning will not be affected.

Where the GAAR applies, any tax advantage gained through the use of the 'abusive' scheme will be reversed.

At present, it is still too early to tell just exactly how HMRC will apply the GAAR in practice. It is therefore possible that some more advanced planning strategies could be at risk of being targeted under the GAAR; although, in general, it seems unlikely that the GAAR could affect any IHT planning techniques which are not already at risk of attack under the associated operations rules (see Section 10.21).

10.23 DEVOLVED TAXES

The Scottish Parliament has had some devolved tax-raising powers since April 2015 and some powers will be devolved to the Welsh Assembly from April 2018. In Section 1.8, we looked at the replacements for SDLT in these nations and more details are available in the Taxcafe.co.uk guide *'How to Save Property Tax'*.

Scotland also has some devolved powers over Income Tax, but these do not really affect any of the issues discussed in this guide (except, perhaps, to slightly alter the impact of the issues covered in Section 8.22). In particular, it is worth noting that the 'normal' UK higher rate tax threshold continues to apply to Scottish taxpayers for the purposes of interest, savings and dividend income and CGT.

As far as IHT is concerned, this despicable tax remains the same throughout the UK. Hence, Scottish, Welsh and Northern Irish taxpayers remain in the same unfortunate position as their English counterparts when it comes to suffering IHT.

Chapter 11

Interaction with CGT

11.1 A QUICK CAPITAL GAINS TAX UPDATE

Before we look at that 'clash of the titans' created by the interaction between CGT and IHT, it may be useful if I provide a quick update on the current CGT regime.

Individuals currently pay CGT at five rates:

- 10% where entrepreneurs' relief is available (see Section 11.5)
- 18% on gains on residential property made by basic rate taxpayers
- 28% on gains on residential property made by higher rate taxpayers
- 10% on other gains made by basic rate taxpayers
- 20% on other gains made by higher rate taxpayers

Basic rate taxpayers pay the reduced rates to the extent of any basic rate tax band remaining available. Generally speaking, therefore, once your combined taxable income and gains for the tax year exceed the higher-rate tax threshold (£46,350 for 2018/19), you must pay CGT at either 20% or 28%, as appropriate, on any further amount of capital gains arising in the same tax year.

Example

Beyoncé has taxable income of £34,350 for 2018/19. After deducting her personal allowance of £11,850, she is liable for Income Tax on a sum of £22,500. This means that £12,000 of her £34,500 basic rate band for 2018/19 remains available.

In February 2019, Beyoncé makes a capital gain of £36,700 on a residential investment property. After deducting her annual CGT exemption of £11,700 she is left with a taxable gain of £25,000.

The first £12,000 of Beyoncé's taxable gain is taxed at 18% and the remaining £13,000 is taxed at 28%.

Anyone with taxable income in excess of the higher-rate tax threshold simply pays CGT at 20% or 28% on all of their capital gains after deducting the annual CGT exemption. (Except where entrepreneurs' relief is available – see Section 11.5)

For further details of the current CGT regime, see the Taxcafe.co.uk guide *'How to Save Property Tax'*.

11.2　THE UPLIFT ON DEATH

Do you remember my opening comments in Section 4.5? I'll refresh your memory: "For CGT purposes, death is often a very good tax-planning strategy."

The reason for this rather dark-humoured remark is one simple fact. On death, the CGT base cost of all the deceased's assets is uplifted to their market value at that date.

Example

In 1985, Jerry set up Killer Limited with an investment of just £10,000. By July 2018, his controlling interest in Killer Promotions PLC (the same company) is worth £100m. Jerry's CGT bill on a sale of these shares would be almost £20m.

Sadly, however, Jerry dies in August 2018, and leaves his entire Killer Promotions PLC shareholding to his son Lee. Lee sells the shares for £102m in March 2019. His CGT bill will be just £400,000 at most.

Lee is treated as if he acquired the shares in August 2018 for a price of £100m. We call this the CGT 'uplift on death'. His taxable gain on the sale in March 2019 is therefore just £2m.

11.3　THE CAPITAL GAINS TAX vs INHERITANCE TAX DILEMMA

Whilst death is very good CGT planning, lifetime transfers generally pose a problem. As explained in Section 4.10, a lifetime transfer of anything other than cash will give rise to a CGT disposal which is deemed to take place at market value.

Hence, in our example above, if Jerry had given the Killer Promotions PLC shares to Lee before he died, he may have given himself a £20m CGT bill!

This creates a bit of a dilemma: the best way to save IHT is often to make lifetime transfers, whereas the best way to save CGT is to hold on to assets until death.

What we really want to do is to minimise the overall tax burden (or, to be more precise, to follow **Bayley's Law**, as per Section 10.2). To do this, we need to start by considering what reliefs the assets concerned will qualify for, both under the IHT regime and the CGT regime.

The three major areas to consider are:

- Business assets
- Transfers to spouses
- The family home

We will look at each of these areas in turn. 'Other assets' which do not fall under any of these headings are dealt with in Section 11.9.

11.4   GIFTS OF BUSINESS ASSETS

Where a qualifying business asset is transferred by way of gift, the capital gain arising may be held over. This provides an effective CGT deferral but does mean the uplift on death will be lost.

Example

Kurt set up Nevermind Limited in 2001 with a share capital of just 100 £1 ordinary shares. The shares currently qualify for both holdover relief and entrepreneurs' relief (see Section 11.5).

In December 2018, Kurt gives 25 shares to his unmarried partner Courtney and they elect to hold over the capital gain arising. In effect, this means that Courtney is treated as if she acquired the shares for £1 each: the same price that Kurt paid for them.

Kurt dies in March 2019 and, fearing a drop in value, Courtney decides to sell her Nevermind Limited shares at their current value of £50,000 per share, or £1.25m in total.

Courtney's base cost for her shares is just £25, so she ends up with a capital gain of £1,249,975. Her CGT bill, at 20%, is therefore £249,995 (assuming she is a higher-rate taxpayer and has used her annual exemption elsewhere).

Sadly, despite its name, holdover relief on gifts of business assets does not actually apply to assets used in a 'business', but generally only to assets used in a trade. What will qualify as a 'trade' can be very difficult to define, but it certainly does not include property investment businesses.

Broadly, the assets which qualify for holdover relief will be:

- Assets used in a qualifying trade (including goodwill)
- Unquoted shares in a trading company
- A holding of at least 5% of a quoted trading company

This time, 'unquoted' does not include shares traded on AIM.

To be a trading company, the underlying business must not include any 'substantial' element of non-trading activities. This is usually taken to mean that non-trading activities amount to no more than 20% of the business, using the tests set out in Section 7.7.

Property used in a qualifying furnished holiday letting business (see the Taxcafe.co.uk guide *'How to Save Property Tax'* for further details) also qualifies, even though this is not strictly a trade for tax purposes.

Partial Holdover

Whilst a lifetime transfer inevitably means that the transferee will not benefit from the CGT uplift on death, it is sometimes possible to achieve a partial uplift without incurring any immediate CGT liability.

This is because where assets are actually sold to the transferee, but for a price less than their full market value, the gain held over is the difference between the sale price and the market value of the assets. The net result is that the transferee is now deemed to have acquired the assets for the price actually paid on the transfer.

Where the transferor's annual CGT exemption is available, a tax-free uplift of up to £11,700 (at 2018/19 rates) can usually be achieved.

Example Revisited

Let us suppose that Kurt actually sold his 25 Nevermind Limited shares to Courtney for £11,725. By using a holdover relief election, Kurt's capital gain can be reduced to just £11,700, which would be covered by his annual CGT exemption.

Assuming that Kurt had no other capital gains during 2018/19, the transfer could therefore still be made free of CGT.

After paying Stamp Duty at 0.5% of £60, Courtney would have a base cost for the shares of £11,785 instead of just £25 as before.

When Courtney later sold her shares, her capital gain would be reduced to £1,238,215 giving her a CGT bill of £247,643.

This simple mechanism would therefore save Courtney £2,352 in CGT; or a net £2,292 after taking account of the Stamp Duty cost.

Where land and buildings are transferred using this strategy, the SDLT cost will need to be taken into account and this will often be quite significant (see the Taxcafe.co.uk guide *'How to Save Property Tax'* for details).

The sale proceeds on the transfer will, of course, remain in the transferor's estate. However, the proceeds could be left outstanding as a loan and the benefit of the loan could be given to another individual as a potentially exempt transfer (using a variation of the 'family debt scheme' which we looked at in Section 6.16). The potentially exempt transfer would be exempt after seven years.

The loan may be deductible from the transferee's estate, but this will depend on whether it is repaid out of the assets of their estate (see Section 2.12) and on whether the property that was transferred qualified for business or agricultural property relief (see Section 7.11).

Restrictions and Formalities

Holdover relief on 'Gifts of Business Assets' is not available for:

- A transfer of shares or securities to a company
- Any transfer to a trust where the transferor, their spouse and their minor children are not totally excluded from any benefit

A claim for holdover relief requires a joint election by the transferor and the transferee (or by the transferor alone where the transferee is a trust).

11.5   BUSINESS PROPERTY RELIEF AND ENTREPRENEURS' RELIEF

As we have already seen, the uplift on death provides enormous potential to save CGT. Whether that saving is achieved at an IHT cost, however, is highly dependent on whether business property relief or agricultural property relief is available.

Another important factor for business assets is the question of whether entrepreneurs' relief is available for CGT purposes.

Entrepreneurs' Relief

Where a disposal of business assets qualifies for entrepreneurs' relief, the rate of CGT applying is reduced to just 10%.

The qualifying rules for entrepreneurs' relief are entirely different to the rules for business property relief or for holdover relief, so it is essential to consider each relief separately in every case.

Broadly speaking, entrepreneurs' relief is available on the disposal of:

i)   The whole or part of a qualifying business
ii) Assets formerly used in a qualifying business which has ceased or been disposed of
iii) Shares or securities in a 'personal company'

A qualifying business for this purpose is generally a trade, although, once again, qualifying furnished holiday letting businesses (see the Taxcafe.co.uk guide *'How to Save Property Tax'* for details) also qualify.

A 'part' of a business can only be counted for these purposes if it is capable of operating as a going concern in its own right and HMRC interprets this point very strictly. However, an 'interest' in a business, such as a partnership share, may qualify.

A disposal of assets formerly used in a qualifying business must take place within three years after the cessation or disposal of the business.

In all cases, the individual making the disposal must have owned the qualifying business for at least a year prior to its disposal, or cessation, as the case may be.

The definition of a 'personal company' for the purposes of entrepreneurs' relief is broadly as follows:

i) The individual holds at least 5% of the ordinary share capital
ii) The holding under (i) provides at least 5% of the voting rights
iii) The company is a trading company (using the same 20% rule as we saw in Section 11.4)
iv) The individual is an officer or employee of the company (an 'officer' includes a company secretary or non-executive director)

Each of these rules must be satisfied for the period of at least one year prior to the disposal in question or, where the company has ceased trading, for at least one year prior to the cessation. In the latter case, the disposal must again take place within three years after cessation.

Entrepreneurs' relief may sometimes also extend to assets owned personally but used in the trade of a 'personal company', or a partnership in which the owner is a partner. A number of restrictions apply, however. Broadly, the relief is only available where the owner is also disposing of at least a 5% stake in the company or partnership, or is disposing of their entire remaining stake, having held at least a 5% stake at some time in the past. The relief is also restricted where any payment has been received for the use of the assets concerned after 5th April 2008.

Finally, each individual may only claim entrepreneurs' relief on a maximum cumulative lifetime total of £10m of capital gains. Thereafter, the CGT rate will revert to the normal rates set out in Section 11.1.

Investor's Relief

A new CGT relief called 'investor's relief' was introduced in 2016, although no-one will be able to benefit from it until at least 6th April 2019. The new relief is available to investors subscribing for new issues of ordinary shares in unlisted trading companies after 16th March 2016.

Shares must be held for at least three years commencing from 6th April 2016 in order to qualify and the investor must **not** be an officer or employee of the company.

Shares qualifying for investor's relief will be subject to a CGT rate of 10%. The relief is subject to a lifetime limit of £10m of capital gains: this is a separate allowance to the limit applying to entrepreneurs' relief.

Where an individual holds shares qualifying for investor's relief, the implications for IHT planning discussed in this guide will be the same as in the case of shares qualifying for entrepreneurs' relief.

Interaction between Business Property Relief and Entrepreneurs' Relief or Investor's Relief

The interaction between these important reliefs has enormous consequences for estate preservation planning. There are three possible combinations which we need to consider, so let's examine each in turn.

Business Property Relief & Either Entrepreneurs' Relief or Investor's Relief Available

These assets can be passed on free from IHT and it will therefore often make sense for the transferor to hang on to these assets and transfer them on death to obtain the CGT uplift with no IHT cost.

If it is not possible to hang on to the original assets until death, the same result can sometimes be achieved by exchanging these assets for 'replacement assets', as explained in Section 7.18. To avoid any CGT liabilities on the exchange, the 'replacement assets' generally need to be one of the following:

i) Shares issued in exchange for shares in the transferor's own company (e.g. a 'takeover')
ii) Shares issued in exchange for the transfer of an unincorporated business into a company
iii) Business property acquired within the three year period following the disposal of the original assets. (E.g. buying business premises to replace previous premises used in the same business or the acquisition of property for use in a new qualifying business.)

Any new business under (iii) above will need to qualify as a trading business. A qualifying furnished holiday letting business would also suffice for this purpose from a CGT perspective, but will not necessarily qualify for business property relief (see Section 7.5).

Assets which qualify for holdover relief on 'Gifts of Business Assets' (see Section 11.4) can generally be transferred during the transferor's lifetime without any CGT liability. However, whilst this avoids CGT on the transfer, it also denies the transferee the benefit of the 'uplift on death'. On the other hand, a transfer of assets qualifying for entrepreneurs' relief or investor's relief will be subject to CGT at a rate of just 10%. In many cases, it will make sense **NOT** to claim holdover relief on the transfer, so that the transferee may benefit from an increased CGT base cost on the assets. This is particularly relevant where the transferee is considering a sale of the asset in the near future (although the potential impact of such a sale when the transferor dies within seven years needs to be considered – see Section 7.20).

Business Property Relief but Not Entrepreneurs' Relief or Investor's Relief

These assets can be passed on free from IHT but would often attract an immediate CGT charge of up to 20% or 28% in the case of a lifetime transfer.

If the Killer Promotions PLC shares in our example in Section 11.2 qualified for business property relief, Jerry would have been able to leave them to Lee free of IHT. As we saw in Section 11.2, Lee was treated as if he had bought the shares at market value at the date of Jerry's death, thus drastically reducing his CGT bill.

In this situation, it will therefore generally make sense to hang on to the assets and only transfer them on death. CGT uplift will be obtained and both IHT and CGT can be avoided if the transferee sells the assets shortly afterwards. At the very least, there should be a very substantial reduction in CGT, as we saw in Section 11.2.

Again, it may be possible to achieve the same results when the assets are exchanged for 'replacement assets' before death. The opportunity to avoid CGT on such an exchange is more limited, however, and item (iii) outlined above may no longer apply in some cases.

Lifetime transfers of these assets will often give rise to immediate CGT liabilities, as holdover relief on 'Gifts of Business Assets' (Section 11.4) may not be available. Even where it is available, the 'uplift on death' will be lost and the transferee will most likely suffer CGT at up to 20% or 28% on the held over gain when they ultimately sell the asset (although there will be a few instances where the transferee is eligible for entrepreneurs' relief and thus pays CGT at just 10%).

Entrepreneurs' Relief or Investor's Relief but Not Business Property Relief (Although it is difficult to foresee a situation where an individual qualifies for investor's relief, but not business property relief, on the same shareholding)

This scenario could apply where:

    i)   Business assets have been owned for one year but less than two
    ii)   A qualifying business has ceased within the last three years
    iii) An individual has shares or securities in a quoted company which qualifies as their 'personal company' for the purposes of entrepreneurs' relief

In the first case, it will generally make sense to hang on to the assets until the expiry of the two year period in order to obtain business property relief.

In the other cases we face a major dilemma. A lifetime transfer of the assets (before the expiry of the three year period in the second case) will give rise to a maximum CGT charge of just 10%, but the opportunity to achieve the CGT uplift on death will be lost and the transferee may face a charge of up to 20% or 28% on the future growth in the asset's value. On the other hand, if the assets are still held at the time of death, IHT will be fully chargeable.

Furthermore, in the second case, it is unlikely that the assets will be eligible for holdover relief on 'Gifts of Business Assets' (see Section 11.4). Even where this relief is available, it only provides a CGT deferral and the 'uplift on death' will be lost.

In practice, it may be difficult to establish the best course of action but an early transfer will often produce an overall saving.

Example

Sanjeev has a large estate well in excess of the nil rate band, including a 10% shareholding in a quoted trading company which qualifies for entrepreneurs' relief. Sanjeev's base cost in these shares for CGT purposes is just £1.

In February 2019, Sanjeev transfers his shares to his daughter Meera when they are worth £1m. He decides not to claim holdover relief in order to secure the benefit of entrepreneurs' relief. His resultant CGT bill is therefore £100,000 (he has used his annual exemption elsewhere). In March 2026, Sanjeev dies when the shares are worth £1.8m. As the transfer to Meera took place more than seven years previously, no IHT is due. If Sanjeev had still held the shares at this time, the IHT arising would have been £720,000.

Meera now sells the shares, giving rise to a capital gain of £800,000 and a CGT bill, at 20%, of £160,000 (she is a higher-rate taxpayer, has used her annual exemption elsewhere, and is not eligible for entrepreneurs' relief). Hence, whilst father and daughter between them have paid £260,000 in CGT, the overall net tax saving for the family is £460,000.

In fact, if we take account of the additional IHT saved due to the £100,000 reduction in the value of Sanjeev's estate when he paid his CGT bill, the overall net saving is actually £500,000.

Clearly, in this example, it was worth incurring a relatively small CGT cost, as the investment was successfully removed from Sanjeev's estate by way of a potentially exempt transfer more than seven years before his death. On the other hand, if Sanjeev had died immediately after his transfer to Meera, there would have been no IHT saving (other than the £40,000 saved due to Sanjeev's CGT bill). The CGT liability would then have been incurred needlessly when Meera could have had a CGT uplift on her father's death.

Worse still, if Sanjeev had left a widow, the transfer to Meera would have used up his nil rate band, leaving no transferable nil rate band to eventually be used against his widow's estate.

Between these two extremes lie an almost infinite variety of outcomes. As a general guide, I have produced the table below. It follows broadly the same lines as the example, but with a few minor modifications. It is based on the following assumptions:

i) There is an existing gain of £1m giving rise to a CGT liability of £100,000
ii) The asset is currently worth £1m and its future value will increase at a rate of 7.5% per annum (compound)
iii) The transferee will sell the asset immediately after the transferor's death and will not enjoy entrepreneurs' relief
iv) The transferee is a higher-rate taxpayer
v) Both the transferor and the transferee will use their CGT annual exemption elsewhere
vi) The transferor will not hold over the gain arising on the transfer
vii) The asset is not residential property
viii) The nil rate band and any transferable nil rate band to which they are entitled would have been fully utilised against other property within the transferor's estate if the transfer had not taken place
ix) The transferor survives just beyond the relevant anniversary
x) The nil rate band remains at £325,000 for the first two years and is then increased in line with inflation at 2.5% (i.e. using the methodology outlined in Section 3.2)

Transferor Dies After	Value on Death	IHT on Transfer*	CGT on Final Sale	IHT if Still in Estate	Net Saving or (Cost)**
< 1 year	£1,000,000	£400,000	£0	£400,000	(£60,000)
1 year	£1,075,000	£400,000	£15,000	£430,000	(£45,000)
2 years	£1,155,625	£400,000	£31,125	£462,250	(£28,875)
3 years	£1,242,297	£346,720	£48,459	£496,919	£41,739
4 years	£1,335,469	£294,880	£67,094	£534,188	£112,214
5 years	£1,435,629	£244,480	£87,126	£574,252	£182,646
6 years	£1,543,302	£195,520	£108,660	£617,321	£253,140
7 years	£1,659,049	£0	£131,810	£663,620	£471,810

* - Includes the additional tax on the estate arising as a result of the transfer (i.e. due to the transfer using up the deceased's nil rate band in the event of their death within seven years). For this purpose, it is assumed that no transferable nil rate band is available to the deceased.

** - Net saving/(cost) takes account of the CGT paid on the original transfer less the IHT saving arising as a result of this cost.

As we can see, under this scenario, the transferor only needs to survive for three years to make the transfer worthwhile.

It is essential to remember that the above savings are based on the assumption that the transferor's nil rate band (and any transferable nil rate band available) would be used up on other assets within their estate. This will not be the case if they would have otherwise left everything to their UK domiciled spouse and the points to be considered in this situation are covered in Chapter 6.

Transferees Eligible for Entrepreneurs' Relief

A lifetime transfer becomes even more attractive where the transferee will also be eligible for entrepreneurs' relief on the transferred asset. In our example above, this might apply if the company in which Sanjeev held his shares became Meera's 'personal company' for entrepreneurs' relief purposes after the transfer.

In practice, this could generally be achieved by ensuring that at least 5% of the ordinary shares are transferred and the transferee is, or becomes, an officer or employee of the company.

The following table sets out the position arising under the same scenario as before except that the transferee now qualifies for entrepreneurs' relief on the transferred asset.

Transferor Dies After	Value on Death	IHT on Transfer	CGT on Final Sale	IHT if Still in Estate	Net Saving or (Cost)
< 1 year	£1,000,000	£400,000	£0	£400,000	(£60,000)
1 year	£1,075,000	£400,000	£7,500	£430,000	(£37,500)
2 years	£1,155,625	£400,000	£15,563	£462,250	(£13,313)
3 years	£1,242,297	£346,720	£24,230	£496,919	£65,969
4 years	£1,335,469	£294,880	£33,547	£534,188	£145,761
5 years	£1,435,629	£244,480	£43,563	£574,252	£226,209
6 years	£1,543,302	£195,520	£54,330	£617,321	£307,470
7 years	£1,659,049	£0	£65,905	£663,620	£537,715

Remember that the £10m cumulative lifetime limit for entrepreneurs' relief applies to each individual. Hence, a transferor and transferee may be able to obtain combined relief on up to £20m between them.

Residential Property

Finally, let's look at the same scenario where the transferred asset is residential property which qualifies for entrepreneurs' relief but not business property relief. This might be the case for a portfolio of qualifying furnished holiday letting properties, for example (see Section 7.5 regarding the status of furnished holiday lettings for business property relief purposes).

We will assume here that the transferee will not qualify for entrepreneurs' relief: perhaps, for example, they might convert the properties to normal residential lettings after the transfer. If the transferee did qualify for entrepreneurs' relief then the outcome would be the same as in the previous table.

Transferor Dies After	Value on Death	IHT on Transfer	CGT on Final Sale	IHT if Still in Estate	Net Saving or (Cost)
< 1 year	£1,000,000	£400,000	£0	£400,000	(£60,000)
1 year	£1,075,000	£400,000	£21,000	£430,000	(£51,000)
2 years	£1,155,625	£400,000	£43,575	£462,250	(£41,325)
3 years	£1,242,297	£346,720	£67,843	£496,919	£22,356
4 years	£1,335,469	£294,880	£93,931	£534,188	£85,376
5 years	£1,435,629	£244,480	£121,976	£574,252	£147,796
6 years	£1,543,302	£195,520	£152,124	£617,321	£209,676
7 years	£1,659,049	£0	£184,534	£663,620	£419,086

11.6   TRANSFERS TO SPOUSES OR CIVIL PARTNERS

As we know, transfers to your spouse are usually exempt from IHT. Furthermore, subject to the wealth warning below, transfers to your spouse are also usually exempt from CGT.

However, only transfers on death will benefit from the CGT uplift explained in Section 11.2. It therefore makes sense to hold on to any assets which are subject to CGT and which you ultimately intend to leave to your spouse so that they can benefit from the uplift on death.

Alternatively, a lifetime transfer of assets to your spouse could be used to get a CGT uplift on their death. You need to be pretty sure that the assets are going to come back to you though!

Wealth Warning

Unlike the IHT exemption, the CGT exemption for transfers between spouses ceases to apply at the end of the tax year in which they separate. Separated couples who have not yet obtained a decree absolute are therefore eligible for the IHT relief but not the CGT relief.

11.7 CAPITAL GAINS TAX AND THE FAMILY HOME

I could write an entire chapter on this subject alone. In fact, I have, but that chapter already appears in the Taxcafe.co.uk guide *'How to Save Property Tax'*.

To put it simply though, your own home is exempt from CGT for as long as you live in it as your only or main residence and for at least eighteen months thereafter. Full exemption will generally apply as long as you moved into the property within one year of acquisition. Any other periods of absence, however, may result in a partial loss of your exemption.

Each married couple or single individual may have just one main residence for CGT purposes at any given time.

Hence, as far as CGT is concerned, any lifetime transfer of your qualifying main residence whilst you are still living there, or within the next eighteen months thereafter, will usually be exempt.

So, what's the problem?

Well, apart from all the IHT problems which we will look at in the next chapter, there are two main CGT problems with giving away your main residence:

- The transferees will lose the ability to benefit from the CGT uplift on death, and
- Unless they move into the property, the transferees will also lose any main residence exemption on the property

In essence, the transferees will be treated for CGT purposes as having acquired the property at its market value at the date of transfer and will be exposed to CGT on any growth in value thereafter.

Practical Implications

A sale of the parent's home at any time within eighteen months of them ceasing to occupy it as their main residence would generally be fully exempt from CGT if they were still the owner at that time.

Furthermore, if the parent retained the property until their death, it would be subject to the uplift on death, giving the children a complete exemption from any gain arising during the parent's lifetime, even if the parent had been absent from the property for more than eighteen months.

Conversely, if a child owns their parent's current or former home, but does not occupy it as their own main residence themselves, it is effectively treated like an investment property and is fully exposed to CGT on a subsequent sale.

The capital gain in such cases will then be based on the property's value at the time that the child acquired it and not at the time of the parent's death. The relevant transfer may be several years earlier when the property's value was considerably less.

The interplay between CGT and IHT on the family home can produce one of three results:

i) The IHT saving may outweigh the CGT exposure which has been created. This is fine and means that the planning is still worthwhile

ii) The IHT saving comes at the price of a similar level of potential CGT liability. Such instances may still be worthwhile, as they may still produce a significant cashflow saving by deferring the tax arising. (This will often be the case where the beneficiaries have no intention of ever selling the property, or at least not for some considerable time)

iii) The IHT saving results in a significantly greater amount of potential CGT. This, clearly, would be foolhardy if the beneficiaries are contemplating any sale of the property in the foreseeable future

The introduction of the residence nil rate band (see Section 3.4) has significantly altered the potential outcomes of this 'interplay' in many cases. Far more cases will now fall into the third category above, meaning that retaining the property in the parent's ownership until death will very often be the most sensible thing to do.

In fact, in most cases where a married couple, a widow, or a widower, intends to leave the family home to their children, there will be little point in trying to avoid IHT on it, as properties worth up to £1m will often be fully covered by the available exemptions from 6th April 2020 onwards. My advice to most such people is therefore to focus their IHT planning on their other assets and keep the family home where it is.

But there remain many exceptions to this, and we will look at these in the next chapter.

Wealth Warning
Where the parent still resides in the property, a simple transfer of the property will usually be a 'Gift with Reservation'. As we shall see in the next section, it would generally be wise to refrain from making any transfer which would be a 'Gift with Reservation', as there would be no IHT advantage but all of the CGT disadvantages would remain. We will look at ways to resolve this problem in the next chapter.

11.8   CAPITAL GAINS TAX AND GIFTS WITH RESERVATION

As explained in Section 4.9, when a transfer falls foul of the 'Gifts with Reservation' rules, it will be ineffective for IHT purposes until such time as the relevant 'reservation' comes to an end.

This has absolutely no impact whatsoever on the CGT treatment of the asset. The transfer which was subject to a 'Gift with Reservation' may still give rise to CGT liabilities based on the market value of the asset transferred and the new legal owner of the transferred asset will lose the benefit of any reliefs to which the transferor may have been entitled, including main residence relief on the transferor's own home.

Generally, with few exceptions, this situation should be avoided as it usually creates CGT problems without saving any IHT.

Example

Tina is an elderly divorcee. In 1998 she gave her house to her son, Robert, but continued to live there until 2016, when she moved into a nursing home. The house was worth £275,000 in 1998 but had increased in value to £725,000 by 2016.

Tragically, Tina dies in May 2018, leaving only a few small possessions with no material value and just enough cash to pay her last month's nursing home fees and funeral expenses. However, as she only moved out of her house in 2016, its value at that date must be brought back into her estate, thus resulting in an IHT bill of £160,000.

To help pay the IHT, Robert sells the house in August 2018. (Let's assume the house is still worth £725,000 at this point.) For CGT purposes, he is treated as having acquired the house for just £275,000, thus giving rise to a CGT bill of £122,724 on top of the IHT bill (his annual CGT exemption of £11,700 is deducted from his capital gain of £450,000; he is a higher-rate taxpayer, so the balance of £438,300 is taxed at 28%).

I have seen this type of situation countless times and it's an absolute tragedy. Had Tina simply held on to the house, Robert would have paid the same £160,000 in IHT on her death and little or no CGT at all. The transfer in 1998 has effectively cost Robert over £120,000 in unnecessary extra tax.

Many families have attempted this type of planning to their cost. To make it even worse, many of these transfers were done to avoid paying residential care fees (see Section 10.10) but, as a result of a number of rule changes and successful cases taken by the local authorities this part of the plan has often failed as well.

In the vast majority of cases, therefore, gifts with reservation are to be avoided like the plague!

11.9 OTHER ASSETS

So what about those other assets, which do not qualify as business assets or main residences and which you're not planning to give to your spouse? Here we are considering assets which do not qualify for business property relief, entrepreneurs' relief, investor's relief, or holdover relief on a gift.

This will make a lifetime transfer of the property less attractive from a CGT perspective. Nevertheless, the opportunity to save IHT by way of an early lifetime transfer remains.

Assets Other Than Residential Property

Returning to the scenario examined in our first table in Section 11.5, the position arising on assets other than residential property where no entrepreneurs' relief is available to the transferor or transferee is as follows:

Transferor Dies After	Value on Death	IHT on Transfer	CGT on Final Sale	IHT if Still in Estate	Net Saving or (Cost)*
< 1 year	£1,000,000	£400,000	£0	£400,000	(£120,000)
1 year	£1,075,000	£400,000	£15,000	£430,000	(£105,000)
2 years	£1,155,625	£400,000	£31,125	£462,250	(£88,875)
3 years	£1,242,297	£346,720	£48,459	£496,919	(£18,261)
4 years	£1,335,469	£294,880	£67,094	£534,188	£52,214
5 years	£1,435,629	£244,480	£87,126	£574,252	£122,646
6 years	£1,543,302	£195,520	£108,660	£617,321	£193,140
7 years	£1,659,049	£0	£131,810	£663,620	£411,810

* Net saving/(cost) takes account of £200,000 CGT paid on the original transfer less the resultant IHT saving arising due to the reduction in the value of the transferor's estate.

Apart from the fact that entrepreneurs' relief is not available, all of the various notes and assumptions made for the first version of this table in Section 11.5 continue to be equally applicable here. I have additionally assumed that the transferor is a higher-rate taxpayer. Subject to these assumptions, in this scenario, as we can see, such a transfer still remains beneficial as long as the transferor survives at least four years.

Residential Property

The position is altered where the assets concerned are residential property, as these are subject to higher rates of CGT (see Section 11.1). Based on the same assumptions as set out above, but assuming that the assets being transferred are residential property, the position is as follows:

Transferor Dies After	Value on Death	IHT on Transfer	CGT on Final Sale	IHT if Still in Estate	Net Saving or (Cost)*
< 1 year	£1,000,000	£400,000	£0	£400,000	(£168,000)
1 year	£1,075,000	£400,000	£21,000	£430,000	(£159,000)
2 years	£1,155,625	£400,000	£43,575	£462,250	(£149,325)
3 years	£1,242,297	£346,720	£67,843	£496,919	(£85,644)
4 years	£1,335,469	£294,880	£93,931	£534,188	(£22,624)
5 years	£1,435,629	£244,480	£121,976	£574,252	£39,796
6 years	£1,543,302	£195,520	£152,124	£617,321	£101,676
7 years	£1,659,049	£0	£184,534	£663,620	£311,086

* Net saving/(cost) takes account of CGT of £280,000 paid on the original transfer less the resultant IHT saving arising due to the reduction in the value of the transferor's estate.

As we can see, under this scenario, it will take five years before a lifetime transfer of residential property provides any advantage.

The position would be different if the property qualified for main residence relief in the hands of either the transferor or the transferee. The situation for a main residence was examined in Sections 11.7 and 11.8, and will also be the focus of Chapter 12.

11.10 CAPITAL GAINS TAX AND TRUSTS

A trust for a 'vulnerable' individual may elect to be taxed as if any capital gains arising belong directly to the beneficiary (except that any capital losses made by the individual cannot be set off against the trust's gains).

However, as explained in Section 8.22, this will generally only apply to disabled trusts, trusts for bereaved minors and a few other trusts where the beneficiary is aged under 18.

Most other trusts (apart from bare trusts and charitable trusts) are subject to CGT at the higher rates of 20% or 28%.

In Chapter 8, we considered the various different types of trust and saw that some of them had their own 'separate life' for IHT purposes and some did not.

With the exception of bare trusts, however, all trusts are treated as a separate legal entity for CGT purposes. This effectively means that, subject to any other exemptions which may be available:

- Transfers into a trust are treated as disposals made at market value, and
- Transfers to beneficiaries from a trust are again treated as disposals at market value

In the case of a bare trust, it is only the transfer to the trust which represents a disposal for CGT purposes. Thereafter, the assets of the trust are generally treated as belonging to the beneficiary for the purposes of both IHT and CGT (but see Section 10.18 for some exceptions regarding trusts for minors).

The Capital Gains Tax Uplift on Death

Assets subject to an interest in possession which fall into a beneficiary's estate for IHT purposes (see Chapter 8) will generally qualify for the same CGT uplift on the death of the beneficiary as assets held absolutely (see Section 11.2). However, the uplift does not apply where property reverts to the original settlor absolutely on the beneficiary's death (but does if the settlor only obtains an interest in possession).

The CGT uplift on death also generally applies to assets in a bereaved minor's trust or an '18 to 25 Trust' on the death of a beneficiary under the age of 18.

Held Over Gains

When any interest in possession which is not within the relevant property trust regime (see Chapter 8) ends on the death of the beneficiary and a capital gain was held over when the same assets entered the trust (see Sections 9.6 and 11.4), that held over gain becomes chargeable.

The held over gain can usually be held over again provided that IHT is chargeable on the occasion of the beneficiary's death or the assets qualify as business assets for hold over relief purposes, as explained in Section 11.4.

Hold Over Relief on Absolute Entitlement

CGT hold over relief is generally available when the beneficiary of a relevant property trust, a bereaved minor's trust or an '18 to 25 Trust' becomes absolutely entitled to trust assets.

There is no restriction on holdover relief when assets are *leaving* a settlor-interested relevant property trust.

Tax Tip

In some cases, it may be worth changing the terms of a pre-22/3/2006 interest in possession trust so that it becomes a relevant property trust (see Chapter 8). Although this will expose the trust to anniversary and exit charges, the ability to hold over any capital gain arising when assets leave the trust may produce greater CGT savings than any resultant IHT cost.

Chapter 12

The Family Home

12.1 WHEN OUR MAIN ASSET BECOMES OUR MAIN LIABILITY

For most of us, the family home is our major asset. In the past, it has also often been the main cause of IHT liabilities.

Now, with both the transferable nil rate band (see Section 6.3) and the residence nil rate band (see Section 3.4) available in many cases, there will be many people for whom the family home is no longer a problem from an IHT point of view.

Many people will soon (from 6th April 2020) have exemptions totalling £1m available to cover their family home, made up as follows:

Nil rate band	£325,000
Transferable nil rate band	£325,000
Residence nil rate band	£175,000
Transferable residence nil rate band	£175,000
Total exemption available:	£1,000,000

As discussed in Section 11.7, many married couples, widows, or widowers, intending to leave their home to their children no longer need to worry about IHT on the family home and would be better advised to focus on IHT planning for their other assets.

It is also important to remember that giving your home away may mean that you are unable to benefit from the residence nil rate band. Selling your home will have a different effect, however, and we will return to this subject in Section 12.16.

But, not everyone fits neatly into the Government's 1950s-style vision of a world where everyone gets married, raises a family and lives happily ever after – until the time comes to hand 40% of everything over to them!

There are many people who, even by 2020, will still not enjoy the £1m of exemption that George Osborne promised us way back in 2007. These people may therefore still benefit from carrying out some IHT planning on the family home.

Who is Still Exposed to Inheritance Tax on the Family Home?

Those who still face potential IHT liabilities on their family home include the following:

- Those with a home worth in excess of £1m

- Those dying before 6th April 2020. Even where all of the exemptions detailed above are available, the maximum total exemption available on a death before that date will be as follows:

Deaths in 2017/18:	£850,000
Deaths in 2018/19:	£900,000
Deaths in 2019/20:	£950,000

- Single, divorced or unmarried people. You have to become a widow/widower in order to benefit from the transferable nil rate band or the transferable residence nil rate band. This does not apply to everyone! Those who never become a widow or widower will only be able to enjoy the following maximum total exemptions:

Deaths in 2017/18:	£425,000
Deaths in 2018/19:	£450,000
Deaths in 2019/20:	£475,000
Deaths thereafter:	£500,000*

  * - subject to any future increases in the nil rate band or residence nil rate band

  Remember also that it remains uncertain whether the transferable nil rate bands will always continue to be available to separated couples.

- Widows and widowers with a property worth in excess of £325,000 and who do not have the benefit of a full transferable nil rate band. Those whose former spouse used some or all of their nil rate band on their death will not be able to enjoy the full £1m of exemption detailed above unless they remarry. In some cases, they may also be unable to claim any of their former spouse's residence nil rate band. See Chapter 6 and Section 3.4 for more details.

- Those with estates worth in excess of £2m and a home worth in excess of £650,000; or £325,000 if they never become a widow or widower. These people will lose some or all of their residence nil rate band due to the tapering provisions (see Section 3.4 for details).

- Those who do not intend to leave their family home to direct descendants. Not everyone has children, and not everyone who does intends to leave their home to those children. If you do not leave your home to your direct descendants (see Section 3.4 for details), or to the right kind of trust for their benefit (see Section 8.6), then you will not be entitled to the residence nil rate band. This will leave your home exposed to IHT on any value in excess of £650,000; or £325,000 if you never become a widow or widower.

As we can see, there are many people who do still need to take action to protect the family home from IHT. The techniques set out in Sections 12.2 to 12.15 will therefore be worthy of their consideration.

As already mentioned in Section 4.9, the major stumbling block to effective IHT planning in respect of the family home is caused by the 'Gifts with Reservation' provisions.

Furthermore, whenever the transferor of **any** asset (but, most particularly, the family home) continues to enjoy the benefit of that asset, there is also the possibility of an Income Tax charge on the 'benefit-in-kind'. The application of that charge, known as the 'Pre-Owned Asset Charge', to the planning methods discussed in this chapter is examined in detail in Chapter 13.

Despite these drawbacks, there are still a number of potential methods for saving IHT on the family home. Many of the methods described in this chapter will also have CGT implications for the transferee. These are discussed in more detail in Section 11.7.

The methods described in Sections 12.8 to 12.11 are only beneficial for married couples where one or both spouses already have a transferable nil rate band available (see Section 6.8).

Any methods described in this chapter which involve mortgages, loans or other borrowings will only work if those liabilities are repaid out of the assets of the deceased's estate, or if there is a valid commercial reason for non-repayment at that time (see Section 2.12 for further details).

12.2   MOVE OUT AND THEN GIVE IT AWAY

If you can afford to, and you are willing to do it, you can simply move out of the property and then give it away. The gift is a potentially exempt transfer which will escape any IHT as long as you survive seven years. Furthermore, as long as you make the gift within eighteen months of the date you move out of the property, it will also be exempt from CGT under the principal private residence relief rules.

If you are prepared to do this, you could then move into rented accommodation, or buy a more modest property. This method will not suit everyone, but it is worth considering in some cases.

12.3   SELL UP AND GIVE AWAY THE PROCEEDS

If you can't quite afford to follow the above strategy, you could, instead, sell your current home, buy a smaller one and then give away the surplus left over cash. All you need to do then is just survive another seven years. If you're feeling really brave, you could even give away all the sale proceeds and move into rented property. Whilst this is good IHT planning, it doesn't leave you with much security in your old age and it might cause some problems with the local authority later if you ever need to go into a residential home.

12.4   RE-MORTGAGE AND GIVE AWAY THE PROCEEDS

If you would prefer to stay in your current home, another way to get most of its value out of your estate, without having to move out of it, is to re-mortgage the property and then give away or spend the borrowed funds.

The outstanding mortgage balance will be deducted from your estate when you die (subject to the rules explained in Section 2.12) and this will reduce your IHT bill as long as you have either:

- Given away the borrowed funds and then survived seven years, or
- Spent the borrowed funds before you die

The major drawback here is the need to service the mortgage debt from your retirement income.

12.5   RE-MORTGAGE AND BUY AN ANNUITY

A refinement to the above is to buy an annuity with some or all of the re-mortgage proceeds. This will enable you to service the debt and give away or spend any surplus.

The drawback here is that in the event of a premature death shortly after purchasing the annuity, a lot of your home's value will have been lost – not to Her Majesty's Treasury but to the annuity provider.

12.6   SELL UP OR RE-MORTGAGE AND INVEST THE PROCEEDS

An even better approach might be to release equity in your property, either by selling or re-mortgaging it, and invest the proceeds in a discounted gift trust (Section 9.9) or loan trust (Section 9.10).

Alternatively, you could sell your property and invest the proceeds in AIM shares (Section 7.28). You would need to limit your investment to the amount you can genuinely afford, as any subsequent borrowings, including any mortgage on a new property, would be deemed to have indirectly funded the purchase (see Section 7.29).

Hence, whilst AIM shares provide the most complete shelter from IHT (after two years), they are probably only suitable where you sell the family home, buy something smaller and just invest the surplus.

A discounted gift trust or a loan trust can be structured to provide an 'income' stream and will be more suitable in most other cases.

All of these investments have the advantage that your wealth is not lost in the event of a premature death.

12.7 SALE AT MARKET VALUE

If you sell your property to your children, or other beneficiaries, at full market value, no 'transfer of value' will take place and hence the property will immediately be excluded from your estate for IHT purposes.

Wealth Warning
Actual payment of the sale proceeds by the purchaser will generally be necessary to make this planning work as intended. Any prior arrangement to give any part of the sale proceeds back to the purchaser will also render this planning void, since the sale would not then have taken place on 'arm's length terms', as required, and a transfer of value will have taken place.

Furthermore, there must not be any obligation on the purchaser to allow you to continue to occupy the property.

The second point above means you will subsequently only be able to live in the property under an informal 'licence to occupy', which is totally at the purchaser's whim. This will not suit everyone!

After the sale, you are free to spend the proceeds, perhaps to support yourself in your retirement. Any future growth in the property's value is also safely excluded from your estate.

As you spend the proceeds and the property grows in value, the reduction in your taxable estate starts to accumulate. These savings also start immediately after the sale and it is not necessary to survive for any period to benefit.

Alternatively, you could combine this method with the method in Section 12.6 and invest the proceeds in one of the IHT 'shelters' suggested there.

On the other hand, however, as time passes there is a danger that the adverse CGT considerations will outweigh any IHT savings. (As we saw in Sections 11.7 and 11.8, the purchaser will be subject to CGT on a sale of the property!)

Another important point to bear in mind is the fact that SDLT will be payable on the purchase of the property. The rates involved could be quite prohibitive in some cases (see the Taxcafe.co.uk guide *'How to Save Property Tax'* for full details).

12.8 THE WIDOW'S LOAN SCHEME & THE FAMILY HOME

The method described in Section 6.12 generally works just as well for the family home as for any other assets. Probably better, in fact, as there is an asset on which to secure the loan and thus give it the necessary commercial substance.

As explained in Chapter 6, however, this method is now only worth exploring in certain limited cases where one or both spouses already has a transferable nil rate band available.

Example

Oscar and Freddie are registered civil partners and equal joint tenants in common of a house worth £1.3m. Each of them already has a transferable nil rate band available from the death of a previous spouse or civil partner.

Freddie dies in December 2018 and leaves an amount equivalent to twice the nil rate band, £650,000, to a discretionary trust. He leaves everything else to Oscar.

No IHT is payable on Freddie's death, since the legacy to the discretionary trust is covered by his nil rate band and transferable nil rate band and the rest of his estate is covered by the spouse exemption.

The trust takes a charge for £650,000 over the couple's house and then passes the title to Freddie's share of the house over to Oscar.

Oscar survives Freddie by just over two years and then passes away in January 2021. At this time, the house is worth £1.4m.

The value of the house in Oscar's estate is, however, reduced to just £750,000 by the £650,000 charge taken by Freddie's discretionary trust (provided that the charge meets the necessary conditions explained in Sections 2.12 and 6.12).

After deducting the nil rate band of £325,000 and Oscar's transferable nil rate band from his previous marriage, just £100,000 of the house's value is subject to IHT at 40%, giving a charge of £40,000.

Without the widow's loan scheme, the whole value of the house would have been subject to IHT on Oscar's death. After deducting the nil rate band and his transferable nil rate band, a value of £750,000 would then have been subject to IHT at 40%, giving a charge of £300,000.

The widow's loan scheme has thus produced a saving of £260,000.

A widow's loan scheme incorporating a loan secured on the family home can usually be put in place for a cost of around £1,000 to £1,500, although this may be more in some parts of the country, or if there are any additional complications. Further details of how to implement the scheme and some of the pitfalls which need to be avoided are given in Section 6.12.

12.9 LEAVE A SHARE TO THE CHILDREN

Another method which may be worth considering where one or both of a married couple are already entitled to a transferable nil rate band is to simply leave a share in the property to your children, who will then, after your death, own it jointly with your surviving spouse. See Section 6.8 for guidance on the value which this share should ideally have in order to optimise the overall IHT position. Any residence nil rate band to which you are entitled should also be taken into account. Remember, as explained in Section 10.6, a joint share in a property held as tenants in common may be any proportion and need not be an equal share.

If your surviving spouse and children then sell the property immediately after your death, there should be no CGT liability – the children will benefit from the CGT uplift on death (see Section 11.2) and the surviving spouse should be covered by the main residence exemption.

Opinions differ, however, on the more common situation which arises when the property is retained and the surviving spouse continues to occupy it.

The surviving spouse's joint share in the property will give them a continuing right of occupation. Some IHT experts think this means that the survivor can remain in the property without paying any rent and the children's share of the property does not need to be included in their estate on their subsequent death.

Hence, as planned, when the surviving spouse dies, their estate would only include their share of the property.

Other experts, however, believe that the surviving spouse's continuing occupation amounts to an interest in possession and that the children's share of the property would therefore also fall into their estate unless they pay rent for their occupation of that share.

Still others consider that a relevant property trust would come into being in respect of the children's share of the property. The consequences of this are explored in the next section.

Unfortunately, at present, it is not yet clear which set of experts is correct and HMRC has refused to comment. Personally, I've always favoured the view of the first set of experts which means the IHT planning will work as intended, although it must be admitted that the position is now far from certain.

If the method does work as intended, it still has the drawback that the children are exposed to CGT on the growth in value of their share of the property after the first parent's death. However, the resultant CGT liability arising will often be considerably less than the IHT saving. Furthermore, if the family intend to retain the property in the long term, CGT is often less of a concern anyway.

So, apart from the possible CGT exposure, everything should be fine as long as you are happy that your children, and, more particularly, their spouses or partners, will all get along OK with your spouse after you're gone.

In practice though, this simple route often causes difficulty and families in this situation have been known to come to blows (both metaphorically and physically). The other joint owners have even been known to force the surviving spouse into selling the former family home against their wishes.

The best way around these practical problems is to use a trust and we will look at this more complex variation to this scheme in the next section.

12.10 CHILDREN PUT THEIR SHARE INTO TRUST

This variation to the method described in the previous section works as follows:

i) After inheriting a share in the property, the children set up a trust, with the surviving spouse as both trustee and beneficiary, and transfer their share into it.

ii) The provisions of the trust are that the property reverts to the children, as settlors, on the death of the surviving spouse.

The drawback to this scheme is that the trust set up by the children will be a relevant property trust (see Chapter 8) and will therefore be subject to anniversary and exit charges.

Nevertheless, these charges may well be substantially less than the amount saved by keeping part of the property out of the surviving spouse's estate. In many cases, where the children's share of the property is worth less than the nil rate band, the structure may, in practice, actually still avoid IHT on the property altogether.

The children will be unable to benefit from any CGT uplift (in respect of the trust's share of the property) on the surviving spouse's death. However, if the trust were then to sell its share of the property, the main residence exemption should be available as the property had been the main residence of the trust beneficiary (i.e. the surviving spouse). The trust could then pass the sale proceeds to the children.

Hence, whilst this scheme may be slightly flawed in theory, it will often still work pretty well in practice.

12.11 LEAVE A SHARE TO A DISCRETIONARY TRUST

In Section 6.11, we looked at the drawbacks to using a discretionary Will Trust and the possible problem of it being treated as an immediate post-death interest and thus falling into the surviving spouse's estate. As explained in Chapter 6, this is now only a problem for certain 'second time around' married couples.

A possible solution to this problem, where it still exists, is to leave an appropriate share in the family home (see Section 6.8 for what is 'appropriate') to a discretionary trust in which the surviving spouse is **_not_** a beneficiary.

As explained in Section 12.9, as a joint owner, the surviving spouse already has a right to occupy the property, so the fact that they are not a beneficiary of the discretionary trust does not make any practical difference to them.

After an interval of at least two years and a day, the discretionary trust can be changed into an interest in possession trust in favour of the surviving spouse. This will be a relevant property trust and hence will not fall into the surviving spouse's estate. Anniversary and exit charges may apply but, as before, these may be avoided if the trust's share of the property is not worth more than the nil rate band.

This scheme is a pretty new idea and, as such, it is currently untested. Furthermore, even the experts are still debating whether it will actually work in practice!

12.12   THE 'FULL CONSIDERATION' METHOD

The 'Gifts with Reservation' rules can be bypassed if, after giving the property to your children, you then pay them a full commercial rent for continuing to live in it. Payment of the rent would also help to further reduce your estate for IHT purposes.

The major drawbacks to this method are the fact that your children would have to account for Income Tax on the rent you are paying and will also be fully exposed to CGT on the future growth in value of the property.

12.13   CO-OWNERSHIP

This method is very popular with widows, widowers and other single parents who have mature single adult children.

Quite simply, you just put the property into joint ownership with one or more of your adult children and then live together with them in the property.

The transfer of one or more shares in the property is a potentially exempt transfer as long as the child or children are living there. It is the children's presence in the property that prevents the transfer from being a 'Gift with Reservation'.

However, if one or more of the donee children should subsequently move out of the property whilst the parent themselves is still in occupation, the only way to prevent the 'Gift with Reservation' rules from destroying this IHT planning strategy would be for the parent to then pay a full market rent for their use of the appropriate share of the property.

It is also important that each party bears their own share of the household running costs. If any child were to pay the full household running costs, or even just part of the parent's share, then a 'Gift with Reservation' would have taken place and the IHT planning will be undone.

Whilst in practice this method works best when the children remain single, there is nothing in principle to prevent it from continuing to work when they marry, or even have children of their own (it just gets crowded).

12.14 SHEARING

The IHT on the property can be reduced by dividing up the legal interests in the property in such a way that there is no 'Gift with Reservation'.

To use this method, the transferor must have owned the property for at least seven years and, if the property is held jointly by a couple, each of them must have owned their own share for at least seven years.

This method is generally only effective when there is no intention of selling the property, i.e. it is to be retained in the family after the original owner's death.

To follow this method, you create a long-term lease over the property which becomes effective some years from now: say in 15 or 20 years' time. You then grant that lease to your children or other intended heirs. The grant of the lease represents a potentially exempt transfer which will escape IHT as long as you survive for seven years.

The duration of the lease needs to be long enough to ensure you will never benefit from your freehold reversion after its expiry. The strategy works best with a very lengthy lease, say for 999 years.

The start date for the lease needs to be chosen on the basis of the donor's life expectancy, but cannot be more than 21 years after its execution.

As the clock runs down towards the time when the lease comes into effect, the value of your freehold interest in the property reduces.

Hopefully, if you time it right, at the time of your death your interest in the property will have minimal value and will easily be covered by the nil rate band (plus any available transferable nil rate band or residence nil rate band).

HMRC has confirmed that this scheme does avoid the 'Gifts with Reservation' rules. This is mainly so that they can collect Income Tax under the pre-owned assets charge (see Section 13.4).

The scheme may also be implemented by granting the lease to a trust with the transferor's heirs as the beneficiaries. The grant of the lease would, however, be a chargeable lifetime transfer (see Section 4.2) and the trust would be subject to anniversary and exit charges. Even so, the scheme may still produce significant savings in some cases.

What If You Live Too Long?

If you are fortunate enough to still be around when the lease comes into effect then, in order to avoid the 'Gifts with Reservation' rules, you could start paying a commercial rent to your heirs (but see Section 12.12 above re Income Tax). Alternatively, by that stage, you may well be happy to move into something smaller!

12.15 THE THREE-WAY SPLIT

Following the introduction of the transferable nil rate band, most married couples should now be protected from IHT on a property worth up to twice the amount of the nil rate band. This scheme may exempt a property which is worth up to three times the amount of the nil rate band (i.e. £975,000 at current rates).

To follow this method we need to make an assumption about which spouse will die first. If we get this wrong, the survivor will have to think again (but should not get an immediate IHT bill). For the sake of illustration, let's assume that the husband will probably die first (statistics would support us on this).

First, if the property is in England or Wales, we put it into a tenancy in common. Next, we divide up the ownership of the property so that two thirds of the ownership goes to the husband and one third to the wife.

On the husband's death he leaves half of his share (i.e. one third of the total) to a life interest trust in favour of his wife, with the remainder to the children. This will qualify as an immediate post-death interest (see Section 8.12) and hence fall within the wife's estate. Most importantly, it will also be an exempt transfer.

The husband leaves the other half of his share (again one third of the total) to a discretionary trust, thus utilising his nil rate band. At some convenient date more than two years later, this trust can be wound up and the property share will be passed to the children. Alternatively, to protect the widow, it may be better to keep the trust going and perhaps pay some modest anniversary charges.

The wife allows an early termination of her life interest and passes that one third share of the property to the children. This will be a potentially exempt transfer and will be exempt from IHT as long as the wife survives another seven years.

Ultimately, when the widow dies herself, her nil rate band can be utilised against her remaining one third share of the property.

As discussed in Section 12.9, some experts would argue that the widow has an interest in possession in the discretionary trust's share of the property and that the scheme would therefore fail. Again, the position on this is not clear.

Before the introduction of the transferable nil rate band in 2007, many people took the view that this scheme was worth a try as there was nothing to lose. Now, however, the scheme generally represents something of a gamble since it means sacrificing the transferable nil rate band.

It will certainly now only be worth considering this scheme where the property is worth considerably in excess of twice the nil rate band, plus any available residence nil rate band.

12.16   DOWNSIZING

The residence nil rate band may also be claimed against any assets or cash which are left to direct descendants, or certain types of trust for their benefit (see Section 8.6), to the extent that these assets are covered by the sale proceeds of a former qualifying private residence sold after 8th July 2015 (see Section 3.4 for details of direct descendants and qualifying private residences).

Such a claim under the 'downsizing' provisions may be made when:

i)   An individual dies with no qualifying private residence, or
ii)   An individual had a more valuable qualifying residence at some time in the past, but after 8th July 2015

There is no need to actually trace the sale proceeds of the former qualifying private residence; it is simply a case of using the amount of those proceeds to derive the available exemption. Nonetheless, the relief may only be claimed against amounts, or the value of assets, which actually do go to qualifying beneficiaries or trusts. Furthermore, only actual sale proceeds (not deemed proceeds) may be used in the calculation of the relief available.

A widow or widower may include any residence nil rate band transferred from their former spouse within their 'downsizing' claim. The maximum amount which can be claimed under these provisions is derived as follows:

i)   Calculate the proportion of the individual's maximum available residence nil rate band which is actually used against qualifying property on their death
ii)   Calculate the proportion of the individual's maximum available residence nil rate band which could have been used if the individual had died immediately before selling the former qualifying residence, based on the assumption that the actual sale proceeds received for the property represented its open market value
iii)   Deduct the proportion derived under step (i) from the proportion derived under step (ii)
iv)   The maximum relief available under the 'downsizing' provisions is derived by multiplying the individual's maximum available residence nil rate band by the proportion derived under step (iii)

For properties sold between 9th July 2015 and 5th April 2017, it is assumed for the purpose of step (ii) that the residence nil rate band for each individual was £100,000 at that time.

Example 1

Billie has been divorced for many years. In March 2017, she sold her house for £80,000 and moved into a nursing home. When she dies in June 2020, she does not own any qualifying property and she leaves her entire estate to her son Duke.

The sale proceeds for Billie's house amount to 80% of the maximum amount of residence nil rate band which is deemed to have been available to her at that time (£100,000). The maximum amount of residence nil rate band to which she would be entitled on her death is £175,000. Hence, she may claim an exemption of £140,000 (£175,000 x 80%) under the 'downsizing' provisions.

Example 2

Frank is a widower whose wife died many years ago with only a very modest estate. In August 2018, he sells his home for £225,000 and moves into a small bungalow. When Frank dies in July 2020, he leaves his entire estate to his daughter Nancy, including the bungalow which is then worth £105,000.

If Frank had died in August 2018, he would have been entitled to a maximum residence nil rate band of £250,000 (2 x £125,000). This included a full entitlement transferred from his late wife. The sale proceeds of £225,000 for his former home thus amount to 90% of his maximum entitlement at that time (£225,000/£250,000 = 90%).

When he dies in July 2020, his maximum residence nil rate band entitlement is £350,000 (2 x £175,000). He therefore only uses 30% of his entitlement (£105,000/£350,000 = 30%).

Frank is therefore able to claim 60% (90% - 30%) of his maximum residence nil rate band entitlement under the 'downsizing' provisions. £210,000 (£350,000 x 60%) of the other assets left to Nancy can therefore be exempted under the residence nil rate band in addition to Frank's bungalow.

Wealth Warning

Where an individual dies owning one or more qualifying private residences, they cannot claim any relief under the 'downsizing' provisions unless they also leave at least one of those properties to qualifying beneficiaries or trusts.

12.17 MAKING THE MOST OF THE RESIDENCE NIL RATE BAND

Thanks to the 'downsizing' provisions described in the previous section, many married couples, widows, and widowers will be able to get the maximum benefit from the residence nil rate band by ensuring that they own a private residence worth at least £350,000 at some stage after 8th July 2015.

To get the maximum possible relief, they will also need to ensure that they:

- Sell the property for actual proceeds (rather than give it away, etc),
- Do eventually leave at least one of any qualifying properties that they own at the time of their death to their direct descendants, or a suitable trust for their benefit (see Section 8.6), and
- Also leave sufficient further sums to qualifying beneficiaries or trusts in order to fully utilise the relief available under the 'downsizing' provisions

The second and third steps can take place on the second death where the couple are currently both still alive. The second step becomes unnecessary where no qualifying properties are held at the time of death.

Earlier Property Sales

The maximum potential residence nil rate band can also be obtained through earlier sales of qualifying property for at least the following amounts:

Sales between 9th July 2015 and 5th April 2018:   £200,000
Sales during 2018/19:   £250,000
Sales during 2019/20:   £300,000

Single People & Unmarried Couples

All of the same principles apply to single or divorced people. All of the amounts are simply halved.

For an unmarried couple, it will be necessary for each person's **share** of the property to be sold for at least the appropriate amount (e.g. for at least £125,000 in the case of a sale during 2018/19). The second and third steps described above will also need to take place on **each** death.

Chapter 13

The Pre-Owned Assets Charge

13.1   WHAT IS THE PRE-OWNED ASSETS CHARGE?

An Income Tax charge is levied on the former owner of any asset who continues to benefit from that asset. In many cases, the charge will also extend to a donor who benefits from the use of assets purchased with funds which they had previously gifted.

Typically, in the case of 'real' property, (i.e. land and buildings), the 'benefit' arises by reason of the fact that the donor continues to live in the property.

The property or other assets subject to the charge are known as 'pre-owned assets' and, broadly, the charge taxes the 'annual value' of these assets as a benefit-in-kind on the former owner still benefiting from them.

For real property, the annual value on which the charge is based is the property's open-market rental value. For most other assets to which the charge applies, it is based on a fixed sum of 5% of their capital value.

The values to be used in these calculations are those prevailing at the date on which the asset first falls within these provisions. The initial value derived can be used for five years before the asset must be revalued.

Any amounts which the former owner is paying for the use of the asset may be deducted from the annual value in arriving at the taxable benefit. These payments must be made under a legal obligation, however, so, in the case of property, a formal lease will be required.

The charge is designed to hit back at a number of IHT planning schemes, but also catches many unintended and innocent victims.

13.2   EXEMPTIONS

Thankfully there are a few exemptions from the charge, which, broadly speaking, will not apply where:

i)   The asset was gifted before 18th March 1986

ii)   The asset was transferred to the donor's spouse, or to a former spouse under the terms of a court order

iii) The asset was transferred to a trust for the benefit of the donor's spouse, or to a trust for the benefit of a former spouse under the terms of a court order. This exemption will cease to apply if the transferee's interest in possession (see Chapter 8) comes to an end before their death

iv) The asset was transferred for the purposes of 'maintenance of family' (see Sections 5.6 and 5.7)

v) There was an outright gift of the asset to an individual, which was wholly covered by the annual exemption or the small gifts exemption

vi) The asset was acquired with funds derived from an earlier gift by the taxpayer which itself would have fallen within one or more of items (i) to (v) above

vii) The asset is, in fact, still in your estate for IHT purposes, or is treated as such due to the Gifts with Reservation Rules (hence, you generally shouldn't get caught for both taxes on the same asset)

viii) The taxpayer's entire interest in the asset was sold on commercial, arm's length terms (even to a connected party)

ix) A part interest in an asset is also exempted if it was sold on normal, commercial, arm's length terms:
   a. To an unconnected party,
   b. Before 7th March 2005, or
   c. For a consideration not in the form of money or other assets readily convertible into money

x) The donor's ownership of the asset ceased as a result of a deed of variation (see Section 16.1)

xi) The donor's continued enjoyment of the asset has arisen only as a result of an unforeseen change in circumstances which has left them unable to care for themselves

xii) The donor's enjoyment of the asset is minor and incidental, such as social visits to the current occupier

xiii) The donor's total annual taxable benefits under the pre-owned asset rules, **before** deducting any contributions paid by the donor, do not exceed £5,000. Note that this is an 'all or nothing' exemption and, if total taxable benefits reach £5,001, then the **whole** of this sum (less any donor contributions) is taxed!

xiv) The asset was acquired with funds derived from an outright gift of money made seven years or more before the donor first enjoyed any benefit from the asset

xv) The original gift of the asset was exempt for IHT purposes under one of the exemptions in Section 3.5 (gifts to charities and other exempt bodies)

xvi) The donor has retained a suitable interest in the gifted asset, such as in the case of a parent who has given a joint share in a property to an adult child who lives with them in that property. This exemption would not apply, however, where the parent gave their adult child cash or another asset with which the child funded their share of a joint purchase

xvii) The donor is non-UK resident

HMRC has also confirmed that the charge should not apply in most cases where a taxpayer has funded life policies held on trust (see Section 10.14). The charge is also excluded where the taxpayer has merely acted as a guarantor in respect of a loan made to another person to enable them to acquire the relevant asset.

See Appendix C for a list of the persons regarded as 'connected parties' for the purposes of the pre-owned assets charge.

13.3   OPTING OUT

There is a 'Get Out Of Jail - But Not Free' card in the shape of an option to elect out of the pre-owned assets Income Tax charge by allowing the relevant asset to be included back in the donor's estate for IHT purposes.

The asset is then treated as a 'Gift with Reservation' (see Section 4.9) and effectively remains in the donor's estate for as long as they continue to enjoy a benefit from it. Hence, in the case of a property, if the donor moves out and manages to survive for seven years, they will have managed to avoid both the Income Tax charge and IHT on the property.

The election to opt out of the pre-owned assets charge should be made by 31st January following the tax year in which the charge would otherwise have first arisen. HMRC will, however, generally accept late elections. Once made, the election is irrevocable.

13.4   IMPLICATIONS FOR PLANNING WITH THE FAMILY HOME

Several of the planning techniques outlined in the previous chapter involve the taxpayer or their surviving spouse having continued enjoyment of their family home. In this section, we will assess the potential impact of the pre-owned assets charge on these planning techniques.

'Move Out and Then Give It Away' (12.2)

No charges should arise as long as the donor never moves back into the property, or only does so due to an unforeseen change in circumstances which has left them unable to care for themselves.

Care must also be taken that the donor never benefits from any other asset purchased with the proceeds of a subsequent sale of the original property.

'Sell Up and Give Away The Proceeds' (12.3); 'Re-Mortgage and Give Away The Proceeds' (12.4) and 'Re-Mortgage and Buy An Annuity' (12.5)

There should be no problems with any of these techniques as long as the donor does not benefit from the use of any asset purchased with the proceeds within a period of seven years after making their cash gifts.

Some concern did initially arise that 'equity release schemes', under which many retired people give their property to a financial institution in exchange for an annuity, might be caught. Thankfully, however, it has been confirmed that no charge will apply where a homeowner has entered a commercial equity release scheme.

'Sell Up or Re-Mortgage and Invest The Proceeds' (12.6); 'Sale At Market Value' (12.7) and 'Widow's Loan Scheme' (12.8)

No pre-owned asset charge can arise under these techniques.

'Leave A Share To The Children' (12.9); 'Children Put Their Share Into Trust' (12.10) and 'Leave A Share To A Discretionary Trust' (12.11)

If the surviving spouse had originally given a share in the property to the deceased, or had given them the funds with which to purchase their share, and had done so before they were married, then the pre-owned asset charge may arise.

Additionally, under the 'Children Put Their Share Into Trust' technique, the beneficiaries under the deceased's Will must be careful not to have any use or enjoyment of the property during the life interest of the surviving spouse. If they were to use the property whilst the spouse's life interest continued, they would face a pre-owned assets charge. Minor and incidental use of the property, such as limited social visits, is, however, permitted.

The 'Full Consideration' Method (12.12)

This method should avoid the pre-owned assets charge, owing to the fact that the donor of the property is making full payment for their continued use of it. It is *essential*, however, that the donor's rental payments are made under a formal lease and are reviewed every five years, in line with the pre-owned assets revaluation rules.

'Co-Ownership' (12.13)

HMRC has specifically confirmed that this method will not be caught under the pre-owned assets charge.

'Shearing' (12.14)

After some initial hesitation, HMRC eventually accepted that this method does work for IHT purposes and therefore can be caught by the pre-owned assets charge.

'The Three-Way Split' (12.15)

As with 'Leave a Share to the Children', there is a risk of a pre-owned assets charge if the survivor had funded the purchase of the property prior to marriage. Otherwise, the scheme would appear to avoid the pre-owned assets charge.

13.5   TAX CHARGES AND DOMICILE

For UK resident and domiciled taxpayers (see Chapter 14), the pre-owned assets charge applies to any relevant assets worldwide, except as noted below. This extends to those with deemed UK domicile (see Section 2.2), or who have 'opted in' (see Section 6.19).

For those who did not have a UK 'Domicile of Origin' (see Chapter 14), but who have subsequently acquired actual or deemed UK domicile, or who have 'opted in', the charge will not apply to any non-UK assets in an excluded property trust (see Section 9.11).

For taxpayers who are UK resident, but non-UK domiciled, not deemed UK domiciled, and who have not 'opted in', the pre-owned assets charge can apply only to any relevant assets situated in the UK.

Chapter 14

Domicile

14.1 WHAT IS DOMICILE?

In essence, your 'domicile' is the country which you consider to be your permanent home. This does not necessarily equate to your country of birth, nor to the country in which you happen to be living at present.

Domicile should not be confused with residence, which is a far more transitory concept (but see Section 2.2 regarding deemed domicile).

At this point, it is worth noting that, technically speaking, you cannot actually have 'UK domicile' but will, instead, have your domicile in England and Wales, Scotland or Northern Ireland. As we saw in Sections 10.11 and 10.12, this can be very important when it comes to intestacy or 'legal rights'.

However, it is usually safe to simply refer to 'UK domicile' for IHT purposes. Nonetheless, we will see some instances where the distinction between the different parts of the UK can be quite important later in this chapter.

It is also worth noting that the Channel Islands and the Isle of Man are not part of the UK for tax purposes, including IHT and domicile.

14.2 DOMICILE OF ORIGIN

At birth, each person acquires the domicile of the person on whom they are legally dependent at that time. That person will usually be their father, but it is their mother if their father is dead or their parents are living apart and they have a home with their mother, but not with their father. The domicile which you acquire at this point is known as your 'Domicile of Origin'.

Throughout your minority, you continue to have the same domicile as the person on whom you are legally dependent. If that person changes their domicile during this period then your domicile also changes and you acquire a 'Domicile of Dependency'.

You only become capable of having your own independent domicile when you reach the age of 16 (or, in Scotland, 14 for a boy or 12 for a girl).

Example
Farrokh was born in Zanzibar in 1946 and lived with both of his parents at that time. His father was domiciled in India and his mother was domiciled in Zanzibar. Farrokh therefore acquired an Indian Domicile of Origin. In 1960, Farrokh's parents moved to England, taking Farrokh with them. They intended to remain in England permanently. At this point, Farrokh therefore acquired a UK Domicile of Dependency.

Re-acquiring a Domicile of Origin

If it ever becomes uncertain which country you regard as your permanent home, your domicile will revert to your Domicile of Origin. Your domicile always reverts to your Domicile of Origin under these circumstances and not any Domicile of Dependency which you may have had.

Domicile and Marriage

Subject to the 'opt-in' election described below, marriage does not generally affect domicile. However, women other than US Nationals, who married before 1st January 1974, adopted their husband's domicile at the date of marriage as a Domicile of Dependency.

Non-UK domiciled individuals with a UK domiciled spouse may elect to be treated as UK domiciled for IHT purposes. See Section 6.19 for further details.

14.3 DOMICILE OF CHOICE

In most cases, a person's Domicile of Origin remains their domicile for the rest of their life. A different domicile can only be acquired, as a 'Domicile of Choice', where a person emigrates and can prove their intention to reside permanently or indefinitely in their new home country.

Acquiring a new domicile for tax purposes, as a 'Domicile of Choice', can be very difficult. This is both good news and bad news since it cuts both ways and HMRC has had just as much difficulty proving that a taxpayer has acquired the UK as their Domicile of Choice as taxpayers have had in proving they have acquired a domicile somewhere else.

To acquire a new domicile, as a Domicile of Choice, it is necessary to not only demonstrate an intention to adopt the new country as your permanent home, but also to follow this up by action and subsequent conduct.

If the taxpayer abandons their Domicile of Choice, without demonstrating a clear intention to adopt a new Domicile of Choice somewhere else, then their domicile automatically reverts to their Domicile of Origin.

Example

Brian has a UK Domicile of Origin. Twenty years ago, he emigrated to Spain and became Spanish domiciled. He declared this intention on form P85, which he lodged with the Inland Revenue (now HMRC) shortly before he departed for the Costa del Sol. In 2018, Brian gets a terrific offer to work in Los Angeles, so he leaves Spain and moves to California. Brian is uncertain, however, whether he wishes to remain in California permanently. As Brian's permanent home is now unclear, his domicile reverts to the UK!

Wealth Warning 1

If you intend to emigrate to avoid UK IHT, make sure you pick the right country first time! Although Brian might eventually be able to establish Californian domicile, this will now be more difficult for him because he has established a 'track record' of abandoning his so-called 'permanent home' and it will be harder to prove that he has no intention of ever returning to the UK.

Wealth Warning 2

Note that I referred to 'Californian' domicile above and not to US domicile. Strictly speaking, domicile relates to a 'territory' rather than a country (e.g. to a State in the USA). In countries with a federal system, like the USA, you will need to decide which territory you are adopting as your new permanent home, not just which country.

This may severely restrict your future freedom of movement. California may be big enough, but what about Rhode Island?

Wealth Warning 3

Another important point to note about emigrating to avoid IHT is that you will continue to be **_deemed_** UK domiciled at the time of your death if you were still UK domiciled under general principles at any time in the preceding five years. (For those who left the UK before 6th April 2017, this additional period of deemed UK domicile was three years.)

As explained in Section 2.2, this may be affected by one of the Double Tax Treaties listed in Appendix B.

Emigrating to avoid IHT must therefore be done early and carefully.

14.4 A GUIDE TO EMIGRATION

There is no set procedure for establishing a Domicile of Choice through permanent emigration. Like many things in the tax world, each individual case will be examined on its own particular merits. Here, however, are a few practical tips to follow:

- Declare your intentions to HMRC on forms P85 and DOM1 before leaving the UK
- Buy a home in your new country
- Take your family with you (including the pets)
- Take whatever steps you can to establish citizenship, nationality, etc, in your new country
- Take up employment in your new country (or, alternatively, establish your own business there)
- Get on the electoral roll in your new country

- Buy a grave plot in your new country (this is given a great deal of importance by the tax authorities when looking at domicile)
- Try to visit the UK as little as possible
- Make sure that your former home in the UK is not available for your use: preferably, it should be sold
- Ensure that residential accommodation is not available to you elsewhere in the UK: if you must visit the UK, try to stay in hotels
- Sell as many UK assets as you can and close your UK bank accounts
- Resign membership of any clubs, associations, etc, in the UK. Ideally, you should try to make a 'clean break' with your previous life in the UK
- Write letters or emails (e.g. to your solicitor) which express your intention of never returning to reside in the UK
- Write a Will in your new country
- Try not to move on again to another territory

Following the above guidelines should generally also ensure you become non-UK resident as well as non-UK domiciled. In fact, non-UK residence is generally a lot easier to achieve. Nevertheless, the statutory residence test (see the Taxcafe.co.uk guide *"Tax Free Capital Gains"* for details) could potentially lead to a few instances where an individual manages to achieve non-UK domicile but remains UK resident for tax purposes.

From 2017/18 onwards, any person with a UK Domicile of Origin who has obtained an overseas Domicile of Choice is deemed to be UK domiciled for any UK tax year for which they are UK resident. Hence, from an IHT planning perspective, it remains essential to also achieve non-UK residence under the statutory residence test, as well as non-UK domicile.

However, I must stress that, in the vast majority of cases, becoming non-UK resident is not enough to ensure you have become non-UK domiciled. The statutory residence test is merely an additional hurdle to be overcome: there is a great deal more involved in obtaining a new Domicile of Choice!

For the reasons explained under Wealth Warning 2 in the previous section, you may need to think in terms of your new home territory, rather than country, when applying the above guidelines (e.g. Queensland rather than Australia).

If you really must retain any connections with the UK (and I don't recommend it), try to make it a different part of the UK. For example, if you have an English Domicile of Origin and you wish to keep a UK bank account, make it an account with a Scottish or Northern Irish branch.

14.5 SHEDDING A UK DOMICILE OF DEPENDENCY

If you have a UK Domicile of Dependency but a non-UK Domicile of Origin, it will be far easier for you to re-acquire your Domicile of Origin than to acquire a Domicile of Choice.

In this situation, you only need to leave your Domicile of Dependency for long enough to be in a position where the country which is your permanent home is uncertain in order to re-acquire your non-UK Domicile of Origin.

Remember also that England and Wales, Scotland and Northern Ireland are all different territories for this purpose. Hence, for example, a person with an English Domicile of Dependency might be able to shed that domicile by moving to Scotland or Northern Ireland, even if they do not intend to remain there permanently.

Shedding a UK Domicile of Dependency will not, however, prevent you from becoming deemed UK domiciled after 15 years of UK residence (see Section 2.2).

14.6 RETAINING A DOMICILE OF ORIGIN

If you are lucky enough to have a non-UK Domicile of Origin it is far, far, easier to retain this as your domicile than it is to acquire a Domicile of Choice.

As stated above, it is very difficult for HMRC to prove that an individual has acquired a new Domicile of Choice. This is especially true if the individual themselves states that it is their intention to return to their country of origin one day.

Example

Thais was born in Brazil, of Brazilian parents. She has, however, lived in the UK for over 30 years, having moved here in her early twenties. Despite this, she has always stated that she intends to return 'home' when she retires. Thais therefore remains domiciled in Brazil.

In **this** case, an 'intention' does not have to be backed up by action but should be more than a vague notion that you would like to 'die in the land of your fathers'. Intentions such as 'to retire to your home country' or to 'return home after your spouse's death' are the sort of thing which would usually suffice.

To confirm your non-UK domiciled status, you should complete form DOM1, declaring yourself to be non-UK domiciled, and submit it to HMRC.

It may also be worth buying a grave plot in the country which is your Domicile of Origin. This is accepted as a very strong indication of your intention to return to that country at some future date.

It is worth remembering that you will retain your Domicile of Origin as long as there is some doubt about where you intend to make your permanent home. It might therefore be sufficient to state that you intend to 'retire abroad' as long as there is some reasonable substance to your intentions. You might even retain a non-UK Domicile of Origin by expressing doubt about whether you intend to live in England or Scotland!

Sadly, as explained in Section 2.2, none of this may actually save any IHT if you are deemed to be UK domiciled for IHT purposes as a consequence of being resident here for more than 15 of the last 20 years. (Subject to the terms of a Double Tax Treaty if you are domiciled in one of the countries listed in Appendix B.)

To ensure that you don't end up with deemed UK Domicile for IHT purposes, you should try to spend five years out of every twenty abroad (or one in four, if you prefer). This does not have to be in the same country as your Domicile of Origin.

Wealth Warning

Non-UK domiciled individuals resident in the UK for seven or more of the previous nine UK tax years may be subject to punitive Income Tax charges unless they elect to suffer UK tax on all their foreign income and capital gains.

Chapter 15

The Inheritance Tax Planning Timetable

15.1 IT'S NEVER TOO EARLY TO START

Most tax advisers will tell you it's never too early to start IHT planning, but when you're struggling to pay a mortgage and make some headway at the beginning of your working career, IHT will probably be the last thing on your mind.

Nevertheless, as we saw in Section 9.3, the earlier you start, the more effective your planning will be, and if you are lucky enough to have the wealth to follow the kind of planning in that section, long term planning will help to pass on more family wealth to the next generation, or even the one after that.

Even if you have little wealth, your first step should be to ensure that any life policies are written in favour of other family members.

15.2 MARRIAGE

First of all, marriage is a good time to remind the family to do their IHT planning by making the exempt gifts set out in Section 5.5. This is also a good time to put money into trust for your own children, even before they're born!

Next, remember to make a new Will. An existing Will is rendered void on marriage or civil partnership unless it was actually made in contemplation of your union.

Once you are married, it may be worth taking steps to ensure that your nil rate band is fully available to transfer to your spouse on your death. As we saw in Chapter 6, this may not always be the best course of action but it is certainly something which you should at least consider.

15.3 BECOMING A PARENT

This is the one which focuses the mind and gets most people thinking about IHT planning.

It's time to step up the ante a little and begin to think about tax efficient trust structures for your children (see Section 10.18). Get your parents to give money directly to your children instead of to you (if you can afford to do without it).

It's time to re-write your Will again as well; you will need to think about how to provide for your children if you die prematurely. Consider what kind of structure you would like to put in place from the choices available (see Chapter 8). Don't forget to appoint a guardian too!

Now that you're a parent, the residence nil rate band comes into play and you should start to factor it into your planning (see Sections 3.4, 12.16 and 12.17).

15.4   ADULT CHILDREN

You can now start giving assets directly to the children without the need for any trust structures. Making use of the annual exemption may make sense, although most of us seem to have little choice anyway!

Normal expenditure out of income can be established to pass on substantial sums to the children and when they marry, you can use the exemptions in Section 5.5.

You may want to consider putting a 'family debt scheme' in place (see Section 6.16).

15.5   YOUR FIRST GRANDCHILD

Time to start looking at trust structures again; as we saw in Section 10.18, gifts to grandchildren are much more tax effective. Bare trusts for grandchildren are really useful and avoid the 'Gift with Reservation' problems which you tend to get with your own minor children.

You may want to re-write your Will again. Think about 'skipping a generation'. What's the point of leaving the money to the children if they're already well established? It might be better left to the grandchildren, so that IHT doesn't come up again for another two generations.

15.6   LOSING A PARENT

If one of your parents dies intestate or with a Will which isn't tax efficient, a deed of variation (Section 16.1) can be used to put IHT planning into place retrospectively.

When your first parent dies, you should consider whether it is better for them to use their nil rate band on assets which might be appreciating in value (see Section 6.7) or for it to transfer to your surviving parent (assuming they are still married).

If you don't need the money, get your legacies transferred to your children (or even grandchildren) instead.

Gifts to charity may also reduce the IHT bill (see Sections 3.6 and 16.1 regarding recent developments in this area).

15.7   STILL TOGETHER

Elderly married couples face a bit of a dilemma under the transferable nil rate band regime. If you're both getting older, it may make sense to start giving away surplus wealth as potentially exempt transfers which will hopefully become exempt if you survive seven years.

Before 2007, there appeared to be no 'downside' to such gifts, as savings could be made as long as you survived at least three years and, even if you did not, there was really nothing to lose (except for 'Gifts with Reservation' – see Section 4.9).

Now, however, we know that if you die within seven years of making any potentially exempt transfer or chargeable lifetime transfer, this will restrict the proportion of your nil rate band which transfers to your spouse. As we saw in Chapter 6, this may have adverse consequences, although there are also times when such transfers will still be advantageous, especially when assets which are appreciating in value are gifted.

You need to weigh up these conflicting factors before making any lifetime transfers which are not immediately exempt. Whilst such transfers may sometimes be beneficial for elderly married people, any potential impact on your surviving spouse's transferable nil rate band should also be considered.

If you do decide to make any lifetime transfers which are not immediately exempt, it will generally make sense for these to be made by the spouse with the longer life expectancy.

15.8   LOSING A SPOUSE

You have two years to put a deed of variation into place to make sure your late spouse's estate is dealt with tax efficiently. Obviously, the key point is to maximise the benefit of their nil rate band, either by having it transfer to you or by using it to pass on appreciating assets free from IHT (see Section 6.7).

If your spouse leaves any property qualifying for business or agricultural property relief, it may make sense to pass this directly to the children in case the relief is later lost. This is often particularly important in the case of a family farm where the surviving spouse may no longer be able to run it. Alternatively, you may want to put a 'double dip' in place (see Section 7.33).

This is also a good time to assess your own financial needs and to start making plans to give away any surplus. Consider your own life expectancy and review the appropriate action set out in Sections 15.10 to 15.12.

15.9   REMARRIAGE

Remarriage provides another opportunity to make some of the exempt gifts outlined in Section 5.5. On this occasion, the ability to make tax-exempt transfers into trust for the benefit of your children may be particularly useful.

If either or both of you is a widow or widower, you may have an existing transferable nil rate band entitlement (see Section 6.8). If so, you should now consider taking steps to maximise the benefit of your existing transferable nil rate band. The methods discussed in Sections 6.9 to 6.12 and Sections 12.8 to 12.11 are all available to save your family up to £260,000.

This is also a good time to consider your new combined estate and decide whether there are surplus assets which can be given away. If your spouse already has an existing full transferable nil rate band entitlement, you will be able to make lifetime transfers without risking any loss of relief. If they have an existing partial transferable nil rate band entitlement, some lifetime transfers may still be made without risk.

Once again, you should re-write your Will, as any previous Will not made in contemplation of your new marriage will be rendered void.

15.10   LIFE EXPECTANCY OVER SEVEN YEARS
(Per Office for National Statistics: men under 83 and women under 85)

There's still time to make potentially exempt transfers which should hopefully have time to become fully exempt. Ending the 'reservation' on a 'Gift with Reservation' will give it time to become exempt also. Remember, if you are single and survive at least three years, some savings may still be made. If you are still married, however, some caution may be required (see Section 15.7, but also Section 15.9 if this is not your or your spouse's first marriage).

15.11   LIFE EXPECTANCY THREE TO SEVEN YEARS
(Men aged 83 to 94 and women aged 85 to 95)

Transfers made now should still benefit from tapering (see Section 4.5), so some tax may be saved if you are single. Transfers by married people at this stage carry a strong risk of having an adverse impact on your spouse's transferable nil rate band unless they are immediately exempt (see Section 15.7 but also Section 15.9 if this is not your or your spouse's first marriage).

For all people at this stage, whether married or not, it's time to really start making the most of the annual exemption, the small gifts exemption and normal expenditure out of income (these are all immediately exempt).

A loan trust or discounted gift trust may make sense at this point, and possibly also gifts of appreciating assets not qualifying for business property relief (but see Chapter 11 regarding the CGT implications).

You may be able to avoid IHT by emigrating. If you survive for at least five years after establishing non-UK domicile, you can avoid IHT on any non-UK assets.

15.12   LIFE EXPECTANCY TWO TO THREE YEARS
(Men aged 94 to 100 and women aged 95 to 101)

Now's the time to think seriously about those AIM shares, but never forgetting 'Dodgy Dave' (see Section 10.2).

Anything which gets your money into qualifying business property (see Chapter 7) may still enable you to save IHT if you can survive two years. Rights issues and transfers of assets into a company under your control may provide immediate savings.

Loan trusts and discounted gift trusts may still save you money even now, as well as other transfers of appreciating property (but watch the CGT situation).

15.13   LOSS OF CAPACITY

If you expect to lose the ability to take care of your own affairs in the near future, it will make sense to appoint a power of attorney.

A power of attorney, or next of kin, can apply to the Court of Protection to make a Statutory Will on your behalf.

The Court of Protection can also authorise your power of attorney to make lifetime gifts on your behalf for IHT planning purposes and is generally sympathetic to applications made for this purpose.

15.14   DEATHBED PLANNING

So, if you've really left it far too late, what can still be done?

Some of this may seem a little flippant and I have no wish to cause any offence to anyone. Tax planning may be the farthest thing from your mind at this point and who could really blame you. Nevertheless, here are some of the things you could think about if time is running out:

Deathbed Marriage or Civil Partnership

The biggest deathbed planning point, if you're still single at this stage, is to marry your partner. No point trying to hang on to your freedom now, just get on with it!

It will almost always be worth marrying at this stage, even if you have very few assets, as any unused proportion of your nil rate band or residence nil rate band will transfer to your spouse.

Last Gasp Gifts

If you haven't used up your annual exemption (see Section 5.2) for this, or the previous, tax year, get gifting. If you've made no previous gifts, one simple £6,000 payment to one of your nearest and dearest will save your family £2,400.

For the rest of your family and friends, there's the Small Gifts Exemption (see Section 5.3). Every person you can find to give £250 will save your estate £100 in IHT.

Remember, however, as explained in Section 4.7, if made by cheque, these gifts will not be effective unless the cheque clears through the transferee's bank account before you pass away.

What About the House?

Although your family may be able to sort things out with a deed of variation (see Section 16.1), it may make things easier for them if you change the title to a tenancy in common now.

Maximising the Residence Nil Rate Band

As explained in Section 3.4, some or all of the residence nil rate band is withdrawn if your estate is worth more than £2m at the time of your death.

Hence, whilst potentially exempt and chargeable lifetime transfers made shortly before your death will not usually save IHT, it may be possible to use them to reduce the value of your estate and thus prevent your residence nil rate band from being withdrawn.

Example

It is May 2020 and Nelson, a widower, is dying. His late wife Sheena died some years earlier, leaving all of her modest estate to him.

Nelson's estate is worth £2.7m, including his home, worth £1m, which he plans to leave to his children, and various cash and savings totalling £700,000.

As things stand, Nelson's residence nil rate band will be completely withdrawn by tapering and the IHT on his estate will total £820,000 (£2.7m - £650,000 = £2.05m x 40% = £820,000).

Instead, Nelson gives all of his cash and savings to his children shortly before he dies. These transfers become chargeable on his death and IHT of £20,000 (£700,000 - £650,000 = £50,000 x 40% = £20,000) will be payable on them.

However, the gifts reduce the value of Nelson's estate to £2m, meaning he will be entitled to a residence nil rate band of £350,000. IHT of £660,000 (£2m - £350,000 = £1.65m x 40% = £660,000) will now be payable on his estate.

The total IHT arising on Nelson's death is thus £680,000 (£20,000 + £660,000), meaning that the lifetime gifts have led to a saving of £140,000 (£820,000 - £680,000).

A married person could easily reduce the value of their estate to £2m by giving the excess to their spouse shortly before they died. This would generally be an exempt transfer (unless the couple had 'mixed domicile': see Section 6.18) and would have no impact on the transferable nil rate band; but it would mean that the deceased's residence nil rate band was available to transfer to their widow or widower.

Where assets other than cash are transferred, the CGT consequences will need to be considered. We looked at these in detail in Chapter 11. However, in some cases, it may be worth taking a CGT hit to save more in IHT.

Example Revisited

The facts are exactly as set out above, except Nelson transfers various assets worth £700,000 to his children rather than cash. The transferred assets stand at an overall capital gain of £500,000 and do not include any residential property. Nelson is a higher rate taxpayer and has used his annual CGT exemption already, so CGT of £100,000 arises on the transfer. Nelson's CGT liability is deducted from his estate, so this increases the total IHT saving to £180,000 (£140,000 + £100,000 x 40%). Overall, the family still remains £80,000 better off (£180,000 - £100,000).

For transfers to a spouse (as defined for CGT purposes: see Section 11.6), there would be no immediate CGT cost but the 'uplift on death' (see Section 11.2) would be lost and this may eventually lead to a higher CGT cost which should therefore be taken into account.

Remember Your Normal Gifts

The exemption for normal expenditure out of income (see Section 5.8) applies to lifetime gifts only. To get that final year's exemption you need to make sure you've made that expenditure before you go.

Spend!

"There are no pockets in shrouds" they say, so why not spend it before HM Treasury gets hold of it.

Any money you can spend which qualifies as 'maintenance of family' (see Section 5.6) will escape IHT. For example, you could spend £1,000 buying clothes for your teenage daughter instead of leaving her a legacy of £1,000 which produces an IHT charge of £667.

You could also think about buying depreciating assets. "How will that help my family?" you may ask, but think about this:

Example

Ian knows he has only a few months to live and wants to give his friend Chas a last gift. What Chas would really like is a new car and the model he has his eye on, a 'Rhythm Stick Blockhead', costs £50,000 new.

Ian therefore buys a 'Rhythm Stick Blockhead' but doesn't give it to Chas straight away. Instead, Ian leaves the car to Chas in his Will.

When Ian dies a few months later, the car, now second-hand, is worth only £35,000 and this is the value to be used for IHT purposes. If Ian had simply given the car to Chas brand new, a sum of £50,000 would have been included in his estate. Hence, by leaving the car in his Will instead, Ian has saved up to £6,000 in IHT.

Contractual Obligations

The liabilities under any contractual obligations existing at the date of your death will be deductible from your estate provided that they meet the rules set out in Section 2.12. Hence, if your beneficiaries would like something done to any asset which is about to pass to them under the terms of your Will, why not contract for the work to be done at your expense?

Review (or Make) Your Will

Whilst you're still of sound mind, there is still time to change (or make) your Will. Maximising the value of your nil rate band should be top of the list if you are married (see Chapter 6 for full details) and you should consider the residence nil rate band if you have children or grandchildren.

As we shall see in Section 16.1, your beneficiaries can always do a deed of variation within the next two years as long as all affected parties agree. What you might need to consider at this stage, however, is whether there are any beneficiaries in your current Will who are likely to stand in the way of any IHT saving measures by refusing to agree to a deed of variation.

Furthermore, as we shall see in Section 16.1, deeds of variation do have some significant drawbacks which can be avoided by making the relevant provisions in your Will instead.

The easiest way to save IHT at this stage is to change your Will to leave some or all of your estate to charity (see Section 3.5). Your existing beneficiaries may not be entirely happy about this, but it's your decision (mostly – see Section 10.12).

If you wish to benefit from the additional relief for charitable legacies which we examined in Section 3.6, you will need to include them in your Will and there are also other doubts over the effectiveness of putting charitable donations in place via a deed of variation which we'll look at in Section 16.1.

All in all, whilst deeds of variation are an extremely useful IHT planning tool, it will generally make sense to put as much of your IHT planning measures in place via your Will as you can.

Go Home or Stay Away

In Chapter 14, we looked at the issues of retaining a foreign 'Domicile of Origin', shedding a UK 'Domicile of Dependency' or obtaining a foreign 'Domicile of Choice'.

In borderline cases, the final outcome regarding your domicile will be heavily influenced by your final actions. To keep or re-acquire a foreign Domicile of Origin, it may be wise to go home to die.

To maintain a foreign 'Domicile of Choice' it will be best if you remain in your adopted country. Buying a grave plot and arranging your funeral in your new adopted country will also be helpful to your cause.

Maximise Your Business Property

Whilst, as explained in Section 7.17, the business property itself needs to have been held for at least two years in order to qualify for business property relief, you can enhance the value of existing business property at any time.

This might, for example, include:

- Paying business debts from private resources
- Rights issues of shares by a qualifying private company
- Transferring assets into a qualifying private company (see Section 7.22 for more details)

Transferring assets to a company may, however, have CGT consequences and these must be borne in mind.

Remember that if you have disposed of qualifying business property within the last three years, you can restore full business property relief by buying replacement property (see Section 7.18), including qualifying AIM shares.

Deathbed CGT Planning

What you generally should **not** do at this stage is to make any disposals which give rise to CGT liabilities. (Although there are exceptions, as we have already seen.)

If you sell assets before you die, your estate will be liable for the CGT arising based on your original base costs for those assets. Subject to this liability, however, the net proceeds of the sale will remain in your estate and will still be subject to IHT.

If you hang on to those assets, the IHT may be a little greater (as there is no CGT liability to deduct) but, as we saw in Chapter 11, your personal representatives or your beneficiaries will be able to sell them later with little or no CGT liability. Conversely, therefore, the best deathbed planning for CGT purposes might be to accumulate more assets – especially from your spouse! (See Section 11.6)

Chapter 16

Planning After Death

16.1   DEEDS OF VARIATION

Perhaps the 'last resort' in IHT planning is the deed of variation.

Deeds of variation are an essential planning tool where a family finds that the terms of the deceased's Will (or intestacy) have an undesired effect for IHT purposes.

Where all affected beneficiaries are in agreement, it is possible to vary the Will in order to create a better IHT result.

As the deed of variation is a legally binding document, it is wise to consult a lawyer when completing it. Strictly speaking, the IHT rules only require the document to be a written instrument, although a formal deed is generally recommended.

Conditions

   i)   The required variations must be recorded in writing within two years of the death (this is the deed).
   ii) All existing beneficiaries affected by the variations to the Will or intestacy should sign the deed. (New beneficiaries benefitting from the variations do not need to sign, although this does no harm.)
   iii) The deed should include a statement that the signatories intend the deed to have effect for IHT purposes.
   iv) Where the deed results in additional IHT being payable on the deceased's death, a copy must be sent to HMRC within six months of the date of the deed. At the same time, HMRC must also be notified of the amount of additional tax due.
   v)   The variation must not be made for any consideration in money or money's worth, except in the case of other compensatory variations to the deceased's Will or intestacy.

It is also common practice for the deceased's personal representatives to sign the deed, although this is no longer required by law.

Variations made by such a deed are treated for IHT purposes as if they had been made by the deceased.

This means that a beneficiary who becomes a party to a deed of variation and, as a result, gives up a right to all or part of their inheritance, is not themselves regarded as having made any transfer of value (neither chargeable nor otherwise).

Deeds of variation may be used to create any type of trust or to implement many of the other planning techniques described throughout this guide.

Deed of Variation Drawbacks

Variations made under a deed of variation effectively rewrite history and are treated as if they had been made by the deceased – *but only for IHT purposes!*

For CGT and Income Tax purposes, the original beneficiary (under the deceased's Will or under the laws of intestacy) is regarded as having made a transfer to the new beneficiary, or to any trust which receives property under the deed of variation.

This could result in the creation of a settlor-interested trust (see Section 9.8) or may invoke the settlements legislation where the new beneficiary is a minor child of the original beneficiary (see Section 10.18).

As explained in Section 3.6, it appears that a deed of variation cannot be used to increase the level of charitable legacies made by the deceased in order to enable their estate to benefit from the reduced rate of IHT applying where 10% or more of the 'net estate' is left to charity.

Furthermore, in a recent case, it was held that a deed of variation which put a charitable legacy in place was invalid. The argument was that by creating an IHT saving for the deceased's beneficiaries, it contravened condition (v) above.

The case involved a charitable trust created by the deceased's family so there were some special circumstances and it is therefore unclear just how widely this decision will be applied in future.

Nevertheless, the decision does cast serious doubt over the ability to use a deed of variation to create charitable legacies and it would therefore be wise to ensure that such legacies are made in the deceased's Will instead.

16.2   DISCLAIMERS

Under a slightly simpler procedure, a beneficiary may simply disclaim their inheritance. Only conditions (i) and (v) in the previous section need to be satisfied and the deed should only be signed by the person making the disclaimer.

The disclaimed inheritance will generally fall into the residue of the estate and will be dealt with accordingly.

This procedure will be particularly useful where nil rate band legacies have been included in Wills made prior to October 2007 and the family decide that it would now be more sensible for the surviving spouse, as the residuary beneficiary, to receive the entire estate.

In addition to its simplicity, a disclaimer has the added advantage that the disclaimed legacy is treated as passing directly from the deceased to the new beneficiary for Income Tax purposes. This is therefore a much better way to pass a legacy directly to the original beneficiary's minor child.

Disclaimer Drawbacks

A disclaimer is not possible where the original beneficiary has received any benefit from their legacy since the deceased's death (e.g. by living in an inherited property). However, it will often remain possible to use a deed of variation to achieve the same result instead – for IHT purposes at least!

16.3 TRANSFERS OUT OF TRUSTS WITHIN TWO YEARS OF DEATH

Transfers made out of a relevant property trust within two years of the deceased settlor's death are treated as if they were legacies made by the deceased directly. Such transfers are exempt from the exit charge (see Section 8.19).

Where the transferee is another trust, it will be treated as if it had been established under the deceased's Will. This provides scope to set up an immediate post-death interest, a bereaved minors' trust or an '18 to 25 Trust'.

In effect, this enables testators to create a discretionary trust under the terms of their Will which can be converted as appropriate within the two years following their death.

Wealth Warning

Once again, these provisions only apply for IHT purposes. Hence, the transfer out of the original relevant property trust will be subject to CGT in the normal way (see Section 11.10). Furthermore, holdover relief is not available under these circumstances.

The relevant property trust will also be liable for Income Tax on any income received prior to the transfer.

16.4 SECOND CHANCES

One might say that the procedures outlined under Sections 16.1 to 16.3 already provide a 'second chance' to get the IHT planning right. However, only one variation under the procedure in Section 16.1 is allowed in respect of any item of property. Similarly, only one transfer of any item of property can fall under the rules explained in Section 16.3.

It is possible for the same item of property to be subject to a deed of variation and to later be transferred out of a relevant property trust within the rules set out in Section 16.3 (or vice versa). Both the variation and the transfer must take place within two years of death to be effective for IHT purposes.

16.5   PET PROBLEMS

Where property is passed to a new beneficiary under either a deed of variation or by way of a transfer out of a relevant property trust within two years of the settlor's death, and the new beneficiary makes a potentially exempt transfer of that same property shortly afterwards, there is a strong chance that HMRC will apply the associated operations rules (Section 10.21). This would mean that the deceased is treated as having left the property directly to the ultimate recipient which, in most cases, is likely to make it fully chargeable to IHT.

16.6   POST-MORTEM RELIEF

Where a beneficiary sells certain types of inherited assets for less than their probate value the beneficiary may claim 'post-mortem' relief for their effective loss. The relief decreases the value of the deceased's estate for IHT purposes and a refund of the IHT already paid may be claimed where appropriate.

The relevant assets must be sold to an unconnected person (see Appendix C for a list of connected persons) on arms' length terms within a specified period after the deceased's death. The specified period depends on the type of asset sold, as follows:

- Quoted shares: twelve months
- Land and buildings: three years
- Related property (see Section 10.5): three years

A claim is not possible in respect of any other assets.

When making a claim, the beneficiary must take account of all sales within the relevant period. Hence, when some inherited assets have also been sold at a profit, it is only the beneficiary's overall net loss which may be claimed.

In effect, the values of all the inherited assets sold by the beneficiary within the specified period are adjusted to their sale price. This is to prevent 'cherry picking', i.e. only claiming for losses without taking account of profits.

Tax Tip
A form of 'cherry picking' can still be achieved by leaving the relevant assets to a discretionary trust in the first instance and then appointing all loss-making assets to one beneficiary prior to sale and within two years of the deceased's death. As explained in Section 16.3, the beneficiary is treated as if they had inherited these assets absolutely, thus enabling them to make the post-mortem relief claim.

The Nil Rate Band: 1914 - 2021

Estate Duty

16th August 1914 to	9th April 1946:	£100
10th April 1946 to	29th July 1954:	£2,000
30th July 1954 to	8th April 1962:	£3,000
9th April 1962 to	3rd April 1963:	£4,000
4th April 1963 to	15th April 1969:	£5,000
16th April 1969 to	31st March 1971:	£10,000
1st April 1971 to	21st March 1972:	£12,500
22nd March 1972 to	26th October 1977:	£15,000

Capital Transfer Tax

27th October 1977 to	25th March 1980:	£25,000
26th March 1980 to	8th March 1982:	£50,000
9th March 1982 to	14th March 1983:	£55,000
15th March 1983 to	12th March 1984:	£60,000
13th March 1984 to	5th April 1985:	£64,000
6th April 1985 to	17th March 1986:	£67,000

Inheritance Tax

18th March 1986 to	16th March 1987:	£71,000
17th March 1987 to	14th March 1988:	£90,000
15th March 1988 to	5th April 1989:	£110,000
6th April 1989 to	5th April 1990:	£118,000
6th April 1990 to	5th April 1991:	£128,000
6th April 1991 to	9th March 1992:	£140,000
10th March 1992 to	5th April 1995:	£150,000
6th April 1995 to	5th April 1996:	£154,000
6th April 1996 to	5th April 1997:	£200,000
6th April 1997 to	5th April 1998:	£215,000
6th April 1998 to	5th April 1999:	£223,000
6th April 1999 to	5th April 2000:	£231,000
6th April 2000 to	5th April 2001:	£234,000
6th April 2001 to	5th April 2002:	£242,000
6th April 2002 to	5th April 2003:	£250,000
6th April 2003 to	5th April 2004:	£255,000
6th April 2004 to	5th April 2005:	£263,000
6th April 2005 to	5th April 2006:	£275,000
6th April 2006 to	5th April 2007:	£285,000
6th April 2007 to	5th April 2008:	£300,000
6th April 2008 to	5th April 2009:	£312,000
6th April 2009 to	5th April 2021:	£325,000

Notes
1. Prior to 1972, there was a slight delay in implementing the increases to the nil rate band applying in Northern Ireland. The dates given above apply to the rest of the UK.
2. Capital Transfer Tax actually commenced on 13th March 1975 but the nil rate band initially remained the same.

Double Tax Treaties

Countries with which the UK Has Double Tax Treaties Covering Inheritance Tax

- France
- Irish Republic
- India
- Italy
- Netherlands
- Pakistan
- South Africa
- Sweden
- Switzerland
- USA

Appendix C

Connected Persons

The definition of 'connected persons' differs slightly from one area of UK tax law to another. Generally, however, an individual's connected persons include the following:

i)   Their husband, wife or civil partner

ii) The following relatives:
   o   Mother, father or remoter ancestor
   o   Son, daughter or remoter descendant
   o   Brother or sister

iii) Relatives under (ii) above of the individual's spouse or civil partner

iv) Spouses or civil partners of the individual's relatives under (ii) above

v)   The individual's business partners

vi) Companies under the control of the individual or of any of their relatives under (i) to (iv) above

vii) Trusts where the individual, or any of their relatives under (i) to (iv) above, is a beneficiary

Additionally, for the purposes of the pre-owned asset charge (see Chapter 13), 'connected persons' also include:

- Aunts and Uncles
- Nephews and Nieces
- Companies under the control of any of these relatives
- Trusts where any of these relatives are a beneficiary

Appendix D

Sample Documentation

<u>1. Memorandum recording a gift (IHT liability remains with transferor in the first instance*)</u>

MEMORANDUM OF GIFT FROM

Roger Meadows of 3 Taylor Street, Penzance

TO

Ian Deacon of 4 Queen Street, Belfast

MEMORANDUM that on 15th May 2018 Roger Meadows transferred by way of gift to Ian Deacon the sum of one million pounds (£1,000,000).

Dated: 20th May 2018

Signed by Roger Meadows:

Signed by Ian Deacon:

* - Note: Any IHT arising at the time of the transfer will be the transferor's liability. In practice, however, most transfers to other individuals will be potentially exempt transfers, meaning that no IHT actually arises at that stage. Any further IHT arising in the event of the transferor's death within the next seven years will usually be the transferee's liability. If this is not desired, a memorandum along the lines of Item 3 below will be appropriate.

<u>2. Memorandum recording transferee's liability for IHT on a lifetime transfer</u>

MEMORANDUM OF GIFT FROM

James Stewart of 15 Castle Street, Stirling

TO

Mary Stewart of 42 Palace Road, Linlithgow

MEMORANDUM that on 16th November 2018 James Stewart transferred by way of gift to Mary Stewart (subject to the payment of any Inheritance Tax) the assets listed in the schedule below to the intent that they have become and are the absolute property of Mary Stewart and IN CONSIDERATION of such transfer Mary Stewart undertook to pay any Inheritance Tax in respect of such gift assessed upon James Stewart or his personal representatives and indemnifies James Stewart and his personal representatives accordingly.

SCHEDULE

- Property at 87 Flodden Avenue, Berwick upon Tweed
- Ten thousand Ordinary £1 Shares in Darnley plc
- The sum of five thousand pounds (£5,000) in cash

Dated: 21st November 2018

Signed by James Stewart:

Signed by Mary Stewart:

3. Memorandum recording a gift (all IHT to be borne by the transferor)

MEMORANDUM OF GIFT FROM

Noddy Hill of 6 Slade Street, Wolverhampton

TO

David Holder of 9 Flame Avenue, Birmingham

MEMORANDUM that on 28th February 2019 Noddy Hill transferred by way of gift to David Holder the sum of two million pounds (£2,000,000). The said Noddy Hill hereby further undertakes that he or his personal representatives shall pay any Inheritance Tax assessed in respect of such gift out of the assets of his general estate and indemnifies David Holder accordingly.

Dated: 28th February 2019

Signed by Noddy Hill:

Signed by David Holder:

National Bodies

Subject to certain anti-avoidance provisions, gifts to any of the following bodies are exempt from IHT:

- The National Gallery
- The British Museum
- The National Museum of Scotland
- The National Museum of Wales
- The Ulster Museum
- Other similar institutions approved for this purpose by HM Treasury
- Other Museums or Art Galleries in the UK which are maintained by a local authority or UK University
- Any library whose main function is to provide teaching and research facilities for a UK University
- The Historic Buildings and Monuments Commission for England
- The National Trust
- The National Trust for Scotland
- The National Art Collections Fund
- The Trustees of the National Heritage Memorial Fund
- The Friends of the National Libraries
- The Historic Churches Preservation Trust
- Nature Conservancy Council for England
- Scottish National Heritage
- Countryside Council for Wales
- Any Local Authority
- Any Government Department
- Any University (or University College) in the UK
- Certain Health Service Bodies

Useful Addresses

Capital Taxes Office

Scotland

Meldrum House
15 Drumsheugh Gardens
Edinburgh
EH3 7UG

England and Wales

Ferrers House
PO Box 38
Castle Meadow Road
Nottingham
NG2 1BB

Northern Ireland

Level 3, Dorchester House
52-58 Great Victoria Street
Belfast
BT2 7QL

Helpline

The Capital Taxes Office also runs a helpline: 0845 30 20 900
(or +44 115 974 3009 if calling from abroad).

The European Union & The European Economic Area

The European Union

The 28 member states of the European Union are:

Austria	admitted 1 January 1995
Belgium	founding member 1 January 1958
Bulgaria	admitted 1 January 2007
Croatia	admitted 1 July 2013
Cyprus	admitted 1 May 2004
Czech Republic	admitted 1 May 2004
Denmark	admitted 1 January 1973
Estonia	admitted 1 May 2004
Finland	admitted 1 January 1995
France	founding member 1 January 1958
Germany	founding member 1 January 1958
Greece	admitted 1 January 1981
Hungary	admitted 1 May 2004
Irish Republic	admitted 1 January 1973
Italy	founding member 1 January 1958
Latvia	admitted 1 May 2004
Lithuania	admitted 1 May 2004
Luxembourg	founding member 1 January 1958
Malta	admitted 1 May 2004
Netherlands	founding member 1 January 1958
Poland	admitted 1 May 2004
Portugal	admitted 1 January 1986
Romania	admitted 1 January 2007
Slovakia	admitted 1 May 2004
Slovenia	admitted 1 May 2004
Spain	admitted 1 January 1986
Sweden	admitted 1 January 1995
United Kingdom	admitted 1 January 1973

The European Economic Area comprises the 28 member states of the European Union plus Iceland, Liechtenstein and Norway.

Appendix H

UK Tax Rates and Allowances: 2016/17 to 2018/19

	Rates	2016/17	2017/18	2018/19
		£	£	£
Income Tax				
Personal allowance		11,000	11,500	11,850
Basic rate band (1)	20%	32,000	33,500	34,500
Higher rate/Threshold (1)	40%	43,000	45,000	46,350
Personal allowance withdrawal				
Effective rate/From	60%	100,000	100,000	100,000
To		122,000	123,000	123,700
Additional rate/Threshold	45%	150,000	150,000	150,000
Starting rate band (2)	0%	5,000	5,000	5,000
Personal savings allowance (3)		1,000	1,000	1,000
Dividend allowance		5,000	5,000	2,000
Marriage allowance (4)		1,100	1,150	1,185
National Insurance				
Threshold	9%/12%	8,060(5)	8,164	8,424
Upper earnings limit	2%	43,000	45,000	46,350
Employment allowance		3,000	3,000	3,000
Class 2 – per week		2.80	2.85	2.95
Small profits threshold		5,965	6,025	6,205
Pension Contributions				
Annual allowance		40,000	40,000	40,000
Lifetime allowance		1m	1m	1.030m
Capital Gains Tax				
Annual exemption		11,100	11,300	11,700
Inheritance Tax				
Nil rate band		325,000	325,000	325,000
Main residence nil rate band		n/a	100,000	125,000
Annual Exemption		3,000	3,000	3,000

Notes
1. Reduced basic rate band and higher rate threshold apply for Scottish taxpayers from 2017/18
2. Applies to interest and savings income only
3. Halved for higher rate taxpayers; not available to additional rate taxpayers
4. Available where neither spouse pays higher rate tax
5. Secondary threshold for employers was £8,112 in 2016/17. Thresholds aligned thereafter

Appendix I

Abbreviations Used in this Guide

CGT	Capital Gains Tax
CPI	Consumer Prices Index
GAAR	General Anti-Abuse Rule
HMRC	HM Revenue and Customs
IHT	Inheritance Tax
SDLT	Stamp Duty Land Tax
UK	United Kingdom
VAT	Value Added Tax